Boss,

There is no possible way I could write this without you being a major part of it. You rescued me twenty years ago without blinking an eye, and gave me an opportunity I will forever be grateful for. Your support have gotten me through some of the lowest points in both my career, and life in general. If I have never told you before, I want you to know I love you, very much! Thanks for always being there.

J. S. P.

A
Compartmentalized
Life

A
Compartmentalized
Life

John Stephen Parker

To order additional copies of this book, contact:
Xlibris Corporation
1-888-795-4274
www.Xlibris.com
Orders@Xlibris.com
64081

THIS IS FOR my greatest accomplishments, Andrea and Jordan Parker. I was not around for everything that you accomplished, and I hope that you will in time forgive me for that. It may have been selfish on my part, but my drive is very deep, and I hope you understand. If I have passed anything on to you, I hope it is this quality and the ability to never be content with what life has to offer. Complacency is a cancer that ruins society. Never believe that one small voice can't change the world because if you think about it, every social revolution started with one person standing up and opening their mouth. Never pass on an opportunity to stand up and say what is on your mind. Remember, Daddy will always love you. To my family, and friends I say thank you for your patience, tolerance, and understanding throughout the years. There was a great deal of experiences that did not incorporate in the book. Some things are so private, and compartmentalized in my mind and heart, that they cannot be written about. Although I have always been a very outspoken man, my private matters run very deep, that words could never convey my true feelings. For this reason, the will remain covered.

To my mother, Jimmy Allen, Bill Quigley, Pete Gallagher, Larry Kindbom, Michele Henke, and Randy Gardner I say thanks for all the years of love, friendship, and support. Through all the compartments of my life, every one of you has been tested, and has always been there when you were needed. Our individual histories are all different and unique, but we have all shared a common thread. You all care about me, and I have likewise always cared about you. Your have all inspired me in various ways, and I will always be grateful for that.

John

FOREWORD

There must be, of necessity, a certain knack in writing a story of a life, even when the writers life in the work. The temptation of the author to saunter down shaded bypaths of personal fancy, to linger in some valley of delight of his choosing, to mount heights and spy out his own particular promised land, is ever present. How much greater then the achievement when a writer, with no straying from the main road, arrives successfully at the finish?

The opening chapter of *A Compartmentalized Life* takes the reader by the hand and introduces him to the long-forgotten time in the city of St. Louis, where historic things have come to pass both socially and with family. This is the story of a lifetime of friendships, love, family, changes in society and lifestyle, and both personal and professional tragedy. Thus the story lengthens with the list of characters, each of whom, in his own proper person, relates his share in the book.

John Parker acknowledges that from the moment he began to gain his own personal beliefs and establish his own foundation for life, he also gained an ability to compartmentalize people, events, and experiences. He has found that this is both a blessing and a curse that had been given to him. Having seen a great deal of life from both end of the spectrum and living through year after year with all the change, both triumphant and tragic, that has compounded his life, he can tell you that he sees in his mind that which his own eyes and the eyes of others doubt.

The reader who enters the walled garden of the *A Compartmentalized Life* discovers that even great people make mistakes, and that even in the face of adversity, people can not only survive, but they can also thrive.

Unknown

CHAPTER ONE

A rooster crows only when it sees the light. Put him in the dark and he'll never crow. I have seen the light, and I am crowing.

—Muhammad Ali

HISTORY AS RECOUNTED

IN MARCH OF 2007 Eddie Robinson, longtime football coach at Grambling University, passed away. He was such a focal point in my whole belief system and my whole philosophy of coaching and on life. I sat back, and I took a hard look at his life. I looked at all the accomplishments that he had achieved in his life, and I realized that there were fewer days ahead of me than behind, so I decided that since I have so many stories and have lived somewhat of an interesting life, it was time for me to put some things on paper. I don't think this'll be my life story because we're going to change the names to protect the innocent, but I think I will also leave in some real names so that the people who have tried to screw me over time realize just who they are.

All my life I've been very misunderstood, but I have a great deal of life stories. It has been a compartmentalized life. Different stages, different loves, different situations that, at times, overlapped into the others. I have always been very good at keeping things sectioned off, but at times, I let my guard down, and it became turmoil. That was how I came up with the title of this book. I've been misunderstood about how I've done things, how I've wanted things, and how I've treated people throughout the years. I thought this was a great opportunity to maybe set the record straight, tell some stories, and God knows I have a thousand of them relating to life, love, relationships, friendships, all of which that, in some shape or form, have revolved around football, which I have been involved in since I was five years old. Hopefully, if I put everything in this compilation that I know I can, this will come off as something pretty good and it will be something that everybody will want to read.

In the mid-1960s, St. Louis, Missouri, was a hopping town. Segregation was still at its height although they had passed that constitutional law that allowed blacks to eat inside at the White Castle and a few of the other restaurants, most of the eateries, in addition to the bus systems and most public transportation systems of St. Louis, were still very segregated. Not legally, but morally. Despite its geographic location, 1960s St. Louis was very much a town with Jim Crow sensibilities more in line with cities in the Deep South than the more racially tolerant northern metropolises. Nearly every aspect of the city's society was segregated. That segregation even extended to Sportsman's Park and then to Busch Stadium, where, until the mid-1950s season, the Cardinals' organization prohibited black patrons from buying tickets in the ballpark's grandstand seats. Back then, St. Louis had its segregated boundaries of the city. Most of the black people lived in the inner city. The south side of the city, better known as the Hill, had an influx of Germans and Italians. The Central West End was mostly inhabited by the more affluent families, or what I always referred to as the chosen sperm. You had the Cervantes family, the Busch family of the famed beer family, were just a couple of those names.

The Fairgrounds Park area was where I lived as a child. The little house at 4241 Ashland Avenue was where I was born. My earliest recollections of childhood that I remember were of it being a very large and versatile house, but when you're three or four years old, it could be as big as the queen's castle in England. I drove by that house recently, and it was still standing unbeknownst to the rest of the neighborhood.

I remember once my mother, Barbara. She was a very beautiful woman, and hopefully, at the printing of this mess you're reading right now, she will still be here. She was a smoker for almost forty years. She told me once that she fell asleep, and the mattress caught on fire. My father was not at home when it happened, so my mom was able to get up and throw the mattress out of the window. One would probably give up smoking after that, but not her. She kept it up for quite some time, until she got sick in the early nineties. But like I said, she was a very beautiful woman. Although she's gained weight in her later years, she was a very thin woman when I was young. I knew lots of my father's friends always found her very attractive.

From what I can recollect, 4241 Ashland was a wonderful place. It was right down the street from 4133 where my grandmother lived. Her name was Mildred Clark, and she was a very tough woman, very strong, very loving, but very strict. She was one of eight children. Her mother, my great-grandmother, was in prison for the murder of my great-grandfather when she was pregnant with her. I guess that will make you inherently tough, when your mother kills your father, and you are born in prison. She was so tough, I actually saw this woman stick her hands into a woodstove one time and turn the hot coals and burning wood with her bare hands. She was tough, but she was a very loving, God-fearing woman. She took care of me during the day while my mother and father worked, and life at that house was an amazing thing every day. My grandfather Herschel was a fun-loving guy, who could never spank me or my rambunctious cousin Brian whenever we got in trouble because he would always start laughing. He always thought he was a carpenter of such, but he was never very good at it.

He managed to make me and Brian two little red chairs one time when we were about four or five years old. He sat these chairs by the upstairs window. The only way to describe these chairs is, short of the straps and the voltage, they were identical to the electric chair used to kill prisoners on death row at the state penitentiary in Jefferson City. My grandmother kind of used them in the same way. If we had to come and sit in those chairs, we knew that the next thing coming was a serious ass whipping, seeing as my grandfather could never whip our asses because he would always start laughing, and his laughter would make my grandmother so angry that our spankings, tree-branch whippings, or whatever else she could find to beat our asses with would become even worse because of my grandfather's comedic routine. This was also when I found out that life has a backdrop of music.

Oftentimes, she would say that she was being loving and doing it out of love although I would question that now in my life because there were times when she loved us nearly to death and, at least, to a great deal of pain. Not really, but when you were taking those beatings, you wanted to die. There were times when she would send you to the yard to get a switch to beat you with. I never understood why in the world you would want to find something to beat your own ass with, and why in the world would anybody think you would come back with anything softer than a pillow, but with her, if you came back with a dried switch—you know, one that would pretty much break on contact—she would go out and grab a very green one off the tree, and she would put her hand on the very end of it and run it all away to the end of the switch, and take every leaf off the switch. It would make that switching sound in the wind when she swung it, and I just knew that I was about to get my ass lit on fire. The sound of that switch would make two things happen: one, Brian and I would cry immediately, and two, my grandfather would begin laughing. We used to listen to Sly and the Family Stone singing "Everyday People." I didn't realize how true this song would be to the life I was going to lead. I would grow to lead a great life meeting a broad range of people, some of which I would love immediately, and some of which I would learn to love over time.

Going back to my 4241 earliest recollections, I actually don't have very many. Most of the people in the neighborhood were like my mom and dad, hardworking people. It was probably not the greatest time in the world for a young black person or for black people in general, but my mom and dad never ever let us see the crappy things from those situations. There were a great number of historical events in those years. In June of 1968, we moved to St. Louis County, in particular Berkeley, Missouri. This was a very volatile time in history, for 1968 saw the death of Dr. King, the death of Robert Kennedy, a high escalation in the Vietnam War, tricky Dick Nixon coming into office, just to name a few events.

My family has never been one to do things quietly, so why would I change now? Let's not forget, I have a family history of a unique member, who had made a huge splash when it came to getting attention with local law enforcement. This goes back to my great-grandmother, who was as cold and calculating of a murderess as you would ever me.

Nannie Peoples lived in Forest City, Arkansas, in the early 1900s. All my much-older relatives remember stories of her being a mean little woman, who was tough as nails, with a short tolerance for foolishness. My grandma Mildred was just like her according to others in the family. On the other hand, my great-grandfather Pony, well, he just happened to be the most foolish man on the planet. I have no idea how he got his name. For some reason, people back then would just have babies and name them anything based on what the last thing they saw was before they had sex, unless it was a nickname for the size of their penis or something. Although I don't really believe you can name someone a "horse" or "donkey," although many of us have been called Jackass. Where else would you ever come up with a name like Pony?

Being the foolish man he was, Pony was also a man-about-town. The funny thing in all this is that Pony is actually a dead ringer for my brother Tony, who also at times has been a man-about-town. Pony liked to drink and gamble. By most recollections, he had never really had a job. Nannie and all the children used to work the farm and fields all day from sunup to sundown Nannie would then come in, feed everybody, put them to bed, and start this whole process again the next day. This entire process was not delayed by pregnancy either. There have been stories of how she would have a baby on Monday morning and be back in the fields by midafternoon on the same day. Clearly anybody that can do that was not going to put up with the foolishness of a man, especially her husband. The other thing that should have been clear to Pony was that one didn't want to fuck around with this woman.

Well, as I said, Pony, being the man-about-town that he was, liked to drink. He also had a fetish for women, and from the stories I heard, his fetish had a tendency to get him in a heapload of trouble. Unfortunately, this trait was also passed down to many of the males in my family. Well, based on the factual conversations told to me by my relatives, Nannie—who was pregnant at the time with my grandmother—was working in the fields with the kids, as she did every day. There was some gossip going around that Pony had another family down the road. There was no proof to it because everybody knew Pony to be the man-about-town but never pinned anything down. One of my grandmother's sisters decided to get proof, and proof was exactly what she got. She was able to verify the rumor. What happened next was varied in history, but as I was told, that information made it clear to Nannie.

Now when I tell you that this woman didn't put up with any bullshit, I will now make it clear exactly what I mean. Nannie got that information in the midafternoon and carried out her day as usual. She finished in the field as she always did. She made supper for the kids as she did every day. Pony, who was drunk regularly, stayed with his schedule of coming home and passing out on the porch of the house. Now I tell you that "hell hath no fury like a woman scorned." That statement could not be truer. Please understand that Lorena Bobbitt had not been alive yet, and the legend of Lizzie Borden had not been written. Nannie

Peoples did not believe in revenge, but she did believe in a process of reckoning. It meant that she would just be evening the score. This man had not only disrespected her as a woman but had broken her heart and soul as the mother of his child. She had just been murdered inside, so what happened next was only her balancing the scales.

As the children sat at the table and ate the dinner that the tired hands of this pregnant woman made after working in the scolding southern summer sun, she made a choice to even the score permanently. While Pony lay passed out on the porch from his usual day of drinking and gambling, Nannie, decided to deliver some swift, clean justice of her own. And being the strong, farm-raised woman that she was, she knew how to use an ax, and use one she did by delivering a swift clean swing—with the power of Shoeless Joe Jackson—and removing the head of my great-grandfather Pony Peoples. She was arrested for murder and taken away to jail. Here was this uneducated little poor pregnant black woman who was calculating enough to separate herself from a person who disrespected her on a regular basis, in what most would say is a final statement of the highest order. But here comes the real question of justice. They arrested her for murder and took her away, but I had some belief, in listening to the old stories, that Nannie Peoples may have been as sly as a fox. This was the early 1900s, and the racial balance of blacks and whites was not a factor. Black-on-black crime was about the same then as it is now. The judicial system doesn't really regard it as something major. It was more of an easy way of getting rid of us by our own genocide. The prosecuting attorney in the case was not going to make Governor of Arkansas by prosecuting Nannie Peoples, and I believe she knew this somewhere in her mind.

JOHN STEPHEN PARKER

The attorney gave her a choice. If you take this to trial, you will probably get life in prison or, worse, the death penalty, but if you plead guilty, they would bring the charge down, second-degree manslaughter. This, coupled with the fact that she was pregnant, added up to about six months in prison. Obviously, she took the plea, served her time, had my grandmother, and went on with her life. Although a man lost his life in this ordeal, you have to admit that was a hell of a deal.

CHAPTER TWO

Don't go around saying the world owes you a living. The world owes you nothing. It was here first.

—Mark Twain

PARKER FAMILY BLUES

I HAVE THREE older siblings who were truly children of the sixties. My oldest brother, Tony, I looked up to very much as a kid. He was a basketball player at Berkeley High School. I would occasionally tag along to practice, or I would spend most of my time crawling up under the bleachers at Berkeley High School. You find all kinds of unusual things under the bleachers at a high school.

My sister, Felice, was more of a flower child. She was into the peace signs and the tie-dyed clothing. She once began to put egg cartons on the ceiling of her room, and she was going to cover the entire ceiling of her room with cartons. This ended very quickly when my father came into her room and found cartons sticking to her ceiling. My brother Mike, more of a middle child, always seemed to take the road less traveled. While all four of us graduated from high school and three went on to college and got degrees, Mike chose his trade school route, went on to be a printer, and probably became more successful than any of us.

We were a very close family growing up. My earliest memories of moving to Berkeley were of my parents repeatedly putting contracts down on homes, in the Berkeley and Ferguson areas. I say *repeatedly* because when most of the white families in those areas that those contracts were put down on realized that a black family was trying to move into the neighborhood, they would all get together and buy the house right out from under my parents. This happened on a number of occasions to my parents. This may come as a huge surprise to some people who read this, but this notoriously happened to black families who only wanted a leg up for their children and their families, and to be able put them in better areas to live, better schools, better classes of people to associate with, and to get them out of the ghettos of the inner city. It still happens today, but it is much more covered up. Kind of like a low-income housing project that all of a sudden decides to go condo, knowing full well that most of the people living there now will have to move because they do not have the financial means to stay.

I applaud my mother and father for stepping out on that limb at a time when it could've been very easy to stay within the confines of the inner city. My parents did not raise children who would be confined, restricted, and who would not speak out and rise up against wrongdoings when they felt there was an injustice. Even as a young boy, I can remember myself being very loud and very mouthy. I've always felt that not only is it your right to question authority, but it is also your responsibility. Often, that scared the daylights out of my mother and father because I'm sure at times they would have preferred me and my brothers and sister to stay in the shadows instead of standing out, but sometimes, you're just born to be a leader. That's funny! They probably would prefer for us to stay in the background because it was safer, but they were never really raised to be that way. Sometimes it worked out the way it was supposed to, and then there were some times where it may have gotten you in just a little bit too much trouble.

My mother was an educated woman with a great deal of street smarts. She worked for a company called Gonterrman and Associates. The owner was a gentleman by the name of Bill Gonterrman. Bill was married to an interesting woman. Her name was Melody. That is a completely different story that I might get into way down the line in this book. If you stay with me, you will find that this will be a very interesting story. Melody's brother Glen, Dr. Glennon Engelmann, was probably one the most notorious serial killers in the history of the city of St. Louis. My mother was a character witness in a murder trial of his in 1958. Bill Gonterman was a very good man who treated my mom very well and very decently at a time in history when not only black people in general were not treated very well, but in particular, black women were treated even worse. If anybody believes me, it's very tough to be black, and in the sixties and seventies, it was very tough to be black, but throughout history, it has always been tough to be a black woman.

Moving to Berkeley in the late sixties, being one of the first black families in the neighborhood, my brothers and sister were some of the first black kids to go to Berkeley High School. My father was the first black police officer on the Berkeley police force. He was a dispatcher. He did that in the evenings and worked at the post office during the day. I remember in particular when we moved to Berkeley how upset my grandparents were. Herschel and Mildred Clark were smart and frugal people. They lived in a two-family flat, what most people refer to as a brownstone in this day and time. It was very convenient and very family-oriented because the upstairs part of the home had my grandparents; my uncle Ted and my aunt Betty and her son Brian lived upstairs, and my uncle Hershel Jr.—everybody referred to him as Sonny Boy—lived downstairs. I remember my grandparents being very upset with my parents because they paid about $16,000 for a three-bedroom ranch house in North County. I think the house payment was about $105 to $110 a month, and I remember my grandmother being very upset because she believed that my parents will always be broke because they were paying over $100 a month for a house. Even after we moved, I still spent my preschool days with my grandparents. There, along with my cousin Brian Preston Clark, I learned many lessons on life.

One of the lessons I learned was that I could not fly. I learned this the hard way because one day, while Brian and I were on the swing set in the backyard of my grandparents' home, we decided to swing on the swing set and see how high we could swing. About that same time, I decided to take a dare. This was probably not the smartest day of my childhood. The dare was to see how high we could swing on the swing set and then jump off in flight. Well, John, being the adventurous person that I am, decided to take the flying leap out of the swing-set seat. I landed face-first in the yard, without much of a measurement as to how far I had actually flown. Although I did manage to nearly knock my teeth out, bloody my lips and nose, and probably give myself a concussion. I say *probably* on the concussion because if I didn't have one when I hit the ground, then I definitely had one after both my mother and my grandmother slapped me upside my head.

One of my greatest memories ever was of Brian's mother, Betty. Betty was a schoolteacher for very long time in the St.

Louis City public school system. She taught for very many years, and hopefully, at the possible printing of this book, she is still teaching, which would be some forty years. This may sound very strange to some people, but we figured out, Brian and I, that all the money in the world amounted to the grand total of twenty six cents. So we would regularly sift through the pillows on the couch, underneath the bed, beg—and I use the term loosely because, really, it was more aggravation to my uncle Ted—for one quarter and one penny. This was most important because with twenty six cents, you can go across the street to Mr. Cook's convenience store and get a package of cookies and a fruit punch. Mr. Cook's store was right across the street, and he was usually out front talking with neighbors. We could yell across the street and let Mr. Cook know that we were on our way for cookies and fruit punch. He would very quickly drop what he was doing and get our snacks ready for us. We always had to take the one o'clock afternoon nap. My grandmother always said it was because we need to get more rest. Later in life, I realized that I and Brian were just loud, rambunctious kids, and this was actually two hours of relief for my grandmother.

Brian and I would play up and down Ashland Avenue. All the way from Newstead to Farragut Elementary School. When it was time to get our hair cut, we had a choice. We could either let our uncle Hershel or our uncle Ted cut our hair, which was always an interesting sight. Often we didn't know whether they were cutting hair or watching *Star Wars* and using the force when they were cutting hair. The line of our hair could often look as though Stevie Wonder or Ray Charles had decided to get a barber's license. The other option was to let Uncle Ted or Uncle Hershel take us around the corner to Mr. Dean's barbershop. If

JOHN STEPHEN PARKER

we were lucky, Mr. Dean would cut our hair. He would always be standing behind us, smoking a cigarette, while he cut our hair. It was always very annoying, but when you're five years old and you had a grandmother like Mildred Clark, you respect your elders.

Now let me tell you what happens if you are unlucky at the barbershop. You receive a haircut from a Muslim man named Mr. Bates. Now Mr. Bates was a very dark-skinned, black man who had very greasy hands. When I say greasy hands, I mean like he would stick his hands into a large jar of Vaseline every morning before he decides to go to work. When he would cut your hair, he would grip your head—and I mean your head, your face, your chin, your neck, and any other body part above your shoulders—to position for him to cut your hair. By the time you are done with your haircut, you needed to go take a shower and degrease yourself because you felt like a big french fry.

But Mr. Bates was a good guy, and he would always do a good job of lining up your hair, but anybody who's ever had a haircut knows that when you line up your hair, you usually use the clippers. These days you have the little mustache trimmers because we have become technologically advanced, and you got that modernization of things. But back in the day, most barbers used a straight razor to line up your hair. The problem with this was when you're a young child of four or five years old, your skin may not be ready for a straight razor. If you put the straight razor on a young child, he is probably going to get razor bumps. The first time Mr. Bates put that straight razor on my head I broke out so quickly and I thought my mother was going to lose it on Mr. Bates.

Now as they say, don't let the smooth taste fool you. My mother was a thin woman with a great sense of humor and a very kind spirit, but she had the ability to be as mean as a snake when the situation calls for it, and she could lay a whipping on you like nobody's business when it was necessary. And believe me, it was more than necessary on more than a few occasions to lay their whipping on me and my brothers and sisters.

One day, my grandfather invited Mr. Bates to come by the house. I came into the room and saw Mr. Bates standing there, and I said, "Hello, Mr. Bates, with your old greasy hands." Very shortly after saying this, I was on my way to the backyard to get one of those switches that my grandmother loved to light my ass up with.

My cousin and I had great times together. Unfortunately, my cousin Brian passed away in 1980 from leukemia. We had some great times growing up in the house. My cousin Brian and I were thick as thieves growing up, and I wonder where we would be today if he were still alive and we were still running around with each other. We would probably be running a small country, turning it into an amusement park or a casino. At this point in time, I began to understand things about life, but I was also getting to be misunderstood. Either way, life moves on.

We lived in 8066 Packard in Berkeley. It was a suburb of St. Louis. It was a great neighborhood. Fortunately and unfortunately, we were the only black family in the neighborhood. Many of the folks were quick to let us know that we were the only black family in the neighborhood. Most of the people in the neighborhood were wonderful people and great neighbors. The Hessmans, the Keenans, the Millers, and many others were great neighbors to us. They knew how difficult it was at that point in time to be the only black family in the neighborhood. They welcomed us with open arms. The Hessman's in particular, were just unbelievable people. June Hessman, who was the closest thing to Jane Wyman that you could ever meet, was a wonderful woman. Unfortunately, there were other neighbors in the neighborhood who let it be known, and I will be sure not to mention the names, that they did not want us in the neighborhood. You find these things out well. When you go out to check your mail and there is a large pile of dog shit next to your mailbox, it is pretty clear that those people did not want you in the neighborhood. My mother could never understand that, and my father would become infuriated by it, but we always seemed to get past things like that. I never really noticed it. You just learn how to deal with it.

For the most part, everybody in the neighborhood got along very well. Every once in a while you got a racial epithet that would be spoken. Occasionally, if there were kids playing with us who were not from the neighborhood and really didn't know who we were, you would get that racial epithet thrown at you just because they had heard it at home. Most of them didn't really know what it meant. They said it because their parents say it, but they really never even knew what it meant. In reality we didn't see any difference. We all played together, went to school together, swam in the same swimming pools, and generally got along great. Occasionally our parents would have disagreements, and you really find out where your neighbor's moral center was during those disagreements. My mother would have card parties with the other ladies of the neighborhood. We had fun growing up.

In those days, Berkeley, Missouri, was a wonderful place. Not like it is today, with airport expansion and highway improvements. All these things virtually destroyed what was once a wonderful city. Some people call it progress, I call it unwanted change. Sometimes progress is staying the same. I realized life had really changed in Berkeley with the final destruction of Berkeley High School. This famed high school produced television stars, professional athletes, famous politicians and, mostly, just your average hardworking person. It was rumored since the late 1960s that Berkeley High School would be torn down because of the airport expansion. Those rumors began thirty-five years ago, only to have the high school be level in 2006. That was the end of the serious era.

Growing up as a kid, we had basic rules much the same as everybody else had. In summertime, you had to be out by 7:00 a.m. if you expected to get picked for a team. And you had to be home when the streetlights came on. One way or another, you would always be in trouble if you were late, either late with your friends in the morning or late with your folks in the evening. I guess we were considered a middle-class family. Although I'm sure my mother and father always considered us as poor, I can't really remember wanting for anything I didn't have, although there are a lot of kids in the neighborhood who had the better bikes and had the better toys and had a few other benefits that we, the Parkers, did not have growing up.

We had a family at the end of the block by the name of Linville. Howard Linville was a great guy. He owned the local Sinclair gas station up in Ferguson. It seemed as though he had two sets of children. He had a set of older ones and, yes, younger ones. His older ones were significantly older in their thirties when we were kids, and his younger ones were my age and the age of my brothers. His younger ones Doug, Don, and Mike had every single toy known to man. It was almost as if this family had stock in the Mattel toy company. I mean, if there was a commercial for the new toy on the television, inside of forty-eight hours, these kids will be playing with it. They always had new bikes, new clothes, new everything. When all the other kids in the neighborhood walk to school in the morning, their mom would drive them to school every morning and wait in the grocery parking lot after school every day.

I attended Frostfield School. It was the only elementary school in the neighborhood, and I say in the neighborhood very loosely. It was actually in the neighborhood called Frostwood, which when you walk to school at the age of six ended up being about three quarters of a mile away from your house. I hated that long walk. It always felt like we would never get there. Over time you figured out ways to cut through people's yards in order to cut some time off. It was early enough in the morning that most of those people were never out of bed yet, so you never had to worry about it. In the afternoon, it always became an adventure because most of those people were wide awake waiting for their own kids to come home, and because you either ended up running from a big dog or being chased by a homeowner, who was not too happy about a little black kid running through their yard. Yes, cutting through those yards became a real adventure.

Occasionally, I would try to time it in the morning to catch the Linville boys riding to school with their mother. She would always feel bad for this poor little black child who was walking to school in the cold while her boys were nice and warm in the backseat of a car. And, boy, did I know how to play it up. My mother and father never knew that I did those things and would probably be appalled by my behavior, but even at a young age, I knew I had a way of getting what I needed to get. I was never a shy kid. I never ever had a problem asking people for help, for assistance, for money, or anything else I knew I could get. I guess that is why I have always been such a very good recruiter and a very good salesman. Fortunately and unfortunately, that has benefited me and gotten me in some trouble from time to time in my adult life. I remember getting yelled at by my mother one day because at 7:00 a.m. on a Saturday, I was already up and out in the neighborhood. I went to wake up the Hessman family, and June Hessman, got out of the bed and, before her own family was awake, made me bacon and eggs. When I was done eating, she then proceeded to call my mother and let her know that I was down at their home. When I arrived home about an hour later, I got the living shit beat out of me by my mother. She could not believe that I was that bold to go wake up this white family early on a Saturday morning and had this woman make me breakfast. I sat at the kitchen table like I was Caesar and had this white woman waiting on me. Mind you, I was only about seven years old. Not bad!

I spoke earlier of the ass whippings that my mother could give. And she was very strategic about those. She could smack you upside your head with some very unique timing. She would occasionally wait until you were walking through a doorway and smack you on one side of your head, only to have the other side of your head bounce off the corner of the doorway. This way, you had a huge bruise with swelling on both sides of your head. You were forced to go to school like that, and you had to try and explain to your friends why you had two big lumps on either side of your head, and heaven forbid you told the truth about it because you never wanted to take any shit from your friends. In this day and time, some would refer to that as child abuse. When I was young, it was simply called discipline. We had the flying projectile shoe that could be placed with the expertise of an NFL quarterback on a third and short play. The funny thing is that now I sit and laugh about those days, but the reality is I had no idea that those days were part of the foundation that would be the backbone of my philosophy for both football and life. I am a person who, to this day, does not have a great deal of friends. I have a lot of acquaintances, people that know me and I know them, but there are only a few people that I can call a deep-hearted friend. Many of them are gone now.

Going back to Frostfield School, in those days, kindergarten was only half a day. You either went in the morning, or you went in the afternoon. When I started kindergarten, I met some very wonderful people. So of those people, I went all the way through high school and actually graduated with them.

When I started kindergarten, my mother signed me up for the morning class. I remember I had to get a physical before starting school. As a six-year-old, I barely passed the physical. Even then, I was a very excitable young man. My blood pressure as a six-year-old was 200 over 100. Now in those days, you didn't put a six-year-old on blood pressure medication. Instead, the doctor's prescription to my mother was for me to "stay calm." If you can actually believe that, we were charged for a doctor to give us a prescription of "stay calm." That had to be the biggest rip-off and most ridiculous prescription in the history of medicine.

I had a sidekick at Frostfield. His name was Charles Pennington. Now Charlie and I were inseparable. One of the reasons for this was because his mother, Jean, was my babysitter during the second half of the day, when school was dismissed. Charlie and I would be excused from school at noon and playfully make our way to his house after school, where we would spend the second half of the day. Jean Pennington was a wonderful woman who took great care of me until five or six o'clock, when my mother would show up and take me home. Charlie and I would spend our days exploring Frostwood. When we wanted candy, we would go up to the IGA Foodliner shopping center. There were only four stores in this shopping center. There was the IGA grocery store, the drugstore, the Ben Franklin five-and-ten, and the hardware store. It was the kind of hardware store that actually had salesmen that took you by the hand and got you everything you needed. They were small and focused. Not like those ridiculous Home Depot stores where people actually die from things falling on their heads. Back in the day, you never heard of people dying at a hardware store.

Jean was wonderful, but Charlie's father, Charles Senior, was the meanest man I had ever met in my life. Charlie and his brother and sisters knew how to take him, but I guess since I was not with him twenty-four hours a day, I just never seemed to know how to take him. He yelled at me one time, and I swear to God, I thought I was going to piss down my leg. I was so scared of him. Later in life, I saw Mr. Pennington before he died, and I realized how great he really was. He was a deacon at Liberty Baptist Church. Charlie ended up just like him. He is now a pastor of a church in St Louis County. What a compliment to his father. I have not seen Charlie in a very long time. The next time I saw him was June 17, 1995. I remember specifically because that was my wedding day. We have since seen each other quite a bit. I often miss Charlie in my life because he is truly one of my best friends in this world.

Somehow I always get away from this but getting back to Frostfield. It was a small elementary school that sat right in the middle of the Frostwood subdivision of Berkeley. At that point in time, Frostwood was still a predominately white neighborhood. I have said a great deal about things being predominately white in those days, and about being the first black family, and the only black here and there. Hopefully, I will not project myself as a racist person. I have very rarely seen color in anybody. I can always recognize an asshole as clear as the next guy can. One thing is for sure, assholes come in all shapes, sizes, colors, and races. Frostwood is now 98 percent black. The property values have fallen. Frostfield has been changed to Berkeley Middle School; it too is 98 percent low-income black families. But back in the day, that place was fun. The teachers there were strict, but you have to remember that these were the times of corporal punishment, and teachers and principals could not only physically discipline you, they were encouraged to do so by your parents.

Our principal was a man by the name of Fielding Poe. He was a man that stood about six feet three inches tall. He had a deep voice, bald head, and a mean disposition about him. When he spoke, people listened. I was sent to his office one day for some reason. I can't remember why, but knowing me, it was probably for some sarcastic remark or comeback that I was usually know for giving. That has become my trademark. When I arrived at the office, I watched Tony Harris, who was in the same grade I was but was at least two years older than me. Some used to say that Tony had a learning disability. That was not true. Tony was just a bad kid that was rotten to the core. He was a bully in every sense of the word, who would take advantage of younger, weaker kids. I mean everything, from just beating up kids to taking their lunch money.

Well, all his bully tactics caught up to him one day, and Mr. Poe got him during one of his famous lunch-money "jackings."

When I arrived at the office, Tony Harris was coming out of Mr. Poe's office with tears in his eyes and whimpering like a baby. You see, Mr. Poe had a paddle in his office, but not just any paddle. It was his fraternity paddle for the Tau Kappa Epsilon fraternity. He had the title of Sergeant at Arms, which basically means he was the disciplinarian of the frat. He was very proud of that. This paddle resembled a small boat oar, and it had a number of holes drilled in it because he liked the fact that when he smacked you on the ass with it, your skin would come through the holes, and it would inflict more pain.

When I saw Tony come out of that office, I knew that he had just felt the wrath of the infamous TKE paddle and that his ass was as swollen as a piece of Bubble Wrap. I also realized that I would rather walk through the fires of hell than to go into that office because I knew that if I go in there, I would just infuriate him until he didn't want to do anything but light my ass up.

CHAPTER THREE

I arise in the morning torn between a desire to improve the world and a desire to enjoy the world. This makes it hard to plan the day.

—E. B. White

EARLY FOUNDATION CONSTRUCTION

FROSTFIELD WAS ALSO where I would also develop my foundational philosophy of coaching football. I consider myself a very lucky person because since I was about seven years old, I knew I wanted to be a football coach. I was never a big fan of professional football. Growing up in St. Louis, Missouri, you were either a natural fan of the Big Red or the baseball Cardinals. I followed the University of Missouri religiously and their famed coaches Dan Devine, Al Onofrio, and my good friend Warren Powers, who I would later work for. Part of my philosophical foundation was also based on the fact that in that time period, not only was I disciplined at school, I had what some would call extreme discipline at home.

I spoke earlier of my mother, Barbara. She was a tough woman on her family. She was often ridiculed by my aunts about how hard she could be on us, but she didn't care. She believed that if you spare the rod, you spoil the child. She learned it from her mother. I do believe if more parents in society today would disregard trying to be friends to their kids, trying to be politically correct, and went back to the days when if you spoke with too much bass in your voice you got that shit slapped out of you, we would not have the issues with kids we have today. If parents would try being parents first and move being friends to about seventh on the list, you would not have things like the Columbine High School (CO) shootings.

Barbara Parker had a cardinal rule when we were growing up. Every morning, she got up at six in the morning. She would make a large pot of oatmeal or cream of wheat hot cereal. By 6:15-6:30 a.m., every able body in the house was moving. By 8:00 a.m., everybody had to be out of the house. Now when I say "out of the house," I mean either you were going to work or you were going to school. The house became a party at 3:00 a.m., which meant "You don't have to go home, but the party is over, and you CAN'T stay here." Her rule was "You will not use my house to dress and rest." I rarely missed a day of school growing up. That would have never flown with my mother. If you had a fever, you went to school. If you were throwing up, you went to school. If you had broken bones, as long as it was not sticking out through the skin, you went to school. If it was sticking through the skin, you pushed it back in, wrapped it up, cleaned up any blood that was on the floor, and you got your ass to school. She would periodically call the house during the day just to see if anyone would answer the phone. We never knew she would do this, but it was one way of finding out who was skipping school. Nobody in our family ever skipped school. You did not want to risk that. She helped to mold my philosophy for a work ethic that, to this day, continues to drive me on a daily basis. At seventy-plus years of age, she still has some type of what she calls a knick-knack, piece-of-change job in addition to her's and her deceased husband's pension checks that she receives monthly. She took a job with Gonterman and Associate in the fifties as an advertising assistant. Because a black woman in society at that time had all the heightened employment value of a piece of whale shit, she could never get an executive job, but Bill Gonterman took a chance on this twenty-year-old woman. Over the period of working there, she married, had four children, buried both her parents, bought and sold homes, was able to fight her way through the segregated times of the world to become the woman that she is. My mother is truly extraordinary, and my lifelong hero. This time period developed not only my philosophy, but introduced me to the people who would remain fixtures in my life even today.

I started playing all the sports that I would eventually come to love while I was at Frostfield. Believe it or not, it was not football. My first love was actually baseball, and my first coach was a man named Glen Shoemaker. Now Glen Shoemaker was a unique man. He lived in the St. Johns/Overland area of St. Louis County. This area was a combination of Mississippi in the 1950s and a larger trailer park. It was mostly of old redneck white people who still referred to black people as "colored," as if we were a load of laundry.

Glen had about five kids. I don't believe that in the season that I was on that team did I ever see those kids clean. He did have a daughter named Patty. She was about four years younger than me and was always crying with snot running down her nose, which made her even grosser. The only thing more I can say about Patty is that she grew up. I saw her some years later when she was graduating from McCluer High School, and man oh man, did she grow up. She was beautiful, and luckily, I was in the age range. We saw each other for a bit, but nothing ever came of it. Nevertheless, Patty was a dirty kid who turned out to be a very pretty woman. I always hoped things worked out for her.

Her father, on the other hand—well, the only thing I could tell you is that he was the second most abusive man I had ever been around with. I saw him yell, scream, slap, and anything else he thought of to degrade his wife and his kids. The other players on the team were scared to death of him, but naturally, being the (1) probably the best athlete on the team and (2) the only black player on the team, he never bothered me. I would pitch every game that year. I pitched three no-hit games that year. My mother, to this day, still has the certificates. I hit twenty-seven home runs in a fourteen-games season.

Now my mother will tell you that I cried my eyes out whenever some got a hit off me. She is not too far from the truth on that. I was and still am a very emotional person when it comes to competition. I love to win, and I hate losing. I don't think that has or will ever change. When I would pitch, it was alarming to me when someone got a hit off me because it did not happen very often. I would throw harder, sometimes out of control, with the intention of striking out as many people as possible. Sometimes, if I got out of control, I hit a couple of kids. This actually worked in my favor because then people came to the plate fearful that they may be hit and were in a hurry to get away from that batter's box. I enjoyed baseball, and to this day, I am still a St. Louis Cardinal fan.

Growing up in Berkeley, I was a friendly kid, but I had a disposition about me. Even then, it would not be easy to become a friend of mine and sustain a friendship with me. In

JOHN STEPHEN PARKER

my neighborhood, I had two friends who would stay attached to me for the next thirty-five years. Randolph William Furch Jr., Bill for short, lived at 8125 Gardner. His mother and father were both teachers. Randy, his dad, taught PE in the University City School District. His mother, Willa, taught home economics right up the street at Ferguson Junior High School, where we would eventually go to school.

I met Bill for the first time during the summer before the second grade because we played on a kid's softball team at Airport School. After the season was over, I didn't think I would see any of those kids again because they lived in a different geographic boundary of Berkeley, but when I walked into Mrs. Crouch's second-grade class, there was my friend Bill Furch sitting there. Right behind me, coming in through the door, was my kindergarten buddy Charles Pennington, and following him was a young kid with a huge anger management problem by the name of Andre Hughes.

Now the unique thing of all this was that not only were all of us in the same class, but all of us were born in the same month. Bill was born on January 4th, Charlie on the 8th, I was on the 16th, and Andre was on the 24th. Mrs. Crouch, who was one of the sexiest teachers we had ever seen, managed to put up with us. She had the greatest legs in the world. Please understand this is the opinion of a large group of seven-to-eight-year-olds. We would sit down in front of her when she would read us stories, and we would actually fight to see who would get to sit right in front of her. Finally, one day, we all got busted when Lisa Elam—who always wore these glasses that suggested that she was born blind in one eye and unable to see out of the other—ratted out to Mrs. Crouch, in front of the whole class, the reason we would half kill each other to sit in front. Mrs. Crouch proceeded to explain to us, *in no uncertain terms,* that her legs and any other body parts of hers were of no subject to us. Not only were we embarrassed, but we all wanted to kill Lisa. I have no doubt that somewhere in life she caught some communicable disease, and her ears fell off. It would serve her right for outing us that day. She managed to take away the wonderful fantasy of four seven-year-old boys.

The neighborhood was beginning to develop more. I use the word *develop* because change seems to always scare people. Summer after the second grade, we had a new guy move into the neighborhood, James Truman Allen III. He was second oldest of a family of four kids. His father worked at Mallinckrodt Chemical Company, and his mother, Marcia, was a longtime nurse at St. Luke's Hospital.

When I tell you things developed, I meant that as you grow, you develop new relationships. Some of them have faded away, and some have stayed with you for the rest of your life. Jimmy's moving in was one of the latter. When we began playing together, it started with baseball. Since Glen Shoemaker had moved on to abuse some other family, that team disbanded. We started a new team. This was my first taste of serious winning, and what a team it was. Myself, Charlie, Bill, Jimmy, and Andre. We had a few additions from the Frostwood area of Berkeley join us. Steve Robinson was a great first baseman and actually be came, like us, one of the best player on the team, and in a way, we probably all believed that. There were many others like Stanley Hayes, Kevin Whiteside, Kamic Fouches, and a couple of others. This was a championship team. Some of us were more, for lack of a better term, *cultured.* The ones in Frostwood were the hard cores. They were always ready to fight at the drop of a hat. Jimmy, Bill, and myself were more of the diplomats. We played for a man named Ron Fozzard. Ron was a bit of a trailer park type guy, but he loved and cared about us. When you didn't have a ride to the field, he would arrange one for you. After the games, he didn't have a lot of money, but he would spend whatever he had in his pocket on ice cream or soda or any other snacks we wanted. His only demand was that we win, which we did.

We played at the Berkeley Khoury League Baseball Park. It was land that was owned by McDonnell Douglas Aircraft Company, over by the airport. We grew up on these fields on a daily basis. Played in dirt, drank the water, breathed the air out there. I say all these thing now because I have a serious feeling of betrayal to both the organization and the MDD Company. Later, it was found that the entire time we were growing up out there, playing on those fields, the state of Missouri had purchased that land from MDD and was using it for toxic dumping. Although I don't know of any of us becoming sick, those fields were shut down in the early eighties and never played on again.

The Diplomats—I, Jimmy, and Bill—became the Three Musketeers. We walked to and from school together. We could get to each other's homes in a matter of minutes. We spent a great deal of time together, but even when we were kids, I always seemed to be the ringleader because I probably had the most freedom.

Bill's parents were a little different. It was almost like they didn't want anybody in their house. I was out of high school before I ever set foot into Bill's house. His mother always thought I ran around with no supervision, and well, I did. I liked meeting people and exploring anything when I was a kid. So I really was not the type of person that she really wanted Bill running around with. Bill was always excited about eating, as if it took priority over a great deal of his life.

Jimmy, on the other hand, had just moved to the neighborhood and didn't really know anybody. We got to be very close. We did everything, from staying at each other's homes, getting into trouble, to digging through the cushions or the washing machine, looking for extra change so that we could walk to McDonald's on Airport Road. If anybody ever went out to eat, Bill's first question was always "What did you eat?" and "How much did you eat?" He could never talk or do anything else if there was a meal involved. It was almost some kind of weird obsession about food.

Those trips to McDonald's were always a treat. We never had a dime to our name when we were kids. We would go through the house, and I mean, we were scavengers. We would find every single penny we could manage to find in the house, the garage, the yard, and anywhere else where there was a possibility of finding minor pieces of change. We would pool our money to get as much food as possible. The standard meal was a Big Mac, fries, and a Coke. If we had enough money, then we would spring for apple pies. Now you have to understand that when I say pool our money, this was I, Bill, Jimmy, and we picked up a tagalong by this time in Jimmy's younger brother Ricky.

Now one of the amusing parts was the trek to McDonald's. We started by going out through my backyard through the weeded path that had been walked down by our many trips. This path led to a creek, which you had to cross in order get to the railroad tracks. Once upon the tracks, you walked down about a quarter of a mile until you got to the grassy yard behind Airport School. You then had to cross a creek on the other side of the tracks, wade through those weeds, which were significantly higher, and then walk through the field and the back of the school yard. You would then come out on Airport Road, just kitty-corner from go old Mickey D's.

The second part that was absolutely hilarious was now that we had ransacked our homes for pennies, the next step was to place an order. There we were, four of the shabbiest-looking kids you had ever seen in your life. If it was cold, we had on worn-ut dirty coats for traveling through the weeds. If it was hot outside, we were usually in shorts and T-shirts, scratches on our legs and burs stuck to our socks. These were remnants from cutting through the weeds. Here we were, ready to—as we used to say back in the day—"grub."

The next thing that happened caught the attention of everyone in the restaurant. In a regular brown paper bag, the kind used to carry lunches, we would have about $6-$8 worth of pennies, and all over the counter they would go. The little girl who had just taken our order was never aware we had these, and when they were finally presented to her, she looked at us like "You have got to be kidding me." We would stand there and watch her count these out, five cents at a time, only to have her occasionally come by a nickel, or a dime once or twice, which brought the biggest look of sarcasm to her face. We did not care. The only thing we were interested in was getting our grub on and making that eventful trek back home. Sometimes, those treks got to be very interesting. We often found ourselves trying to avoid an oncoming train.

Growing up in Berkeley with Jimmy and Bill was a whole lot of fun. It's amazing, the experiences that we all share. Although Bill was a little bit different, the three of us got along just like brothers. And just like brothers, there was the usual animosity. Sometimes, we ended up in the same class in school. But even when we didn't, we still manage to find each other when school let out. We would cut through this area that we called the farmer's field. This always cut at least thirty minutes off our trip to and from school. When we got to the end of the field, again we got to a point where we cut through backyards, which would bring us to the back of Bill's house. From there, Jimmy would walk up the street, and I would walk around the corner.

We did everything together. We played baseball on the same teams in the summer. We played football on the same teams in the fall. Sometimes, you don't realize when you're nine or ten years old how close you actually get to people in your life. Little did I know that these two people would be involved in my life, even today.

CHAPTER FOUR

*Ideas are refined and multiplied in the commerce of minds.
In their splendor, images affect a very simple communion
of souls.*

—Gaston Bachelard

TRANSITION HAS ITS PAINS

BY THE TIME our six years were finished at Frostfield,
something began to take effect in the St. Louis area. It
was the mid-1970s, and although it had already affected many
major cities in the country, forced busing was about to take effect
between the St. Louis City and the St. Louis County schools.
Back then we didn't really know why or for what reason they were
doing these things, but as we've gotten older, I realized that this
was probably one of the biggest crimes in the history of education
in the state of Missouri. I understand desegregation because there
is always a huge difference between the educational systems of
the city schools versus the benefits of attending a county school.
This was also the swan song of the Berkeley school district.

The Kinloch school district was dissolved in the early 1970s.
It merged with what was then a slowly dying Berkeley school
district. The Ferguson Florissant school district was one of the
largest in the state of Missouri. The city of Ferguson sat adjacent

to Berkeley. It was mostly working-class white people. There were not many, if any at all, black people in Ferguson at that time. The ones that were there were mostly good-hearted people who had no idea that they were about to go through a significant change in their neighborhoods.

I spoke earlier of the tumultuous times that black people had when they moved to St. Louis County. Ferguson was one of those cities that was not quite accepting of change. When my parents first tried to move the St. Louis County, they attempted to buy homes in the Forestwood Park area only to have the white families in those neighborhoods pool their money and purchase a home from under my parents. The next home they attempted to buy was in a very exclusive subdivision, right on Florissant Road. The name of the subdivision was Pembroke. It was a very affluent subdivision where many of the significant public figures of Ferguson resided. One of my high school friends Tom Blake, whose father was a physician, lived in Pembroke. They were nicer homes, mostly ranch-style, with basements. They were very large, and some even had swimming pools. Back then, Pembroke had its own security force, which patrolled their streets regularly. They even had their own lake, which had about seven or eight homes right on the waterfront. As forced busing began, Ferguson began to get an influx of black families. Berkeley already had its share, as it was beginning to get a reputation as a bad suburb of the city of St. Louis.

When the migration from Ferguson began, just as it did in every major city in the country, most of the residents who were white began to migrate west to the city of St. Charles. This was the new promised land. New housing developments were beginning to sprout up, and these homes had very large lots. Black people had just begun moving to St. Louis County. Those homes were in the mid-$20,000 to $30,000 range. The homes in St. Charles were moving into the $60,000 to $70,000 range. Now the people who moved to St. Charles County can say whatever they want to say. I am sure that many of these people had all kinds of reasons to move out there. The truth of the matter was, most of the people that move to St. Charles in the early to midseventies move there because they were trying to get away from black people. They were afraid of everything, from simple change to that crazy myth of property value going down because the dirty "niggers" had moved to their neighborhood. Why else would you move to an area outside of the city where the only main artery in and out of was Highway 70, which, at that point in time, was composed of only four lanes?

My memories of that neighborhood, of Berkeley in the early days, of the many relationships that it gave birth to, would not be complete without my telling you about my friend and mentor Mr. Pete Gallagher. Pete was a graduate of Berkeley High School, who had more pride in Berkeley Senior High School, and in the city of Berkeley than any person I ever met. His elementary school, Holy Ghost Catholic School, sat down on Wabash Avenue, down by the North Fork and Western Railroad Depot.

When I was seven years old, I was walking home from school one day and here comes this young white guy jogging along with his dog. He stopped and asked me who I was, and I told him. He asked me where I lived, and by the time we started talking, we were only about two hundred yards from my home. In this day and time, when a twenty-five-year-old man stops to have a conversation with a seven- or eight-year-old little boy, most people would consider him a pedophile. With Pete, there was a genuine interest. That was the beginning of what I would call an extraordinary friendship. When I had baseball games as a kid, Pete was there. When I had football games on a Sunday afternoon, Pete was there. He watched me grow up and was always there. I remember learning how to drive a stick shift when I was eight. Pete and I attended a St. Louis Cardinal baseball game one day. I specifically remember it was Poster Day at Busch Stadium. I remember Pete getting very intoxicated at the ballpark. Believe me, this was not a rare thing. That guy loved to have a beer. Pete had just bought a little British Triumph Spitfire convertible. That was a great car. He drove it to the ballpark, but I remember having to drive it home because he was a bit too lit up and could not get us home. I got my first driving lesson that day.

I had a lot of firsts with Pete. I had my first drink with him. It was during basketball season. Back then, Pete worked for the Business Products Center on Washington Avenue, in downtown St. Louis. Back in the day, that area was a shopping hotbed in the forties and fifties. Lots of warehouses, the Brown Shoe Company, and St. Louis Board of Education were just a few of the occupants of this neighborhood. Today, this area has been refurbished and updated. Most of the buildings have been turned into loft apartments and condos. Pete was a top salesman for the company for many years. Whenever fall would roll around, Pete would always assemble a basketball team. Pete was a huge basketball fan but somewhat of a frustrated athlete. He was not a very big man. Short, skinny, but he had a quirky disposition about him, and if you pushed him, he would definitely be ready for a fight. He would always sponsor a team, mostly of guys he had known for a long time, and some of which he had gone to Berkeley High School with. Two of which were Bob Huntze and

Charlie Humphrey. I knew Charlie because he was a PE teacher at Frostfield when I was in school there. They would play ball just about anywhere. They played on a Thursday night league at Berkeley Junior High. They played in a Saturday league at Ferguson Junior High, another at Crosskeys Junior High, and even at the Wohl Community Center in the heart of the black community. Pete was fond of all sports, but he was a basketball fanatic. He had a big heart, and he really loved kids, especially this annoying black kid who I am sure got on his nerves, and probably his wife Donna's on more than one occasion. Although I have aged and now have kids of my own, I can truthfully say that there would be no John Parker without a Pete Gallagher.

When the boundaries of the school district were changed in the midseventies, not only did it separate a lot of friends, it separated people from a knowledgeable culture that they had been familiar with. Frostfield ended for Jimmy, Bill, and me. Before it ended, we were all scheduled to attend Berkeley Junior High. With the changing of the district boundaries, the three of us had our schedules changed, and once again, we would continue to walk to school, right up January Avenue, to Ferguson Junior High. This also brought a huge change in culture. We would now be attending school with many of the affluent kids in the Ferguson area, and also with the racist families that lived in many of those subdivisions. I say this as if things were about to be turned over in our lives, which is not completely accurate. There were some outstanding people that were about to come into our lives, my life in particular. Little did I know that junior high was about to be the major turning point. Not only would I meet what would become the long love of my life, I would be influenced by the most important factor in my coaching life and my entire world surrounding football. The next three years would be set as the cornerstone of a life and a career, which has at times gone astray but, for the most part, has been focused on the preparation of young men for life, both on and off the field.

If you have not noticed, I have spoken about my family and, in particular, my mother with great respect and admiration. She has always been one of the most influential people in my life. The person whom I have not had much to say about is my father. Stay tuned!

CHAPTER FIVE

We will that all men know we blame not all the lords, nor all those that are about the king's person, nor all gentlemen nor yeomen, nor all men of law, nor all bishops, nor all priests, but all such as may be found guilty by just and true inquiry and by the law.

—Jack Cade

JWP: THE MAN, THE MYTH

JOHN WESLEY PARKER, born August 5, 1931, to Geneva Parker. My father, well, he was a hard man, raised by hard people who had a knack for criminal activity. The stories I have heard about my father's childhood and adolescence were not very attractive. He was a bit of a thug growing up, with a bad temper. He had a brother named Frank who was a drug addict, mostly a heroin user. Frank was also a thug, who had spent a little time as the guest of the state of Missouri. He was always nice to me and my brothers and sister, but I had a cousin Richard whom I found out later in life was gay. Richard told me that Frank used to rape and sodomize him as a child repeatedly for years so that the only affection that he knew was from men. It was acknowledge when later I found that my father was just as much a molester as my uncle was. I will not go into the extreme details of it because as much as this book is therapy for me, it is also a confession.

When I was seven years old, I was molested by my father repeatedly during the summer. He would enter my room in the morning after my mother would go to work. This was one reason I loved spending the night at my friends' houses and hanging around Pete or anybody. It might be one reason I was so involved in sports. I knew when I was playing anything, it would keep me from being at home, which gave less opportunity for things to happen. After a while, he caught on to what I was doing and then he came up with some crazy rule that if I left in the morning to go play, I had to be back in the house by twelve thirty in the afternoon. He always told my mother it was because it was too hot outside for me to be out. Later in the summer, I made a habit of disobeying him about being in the house by twelve thirty, so instead of molesting me, he changed the script and began beating me for disobeying him. To me it was the lesser of two evils. I could either be molested, or I could just get the hell beaten out of me. What a great bunch of choices for a seven-year-old.

My mom told me one time that my father's brother Frank was giving my father a bunch of shit one day while sitting at my grandmother's kitchen table. Evidently, this went on for about fifteen to twenty minutes, and the whole time, my dad's temper was beginning to rage. Now both my dad and my uncle were known for carrying small handguns back in the day. For some reason, they thought it was really cool to carry concealed weapons. Well, on that day, my uncle Frank was giving my father some shit and my father decided to snap, and when he did, he also unloaded his pistol. No, he didn't kill him, but he did unload that

.38 revolver into the wall at just about Frank's head. Just one of the many eventful moments in my father's family history.

My father, as I said, was a very hard, mean man. Maybe it was because of how he was raised. He gave me some lame excuse about being a soldier and being raised during three wars (WWII, Korea, and Vietnam). As far as the soldier part goes, I can only say that we were safe from the North Koreans because my father had the United States well covered at Fort Rucker Army Base in Georgia, or where ever he happened to be stationed at the time, and he would kill all the "bastards" if they attacked us here. Then again, it could have been because he was just an abusive asshole. As we progress through this text, I leave it to you to draw your own conclusions.

My earliest memories of my father's abuse was of his putting me and my brother Mike outside so that he could punch and slap Mother repeatedly. I cannot remember what the argument was about, but I can remember listening outside the back door of our house in Berkeley. Listening to my mother asking "Why are you hitting me?" I remember the side of her face looking like a tenderized steak. She went to work like that, and I can only imagine the embarrassment she felt walking into Gonterman and Associates, looking like that. Her boss, Bill Gonterman, took her to the doctor and got her x-rayed. I guess that only added to the distain I had for my father. It grew significantly over time.

I think back to my baseball days as a kid. People used to ask me why I could hit so well. I would tell them a story. When you are going through it, you learn to deal, but now as an adult, you know that it was a version of child abuse. I hit the ball so well because I learned to not be afraid of it. I learned not to be afraid because as a young boy, at about six or seven years old, my father would put my coat on me and place me up against a chain-link fence and throw baseballs at me. I would get hit over and over in my back, head, legs, and even in the face. It was general torture, and there was never any letting up. Once, my mother pulled into the driveway during one of the pain-tolerance episodes. She looked over to see what was going on and saw me utterly terrified at what was happening to me, except there was nothing she could do. My father was very controlling, and when he was in charge of a situation, he would never listen to anybody. She went in the house and left me to handle that situation on my own. After about the fifth episode of this, I learned not to be afraid. When I would stand in the batter's box with a bat in hand, as far as I was concerned, if the pitch was close, I would make contact. When you can hit home runs year after year in a sixteen-game season for five or six seasons in a row, you must be doing something different, or at least thinking different. I struck out less than half a dozen times in my entire baseball-playing days. This was because I could hit anything that was pitched at me. Not sure if it was a defense mechanism or just a sense of confidence in standing in the batter's box. I guess I can probably in some sick way thank my father for the physical abuse of the target-practice days in the backyard.

He was very no-nonsense on many things like this. He taught you how to swim by throwing you in the deep end of the pool. While you were struggling, he would be standing there very calmly, just saying "Get to the side." I can remember almost drowning in the pool because my swimming lesson was so traumatic. My father was a great swimmer and actually taught at the YMCA, but with us, it was different. His belief was that he wanted to find out if we had life-survival skills, so he would throw you in the deep end and tell you to basically "stay alive." He would then teach you how to swim, if you still had intentions of learning.

He once tried to teach my mother how to drive a stick shift transmission vehicle. He, my mother, and I drove into the city in a 1969 Volkswagen Beetle. About nine miles from home, he decided to just stop the car and get out. My mother abruptly asked, "Where are you going?" My father's response was very simple. He said, "You wanted to learn how to drive a stick, well, get yourself home." With that being said, he got out and started walking back home. My mother got behind the wheel and got her baptism-by-fire lesson of driving a stick shift, and what a lesson it was. I almost got whiplash riding in the backseat that day. Not sure what it is like to bull ride, but that little car was bucking and jerking back and forth. My mother drove all the way back to Berkeley crying her eyes out in first gear because she could never find the friction point in switching gears.

My father was not a good man. He was, in my opinion, much more of a monster than he was a man. When I was a child and we moved to St. Louis County, he was working at the post office in Berkeley. He was also a police officer in Berkeley. The only black police officer on the force. He was a violent man who would discipline and control with a belt or a punch and, occasionally, even with a gun. He once stuck a gun to my brother's throat because he was mad about something. I have no idea what it was, but it was also not the meanest thing I saw him do and certainly not the most monstrous thing I had heard about from him. I remember once when I was in the fifth grade at Frostfield. My father was the chief of police in Kinloch. He had an altercation with a man on the street once and ended up breaking the man's jaw. He got sued, and although it was thrown out of court, it was still much publicized. For the first time, I understood what it was like for my brother growing up in Berkeley as a kid.

Every teacher at Frostfield knew who my father was, and you can be assured that they let me know. When I was younger, he worked at the post office depot in Berkeley. I told you earlier that he was a bit of a criminal. How they ever allowed him to become a police officer and carry a gun was unbelievable. It was a fact that the judicial system in Missouri was very generous. While he was working at the post office, he was arrested for stealing out of the U.S. mail. Last time I checked, this was a federal offense, and you ended up in the Federal Penitentiary in Leavenworth, Kansas for federal crimes much less than this. He was fired from the post office and sentenced but never served a day in jail. He hired one of the best criminal defense attorneys in the state of Missouri, Mr. Donald Wolfe. Don pleaded the case down to a minor sentence, which consisted of a fine that was to be paid. I remember my mother working a second job at JCPenny department store to pay off the fine. What an admirable woman she is. My father was a very matter-of-fact person, and if there is one trait that I am not real proud of having, that is it.

Although my sister will never speak of it, I have a distinct belief that she was mistreated as a child also. I know that theirs was an even more volatile relationship than mine was with him. I remember that she didn't even want him there when she graduated from college. I was molested by him as a child on more than one occasion. I have never ever spoken of it to anybody, not even my mother, but it happened. This is not something that I imagined or blocked out of my mind. I just never spoke of it.

People say that you should not hold a grudge against people because it will consume you, and the only person that it hurts in the long run is you because the other person usually doesn't know, and for sure, the other person doesn't care. This may be why I have had problems in my own relationships. He beat my mother on more than one occasion that I can remember. He was a very high-strung, aggressive person. He yelled a lot and was a major control freak. My mother, over time, gained her own independence. My father became the chief of police in Kinloch, Missouri, which made him believe he was even more powerful. When he arrested people, he not only arrested you, but he humiliated you in public. He would physically arrest you and others at the same time and then publically march you down the street to jail. This gave him the persona more of Matt Dillon of *Gunsmoke* than of a police chief in a suburban municipality. Not to mention it played into his ego, which never needed to be played into. I remember as a child he would come to my games, but he would never take me there or give me a ride home. I always had to ride my bike to and from the games. If it was after the game and there was another parent available, I would put my bike in the trunk and get a ride home with them. While he was attending the game, he would always make a spectacle of himself. He was loud and boisterous and really quite embarrassing. Now I know how parents are at games. They cheer and root for their kids, but my father's attendance always went more toward humiliation than encouragement. I hated it more than anything. What I hated even more was the humiliation I received when I got home. This was the kind of person he was.

CHAPTER SIX

You have to wait for people to program you. The only difference is the amount of people that you're going to reach but that's going to even out in the next two or three years anyway. Computers are being bought faster than televisions right now.

—Chuck D.

NEW ADDITIONS

I HAVE SOMETIMES realized that my demeanor with people could be better, but I am who I am. I began to realize that early on at Ferguson Junior High. Every morning, I would meet Jimmy, Bill, and by this time, we had a couple of additions to the group. Ronnell Lloyd had moved to Berkeley at the end of the previous year. He was the youngest of a large family. He was a city kid, who, at first, had a hard time adjusting to the county. So much that he would ride his bike down to his old neighborhood to see his old friends. I actually took that ride with him once to the 5800 block of Wabada. It was hard on him first moving because he was a city kid, and there is a much different social culture in the city of St. Louis compared to the county. Ronnell was an outstanding athlete. I had never seen anybody run like he could.

The other guy that joined us was Ronnie West. Ron was an obnoxious fat kid that lived up the street from me. He always wanted to be cool and one of the "in" guys. He was a crybaby who tried really hard to be a bully, but could never be one because he was way too much of a pussy. We would all walk to school and engage in some very interesting conversations. During these conversations, you figured out real fast just how much of a difference there was in all of us. Me, Jimmy, and Bill were clearly more intelligent and more conscientious about things. Ronnell was a great person, but school wasn't really his thing. Ron was just a complete idiot who wanted to be a thug but was way too much of a pussy to be one.

This was also when we began to meet other people who would influence us as individuals and when football began to be a major factor in my life. Classes at FJH were different. I had a math teacher named Mrs. McDonald. She was actually the grandmother of singer Michael McDonald of the legendary Doobie Brothers rock band. I also met a girl who would remain, even to this day, one of my closest friends. Her name was Michele Henke. She lived in old-town Ferguson in a house that was one of the original homes in Ferguson. It backed up to two landmarks of the community. One was Gasen's Drugstore, and the other was Mimi's Subway Bar. Her mother, Mary, was a teacher at St. John and James Catholic Church and School. Her mother was a wonderful woman. I use the term *was* because she died on my birthday in 2004. That was the end of a true era. Michele's father, on the other hand, was a son of a bitch of the first order. He was a drunk who abused his wife and daughters sometimes sexually but mostly physically and mentally. Michele and I would become close, probably because we had similar situations.

The other person who I would meet and ultimately gravitate to was a man named Bill Quigley. Bill was the junior high head football coach, and PE teacher. Bill was a very intimidating person. He demanded respect from people, and when he did not get it, he would let you know. When he did called roll for his class, you had to answer "Here, sir," or he would not acknowledge you even being there. Q, as I have always called him, was the motivating factor for me becoming a coach. I never realized how much of an influence he was not only on me but on a great many of my friends. Q was as hard as nails when it came to the game, even a little sadistic. He would always show us little tricks of the games to do after the play was over. It was like that scene in *The Longest Yard* with Burt Reynolds, where they are instructing the team on the use of brass knuckles and how to break an arm or a leg while tackling someone. Q always called it giving a guy the business. The one thing he taught me and every guy that ever played for him was a caring and total dedication to the game. When you won, you celebrated, and when you lost, you cried. That is how you learned about the game and how to have feeling about it all. Bill instilled a sense of pride and loyalty in every player that ever had the privilege of playing for him. He never wanted to hear about how good you thought you were. His whole thought process was "you show me, and I will believe it when I see it."

He loved all his players, even the ones he would rip on a daily basis. And boy, could he rip a kid. And when I talk about the sadistic side, I remember we had player named Sam Dew. Now Sam was a great guy that weighed about 105 pounds. He had a lot of heart but not a great deal of ability when it came to football, but he tried hard. Well, we had a machine called the blaster. It was an upright stand that had six pads on it that swung open like doors on an old saloon. The only difference was that you could adjust the tension on those pads so that it would add resistance when you ran through the machine, and Q would turn that tension up so that if you didn't hit that shoot with enough force and keep your legs driving, you would either get kicked back, or worse, you would get hung up between the pads.

Well, this was about to be a bad day for Sam. Sam started toward that blaster this day with all the intention of getting through it. Unfortunately for Sam, it was not going to happen, and the worst happened, and he got hung up in there with his feet off the ground. He looked as though he was being tortured. That was about the same time that Q looked at me and said, "Parker, get him out of there." I said, "How do you want me to do that?" He said, "Knock him out." So I got a healthy head of steam up and started toward Sam. I then placed my helmet in the center of his back at full speed because if I did not, I would be the next guy hung up in that predicament. Well, Sam went flying out of the blaster as I made contact. He was hurt, but he wasn't injured, which meant he would be back again the next day. I remember the feeling of making contact with Sam, and the satisfaction of being able to knock the utter shit out him was a feeling that I knew I was going to love for a very long time. There were no hard feelings ever between me and Sam about the day. In fact, Sam and I became great friends. To this day, Bill Quigley and I are very good friends. I even asked him to join my staff one time. He declined, but I would have loved having him work with me to build a team.

This was also a time in my life where I would experience the love of a girl for the first time. I mentioned Michele Henke earlier. You have to understand that up until this point in my life, I was

Good Time Charlie. I had a great time in school, in sports, and yes, I noticed girls, but the fact was that I never believed that they noticed me. I was a good guy but one of the funny ones who was trying to hide the fact that he/she was an awkward kid. People will say different, but I have never believed that I was ever a major ladies man or, as they would say back in the day, a "player." I could always have a conversation with just about anybody, about anything at anytime.

I met Michele for the first time in the seventh grade. She was one of seven children with four older brothers. She was a lot like me, as I said. She had a wonderful mother, like me. She had an abusive father, like me. She dreamed of a better life for herself, like me, and she was willing to go out and get it the best way she knew how. When you come from situations like that, you look for ways out or for someone to rescue you from it. Like me, she was a poor kid but didn't really know it. We all thought because we had roofs over our head that everything was OK, but the truth was that both of our parents shielded us from those things to allow us to try and be kids. We have gravitated to each other since we were thirteen years old, but when the freshman year of high school rolled around, all that changed, and little did I know, it was going to change for the rest of my life.

During the freshman year, football went great. You play a limited schedule of six games. That year, I caught seven touchdown passes for Q. Basketball came around, and although I was a starter and played basketball all through high school, it was never really a love of mine. I did it because I was an athlete, and athletes love competition. Tom Bolche was my coach, and he was a good guy. When that was over, I started track with Coach Joe Hunt. Joe was a man who would joke with all the kids all the time. He was a good coach who knew how to get the most out of all his players. Just like in football, we knew what had to be done, and we got it done. This time, we had a new addition to our team. His name was Nolan Morgan. Nolan was a kid who lived on the Freguson-Kinloch border on Dade Avenue. Nolan and I first met on the baseball fields of Ferguson. He played in an age-group above mine until I decided to move up. We competed against each other in basketball also. We fought hard against each other, but we were always very caring and respectful of each other off the field. Kind of like Magic Johnson and Isaiah Thomas.

Going back to Michele. Sometime around the middle of my freshman year, I found myself hanging out with a couple of new people. John Snead, Brian Burroughs, and David Poenicke were three guys I met at FJH. We would run around Ferguson on Friday nights. Occasionally, we would go and place toilet paper around someone's house and things like this. Many times while running around, we found ourselves running into the usual crew of girls, which consisted of Susan Hughes, Cindy Thompson, Kim Ferrante, Debbie Schneider, and Michele. While everybody was hanging out laughing, Michele and I would always focus our attention on each other. Finally, one day, we decided to be vocal about our feelings for each other. That was good, and in a way, it was bad. I remember the first time I kissed her. I had no idea what I was doing or even how to do it. Not sure if she was all that knowledgeable about what she was doing. I do remember feeling something that I had never felt before in my life. Not sure if it was my heart pounding in my chest or the erection that was pressing against my Levi's 501s. Either way, I knew right then and there that my life would never be the same, and that Michele Henke would be a major part of my life forever.

Our relationship blossomed, and people can call it puppy love or having a crush on each other. You can laugh about it, as many people did have who knew us then, but the truth is you just know when something is more than a passing deal. Thirty years later, we are still as close as we were when we were kids, probably even closer, even though we both have lives and kids of our own now. The relationship blossomed for quite some time. You also need to realize that there was something else different about this relationship. Michele was a white girl from Ferguson, and I was a black kid from Berkeley. This was the late seventies, and although segregation was over, this was probably not the most popular and accepting thing to do. We were blazing a trail that not many people were happy about. The same people that were our so-called friends were the same people who would not stand beside us. I really didn't give a damn what anybody thought, but that is who I am. I never gave a shit about what anybody thought. I loved her, and that was the only thing that mattered. We would sneak away to see each other as often as we could. This was all that we had and it was tough, but it was enough. That was until her father found out about us.

I got a call from her one day, and she said that we could not see each other anymore. I understood why, but at the same time, I didn't understand. Her friends cornered me one day thereafter and told me that her father, when he found out about us, beat the shit out of her and made it clear that "she would not be seen with any niggers." He was a drunk who took pleasure in abusing his family, and as much as I loved her at that time, I had to let her go. I would not allow her to be abused because of me or a relationship with me. I loved her too much for that to happen. For the next thirty some odd years, I loved her and have always been her friend from afar, because that was all I could do.

FJH helped lay a foundation for me as a coach and as a person. The relationships I developed there with the teachers and my friends, some of which I still have today, have gotten me through some really tough times in my life. This also was a great boost that projected me into a brand-new world. The world of McCluer Senior High School.

CHAPTER SEVEN

Calamity is the perfect glass wherein we truly see and know ourselves.

—William Davenant

LIFESTYLE CHANGES

McCLUER SENIOR HIGH School was erected in the late fifties. Up until then, all kids in Ferguson attended Ferguson High School. The city of Florissant, which sits to the north of Ferguson, did not really exist yet, so there was no need for a high school out there yet, and the ones that lived really far out went to Hazelwood High School. Even after McCluer was built and old Ferguson High became Ferguson Junior High, McCluer played their home football games on the football field at the old high school. McCluer grew very rapidly. By the late 1960s, the school had over five thousand students in it. This made for some very good athletic teams as you had a huge number of potential players to select from. In 1968, the Missouri High School Athletic Association created a Missouri State Championship play-off system. It consisted of a number of play-off games, ending with a championship game. McCluer won both the 1968 and 1969 state championship games. The head coach at the time was a man named Bob Johnson. Bob had actually been the head coach at the old high school since about 1950. When the new high school was built, it was only natural that he became the head coach.

McCluer was a huge campus in comparison to other large high schools in the St. Louis area. It was a combination of five separate buildings tagged as M1-M5, with the center point being a gathering point called the triangle. This was where everybody who was anybody hung out before class began and during the lunch periods. Every morning, I would get to the triangle as early as possible so that I could see Michele. Even though at this point in time there was nothing more than a good friendship between us, I would still get there just so I could see her. Jimmy and Bill were still huge factors in my life, but as happens in everybody's life, you meet new people when you go to high school. It didn't separate us but gave us an opportunity to bring more people into our circle.

About this time, I became very close with John Snead. Now you want to talk about two totally different people. John and I were a complete odd couple. John was the son of Brad and Jo Snead. They were a middle-class white family from Ferguson, straight out of a Norman Rockwell painting. Brad was a retired army officer, and Jo was a substitute teacher and housewife. There were two sets of Snead kids. There was Martha, who was just a sweet girl. I could never understand why Martha never got married. There were a lot of guys out there who could do significantly worse than hitching up with her. John was next followed by Sarah, who I considered one of the most beautiful girls I had ever laid eyes on. My mother thought the sun rose and set on Sarah and could never understand why I never made a play for her. It was because of the relationship I had with John and his entire family. It was something I never wanted to ever screw up.

Getting back to the family. The second half consisted of David. A very smart guy who was at one time a college career student. Then there was Kate. I remember when she was little, when she was bad, Mama Jo (as I called her) would give her a swat on the butt and send her to her bed. When she was in high school, Kate would make banana bread every Christmas, these little loaves of bread. I would always come over to the house, and whenever I would leave, Jo and Kate would always bag up at least a dozen loaves of bread. It was so good that only a half dozen of those would make it home. They always found that amusing.

Kate grew up, and I mean really grew up. I saw her at Christmas one year after she had graduated from college, and boy oh boy. The same little girl who used to make me banana bread had baked herself into a beautiful, sexy woman. I actually had a hard time trying not to look at her. Finally, the last one was Andrew, the rooster as I always called him. He was the typical Snead. Blond hair, blue eyes, pretty, smart, straitlaced. At least he was when he was young. Let's just say we all develop bad habits as we get older.

Even with all my longtime friendships with Jimmy and Bill, the Snead family and their household was my second refuge in a very unstable period in my life. At this point in time, my own house was in a shambles. My father, whom I could hardly stand to be in the same room with, was not only abusive to his family, he was also a man of infidelity. He had been having an affair with a woman named Lorraine for quite some time. Ironically, she lived in my old baseball coach's house, Ron Fozzard. My father was the kind of guy who would go out for smokes and come back hours later. I remember on Christmas, he never even came home on Christmas Eve because he was out all night. The next morning, there was nothing under the tree. My brother Mike had begun working as a printer for a company and was making very good money. He knew how much I wanted to play football and try and build up my body, so he bought me a weight bench and some weights so that I could work out. My dad showed up in the morning at about eight. Neither me, my brother, nor my mother said a word to him. We just sat at the kitchen table staring at the bowls of cereal we were eating. I could see the total disgust on my mother's face.

My father was the kind of guy who would come in and sit down and then make an attempt to make everybody feel sorry for him. He would start sniveling and crying out loud as if he was so pitiful that you had to feel sorry for him. I guess that was the beginning of my black-and-white attitude about things. Either they are one way or they are the other. There has never really been a great deal of gray area with me, and even at fifteen or sixteen years of age, I had little use for excuses. Not to mention right after he put on this pathetic performance, he got his coat on and walked right out the door. I assumed right back to Lorraine.

My mother was a very tolerant woman who would put up with almost anything to keep her family together. She considered leaving him when I was about in the seventh or eighth grade but changed her mind at the last minute. On this occasion, the situation was going to change. He told her that he would be at work during the day, and by this time, my mother had retired from Gonterman and Associates. She was now an administrator at Emerson Electric Company in North County. She decided to take the day off and follow him to verify her suspicions. She was successful, finding him at Lorraine's home. That evening, he came home and tried to say that Lorraine was someone else's girl and he was trying to work out a problem between them. It was not going to work this time. She told him it was done. He tried to plead his case, but my mother was not hearing it. She went on with her daily life, but behind the scenes, she was already planning her departure. Everything was going normally until the day my mother walked into the house and said to me, "I am leaving now, this is your house, you can stay, or you can go with me now, either way, I am leaving now." She had already secured an apartment in Ferguson and was ready to go right now. Right then I had a decision to make, and I made it. In a matter of about thirty minutes, we had packed our things and left. I ran up the street two houses and got my friend Brian Bacott. Told him what the situation was, and without any questions, he got his truck and loaded my mom's things and my things into the truck, and away we went. One thing about John and Brian was that they were very loyal.

Mom and I moved to the Mason Deville apartments in Ferguson. It wasn't exactly paradise, but it gave her a sense of peace. It was a two-bedroom, one-bathroom, and second-story apartment. The rent was $185.00 a month. I had my own room and my own closet, which was something I never had, but my mother and I didn't have much else. She took two forks, two knives, and two spoons. The same for plates and glasses, also one pot and one skillet. I took my bed and frame and my dresser. My mother took an old mattress and put it on the floor and an old chest from the garage. It wasn't much, but it was now home. I forgot. We had no furniture. Only a big wing-back chair and a thirteen-inch black-and-white television. We had nothing, to speak of. Most of my friends didn't even know this was going on. Jimmy and Bill didn't even know. One day, we were living in Berkeley. The next day, we were living in an apartment in Ferguson.

During this time, John and I had gotten to be very close. His father and mother always welcomed me into their home with open arms. I even began to call them Mom and Dad. John and I hung out all the time. If I was not at home, I was at John's. He was a very straitlaced guy. That was not to say that he could not have a good time, but John was a brain. I mean, National Honor Society type. He went to Georgia Tech University on an engineering scholarship. When we were in junior high, I hated math, mostly because I was never any good at it. Not to say I was not an intelligent person, but I believe math is the reason God created calculators. When it came to algebra, you may as well have been trying to teach me Chinese in Italian. I stunk at it, but I was resourceful enough to find a way to pass a course that I knew long ago I was never going to use. So I paid John about a buck every two days to do my algebra. It would take me hours to do that shit, and I knew I would remember nothing about it. It would take him about five to ten minutes. I would have it all correct and handed it on time.

Now I know what you are thinking: "What would you do when it was test time?" Well, I told you I was a good salesman. That was the time that I sold my teacher of the lame excuse of test anxiety and that I would always freak out when it was time to take an exam. She bought it, and understood. Boy, was I good. When it was time for geometry, I found that it was easy. I learned about geometry by shooting pool. I have forgotten most of it now, but back then, I could remember nothing but angles.

The impeding separation of my parents was volatile. My father was not the kind of person who accepted rejection very easily, even when it was his own fault. It was his doing that they were apart. My father cheated on my mother for years on end. There was always a Lorraine somewhere in my father's life. Something on the side that kept him somewhat excited about life. My mother was all about responsibility and loyalty. She was about hard work and accomplishment. Discipline was her foundation. My father was Good Time Charlie. He had a group of old friends whom he used to party with back in the day. My mother had a good time, but she always knew when to come home. My father, on the other hand, drank like a fish and smoked like a chimney.

When we first left, things were not too bad. He would call and bother her, but he was never violent. But the longer she stayed gone, the more he began to realize that she was not coming back, and the violence escalated. One time, he came over and slashed all the tires on her car. He would wait for her in the parking lot when she came home from work. He would follow her. In these times, it would be called stalking, but back in the day, you could get away with it.

I really didn't have anybody to talk to at this time. The love of my life, Michele, had pretty much left me behind. We would occasionally run into each other, but she had fallen in love with a complete asshole named Terry Shannon. Terry was the son of the longtime director of athletics at McCluer High School, Ed Shannon. He was your typical little white boy with a complex. He was a short, weasel-looking guy with a Napoleon complex. He thought he could rule over her with an iron fist. He even brainwashed her into graduating early from McCluer and leaving her friends. She was so in love with him that she was willing to change her entire educational plan to try and be with him. Later in life, I realized that she was doing what she needed to do to get out of her home life. We still talk about it today, and she tries to deny it, but she knows the truth deep down although she always gives that ridiculous excuse about having nothing to stay there for, or some bullshit like that. She left to be with a guy. I know it is the truth because she hates it when I call her on it. We had been in love with each other since we were fourteen years old, and other than me, Terry was the only other person that she would give herself to totally. She knew it, I knew it, and worst of all, Terry knew it, and he never failed to make me aware of his disdain for me. One time, when we were about seventeen, he gave her strict orders that she was not to have any contact with me whatsoever. The shitty thing was, she abided by these orders, which I could not believe.

Michele was a Henke. You have to understand what that means. These were some of the most stubborn, obstinate, and flat-assed tough people on the face of the planet. Her older brother Joe, whom I worked with when I was an assistant coach at McCluer when I first started coaching, was cliff diving on the Missouri River one year. He dove off a cliff and into about four feet of water and broke his neck and survived. He was actually the valedictorian of his class and gave his speech from the hospital bed. Henkes were tough, and I always believed that Michele was the toughest. She had to be if she was going to take the chance of having as close a friendship with a black kid from the other side of the tracks, full well knowing what her family, mainly her brothers and her dad, would do if and when they found out. When she made a decision to run off in college, chasing after a guy, I knew something in her had changed. Especially this guy. What a waste, but I never gave up on her.

Anyway, with my mother, there was a sense of relief finally, but it was long from being over. My father would continually harass my mother and me. There were times that I was at the end of my rope. At that point in time, I would turn to the Sneads or to Pete and Donna Gallagher. I spoke earlier about Pete, but as I got older, it became more of a brotherly relationship. Pete and I would hang out, mostly with his friends. I learned a great deal from him and his gang. There was Glen Merhoff, the South County toe sucker. Mike Stroot, Bob Huntze, and Rick Pilgrim just to name a few. They were all old Berkeley boys. There was one guy named Bill Nolan and his wife, Jean. Jean was a gorgeous woman with a fantastic body. I remember crashing one of Pete and Donna's famous yard parties when I was about ten years old. Pete had one of the only round "Dough Boy" type above-ground swimming pools left in North County. I remember looking in that pool and seeing Jean floating across the pool with two wineglasses, with wine in them, sitting on her tits. That was one of the most amazing things I had ever seen in my ten years of life, and it was pretty exciting to many people there, as they all started cheering.

Escaping to Pete's or John's was easy and very comfortable to me. I have no doubt that on occasion, I was the houseguest that would not leave, but I think they realized that I was always on the verge of losing my mind because of my own home life, and they allowed me to stay around as long as I wanted. I can remember John and me running around until eleven at night and then just standing in his kitchen shooting the shit until I would go home. Whenever I would walk in the apartment, my mom would just ask me if I had been at John's and I would say yes. She would then just go on back to sleep. She realized that the stability of the Snead house was what I needed. She was working hard at trying to pull herself up after leaving my father after thirty years of marriage, and believe me, I use the term *marriage* very loosely. It was very tough on her. She put up with a great deal of shit for a very long time partly because of us and partly because she has always had this obligatory need to want to take care of someone. Now she was finally free, but at the same time, she was truly on her own. Well, not really. She still had me for what it was worth.

Things at McCluer went about as they should in high school. After Michele, there was no love interest, mostly because I knew nobody was ever going to measure up to her and the feelings that I have always had. I buried myself in athletics. Football, basketball, track, and baseball during the summer. By the time my junior year rolled around, I dropped baseball, and although I still played basketball and ran track, I began to focus all my efforts on football. My mother allowed me to do that also. I was not a very big player. When you are five feet eleven inches tall and weigh less than 150 pounds, you had better be able to run. That is one thing I could always do and do well. You also have to understand that school was never a huge priority for me. High school was never about really knowing anything. It was more about great memorization of facts. Now I am not saying that I was dumb, but I always felt that I had better things to do with my day than sit in a bunch of classes, half of which I was never going to use. I did what I had to do in order to get what I needed to get out of them. I studied when I felt like I needed to, but you were never going to find me in some library somewhere, with my face in a stack of books on a Friday night. I learned how to play the game, which is really what life is all about: one big game that you have to learn how to play.

Junior year wrapped up. I was now living in a small apartment instead of a house with a pool. My father was still occasionally harassing my mother although at this point she had begun dating a man from her church. His name was Millard Johnson. I first met him when I was about nine years old. He was a deacon at her church. He was from Robertson. It was an all-black community adjacent to the cities of Berkeley and Hazelwood in St. Louis County. The fact that my mother was dating was infuriating to my father. It was a sense that this was truly over. When they finally divorced, it was total closure. My father went through some type of depression, always threatening to kill himself, running around looking for sympathy from anybody who would listen. Truth was, he had burned so many bridges with the way he treated my mother for all those years that nobody wanted to hear his crap. He was now reaping what he had sown for years.

JOHN STEPHEN PARKER

CHAPTER EIGHT

*Most of us readily take things for granted that at an earlier
time remained to be discovered.*

—Robert A. Dahl

BEGINNING OF THE END

I WAS DETERMINED to make my last year at McCluer
a great one. Michele had run off to the University of
Missouri, chasing after Terry Shannon, so I was again with no real
girl in my life. There was Melissa Horvath. She was a freshman
girl who had just come up. That was a change at McCluer now.
The junior high had become a middle school, and they moved
the ninth grade up to the high school, which made it even more
crowded.

Melissa was more of a little sister than she was a girlfriend. She
was fun to hang out with, and I spent a great deal of time at her
house with her family, but there was never going to be a long-term
relationship with us. There were always girls in my life. Debbie
Schneider, Susan Hughes were two who have always been in my
life since junior high. To this day, we are still close. Angie Qualls
and Cheryl Nowlin were also good friends of mine. I found out
much later in life that Cheryl had always had a thing for me.
That was funny to hear. I was always actually more attracted to

Angie because she had the crazy, wild thought processes of John Parker. We also had the same misunderstood personalities. Lots of people thought Angie was promiscuous. You know how people, especially young people, can be catty about things. I think it stems from jealousy more than anything. Angie was a cool, popular lady who was real. To this day, Angie and I are great friends, and we will forever have each other's back.

I concentrated on football. It was now my senior year. I had never been to a school dance, a homecoming dance, or any type of school function like that. As far as I was concerned, homecoming was over when the football game was over. I concentrated on athletics and trying to graduate. Although Michele had gone on to Mizzou, she was still very much on my mind every day, but for some reasons, things began changing for me. I was no longer the skinny little kid. I was growing up, and girls were beginning to notice me. Well, not to say they were not before, but now it was obvious. Pretty much overnight, I became the "man" when it came to women, and although there had not been any steadies, there were a great deal of hookups but not defined in the same way it is today.

I noticed this girl who played in the band and was also a women's basketball player. Her name was Susan Walters. Little did I know that for the next six to seven years, this woman would be a major part of my life. Susan was one of three children. Her father, Harold, was a Boy Scout leader. John Snead was actually in his troop. Susan and I got to be good friends and then much more. The first time her father met me, he shook my hand and said hello. He was Mr. Friendly. That was the last time it ever happened. Once he realized Susan and I were romantically and emotionally involved, he never really spoke to me again. You

JOHN STEPHEN PARKER

have to understand that Susan's family was very well-off. They lived in an affluent section of North County, between Ferguson and Florissant, called Calverton Park. There were absolutely no black people in Calverton Park. The first black to move into the neighborhood was Vernon Mitchell, the principal at Berkeley High School, and that was not until the mid-1990s. So when Harold saw his only little princess hook up with the black football player from across the other side of the tracks, he was not happy at all.

Judith, her mother, was a nice lady and a great cook. She was a cook at this small eatery in old-town Ferguson. She was a bit more accepting of me although that could have been alcohol induced. You see, Judith was an alcoholic. She could drink wine with the best of them. She would fix these great meals and drink the whole time she was cooking. By the time dinner would roll around, everybody would eat, and she would pass out at the dinner table. She was also very codependent on Harold. She had a degree, but when it was time to go out into the real world, she said "Hang on." The real world, in my opinion, was real scary for her. Fortunately for her, she met a man who said "Hang on, you don't have to go." From then on, she has been well taken care of. Susan came very close to slipping into this same rut and becoming codependent.

Football was primarily the focus. I was not the greatest student in the world, but I wanted to go to college. By this time, my mother and father were divorced. Mom and I were settled in the apartment, and she was working at Emerson Electric. I knew if I did not have a great senior season, it would be difficult to get any scholarship looks. I trained hard prior the season. This was probably when the whole discipline and attitude adjustments were made within my own constitution. I was determined to not only put McCluer High School on the map, but to also be sure that I got enough publicity that colleges would give me offers.

One of my coaches whom I had the utmost respect for was Norris Stevenson. Norris was the first black football player at the University of Missouri, and he was drafted by the Dallas Cowboys. He was a professor and the head track-and-field coach at Florissant Valley Community College. He came on board as an assistant at McCluer during my senior year. What a great staff addition. He was our defensive coordinator. How he selected people for positions on defense was as simple as I have ever seen. If you were over 235 pounds, you were automatically a defensive lineman. Anybody from 185 to 225 pounds were linebackers, and when he selected the secondary, he said, "I need the four guys who would run the 4 × 100 meter relay on the track team." Well, that put me, Nolan Morgan, Bill Furch, and Kevin Lowell in the defensive secondary. Kevin was the only junior in the secondary and the sole white boy. We used to call him the pale rider because he would always tackle you from the back by jumping on your back and riding you down to the ground.

We opened up that year against the archenemy, McCluer North. In the early seventies, McCluer had some five thousand students in it. At that point, it was evaluated that a new high school was needed. So some two miles away, they built McCluer North High School, home of the North Stars. It was a modern high school, which resembled a shopping mall. Open hallways, larger classrooms, state of the art, and with it came an elitist attitude with anybody who went there, as if they were somehow better than the original. There was not a more heated rivalry in the state of Missouri than the McCluer Comets versus the

McCluer North Stars. And I mean we hated each other. Our players, our coaches, our parents all hated each other. When we played each other in anything, especially football and basketball, both the Florissant Police and the St. Louis County Police would line the sidelines, fully expecting an all-out brawl to break out at some point.

When it was announced that we would open up the senior season against the North Stars, we knew we better be ready, and we better bring our A game. I trained harder that summer than I ever trained in my life. Not only because I wanted a scholarship, but also because there was a loudmouthed prick on their team by the name of Vernon Whitlock whom I was hoping I would get at least one shot at during the game. We worked out at the same gym in the summer, and he was running his mouth about how great he was and how he was going to run for 150 yards against us. I was determined not to let that happen. Every time I saw him, he had something else to say. It got old but was great motivation.

We opened up Labor Day weekend that year. In those days, you played at 1:00 p.m. on Saturday afternoons. Not many of the stadiums we played in had lights. You were only guaranteed of two night games every other year. Ritinour High School had lights, and Riverview Gardens High School, better known as the View, had lights. They had lights at Berkeley High School but were unable to use them because when they expanded the Lambert-St. Louis Airport, the football field now backed up to Runway two west, and the lights from the football field interfered with the lights from runway and confused pilots that were landing commercial jets. In later years, those early-season 1:00 p.m. games were moved to 10:00 a.m. because it was hot and some kids became pussies and didn't want to play if it was too hot. They even made it a state law that you had to take water breaks. Hell, Bill Quigley just told us, "When you get thirsty, move your tongue around in your mouth long enough and you will create enough spit to quench your thirst," and that was what we did. Somehow, over time, video games and mothers have turned kids, mainly boys, into the biggest generation of pussy-pansy bastards I have ever seen. In those days, Bill Quigley, Bob Johnson, Mike Ballard, Mike Mueller, Sam Hastings, and Norris Stevenson were not having it.

We marched into our stadium that Saturday afternoon, with me, Nolan, Keith Word, and John Bredenkamp leading the way. Mike Ballard was our head coach. Mike had one leg because he had the other one removed because of cancer. He was a tough son of a bitch who had one of the hottest wives around. Diana Ballard was unbelievably beautiful. She died some years later in a plane crash. If there was an injury on the field, Mike would walk up to you and look you right in the face and say "Get up, nobody cares, nobody gives a shit about you being hurt, and we don't have time for it." If you continued to lie there, he would yell, "Move it up ten yards" so that we could continue to practice while you lay there. Hard-core guy, but when you got to know him, he was a great guy.

Mike came up to me before the game and said, "We are throwing you the ball on the first play of the game. There is no pressure, but if you drop it, I promise you will never touch the ball again this season." Now I didn't feel any pressure. Bill Quigley used to tell me that "pressure is something that you feel when you don't know what you are doing." I felt no pressure. I was a very good receiver. My hands were then and are still as soft as a baby's ass. I was scared of not touching the ball the rest of the season because I knew Coach Ballard was a man of his word.

Harry Linnenbom was our quarterback. Harry was a strange bird who always thought he was a better athlete than he really was. He was one of those guys who never really fit in at high school. As tough as it was to be a kid in general, it was probably tougher on Harry. He was a trashy poor white kid who lived behind the cement factory in Ferguson. He tried hanging out with the cool kids, but nobody would ever let him in their circle. Funny that the starting quarterback couldn't fit in, but Harry never could. He really had some psychological problems also. One day, he came to practice drunk on his ass. I never did understand that. Mike Ballard's practices were hard enough. I could never imagine trying to go through one intoxicated. Guess it all came to a head one day about five years later when Harry stuck a gun in his mouth and finally became part of the ultimate "cool kids club."

That day was something out of a Hollywood movie. We took the ball on our own twenty-three yard line. Harry called the play, and I remember it like it was yesterday. The play was slot I right angel pass, on 2. Harry asked me, "You ready?" I told him, "I'll let you know from the end zone. Just put it out there and let me run for it." The ball snapped, and I started on an out cut and then turned up the field. Mike Mueller was the defensive coordinator for McCluer North because they had passed him over for the head coaching position at McCluer. Later, he would become the head coach at McCluer and take a team to the state championship game. When I turned up the field, I heard Mike screaming, "There goes Parker, there goes Parker," but his screams were too late. Harry had already laid the ball up for what would be a seventy-seven-yard touchdown pass on the very first play of the game. That was the beginning of the end for North that day. The final score was 19-3. I had two TD receptions that day, and Bill had one. We held Vernon Whitlock to a minus thirteen-yards rushing and sacked their quarterback seven times. More importantly, I was on my way to the college scholarship I badly needed, as I was named St. Louis Post Dispatch Player of the Week.

That would happen a couple of other times that year, with wins over Ritneour, Hazelwood West, and Pattonville. The life-changing game for me was the night game against Riverview Gardens. Going into the game, we were both undefeated at 5-0. They were a team of mostly hard-core black kids for the north side of St. Louis in an area called Castle Point. The rivalry went back to the late sixties when Bob Johnson was the coach at McCluer and Gerry Nordman was the head coach at the View. These two guys very much hated each other but very much respected one another also. McCluer won the first two state championships in '68 and '69 respectively, but during the '69 season, there was a controversial 2-0 win over Riverview Gardens that propelled McCluer into the state play-offs and left a very bad taste in the mouth of Coach Nordman, and he never let any McCluer team that ever played in Rams Stadium forget it. Coach Nordman would do things like turn up the heat full blast in the visiting team's locker room so that you were forced to sit outside where the crowd would walk by and heckle you and cause problems.

The View was full of athletic talent every year, but they were much undisciplined both on and off the field. They would have great athletes, but one day, they would get into a fight and get suspended or skip a class or do something stupid that would render them ineligible for a game or two. We knew our hands were full. They had a running back named William Peoples. He could run like a scalded dog. He ended up going to Drake University to play. They had a linebacker named Hank Berry. The kids called him Big Bank Hank after the famed lead singer of the rap group the Sugar Hill Gang. Hank went to Missouri on a full ride. Ben Broadnax was their talented running quarterback. Johnnell Moore was a great outside linebacker. They were loaded with talent. Well, something happened in that game just before halftime. I got hit after making a catch, and somehow, everything went numb, and the lights went out for a while. When I woke up, Mike Ballard was standing over me, telling me not to try and move. They were sending an ambulance to take me away, all against my persistent pleadings that I was OK and this was not necessary. They took me away in a neck brace just before the half. My father and mother followed closely behind in his car. After the doctor did his diagnosis and released me, I returned to Rams Stadium.

The third quarter was about halfway over when, out of the dark corner of the stadium, I came running through the back of the end zone. I remember the crowd going completely nuts. There is nothing in the world like the sound of twenty thousand people screaming your name and cheering you on to do well. It becomes so emotional that you don't want to let those people down.

When I ran back through that crowd, all I could think of was "Make a statement now." So the first thing that needed to be done was I needed a big catch. Two plays later, Harry laid one right down the middle of the field for me for a sixty-five-yard TD. All the pain in my neck was gone immediately with that catch. Although we went on to lose that night, 28-21, I had secured what was to become a future in football at the collegiate level. More importantly, I taught myself that no matter how hard you get hit, you always get up and you continue to get up. As you continue to read this, it is clear how this has always been a foundation of my philosophy for life, and something I have tried to instill in not only my own children but in the thousand of players that I have had the pleasure to influence in my career and in my life.

The season ended, and I was selected for both the all-conference and all-STL metro teams. I was waiting on the all-state selections to come out because I would be assured a scholarship if my name was on that list. The list came out, and my name was on it, but unfortunately, I was listed as a third team selection. I was devastated and disappointed beyond belief. I believed at the time that my chances of going to college were pretty much null and void. Funny though, I began working out and running even harder then. Basketball season rolled around and with a whole different set of people. Truman Gilbert was the head coach. He was kind of a reject from the sixties, with a Beatles haircut. He never played basketball. He was actually the manager for the same team that Pete Gallagher, Bob Huntze, and that crew played for at Berkeley High School back in the mid-1960s.

Now I would never say that in order to coach, you had to have played the game. There are many coaches in many different sports that have never played at either the college or professional level but are great coaches. Unfortunately, Coach Gilbert was not one of those guys. He tried his ass off though. He also didn't have the greatest talent in the world. My junior year, I knew it was going to be a bad season when on the first game of the year we came out for warm-ups and Tony Russo tripped over his warm-up suit and fell in front of the home crowd. Senior year was better. We had graduated Doug Clark, or Box Head as everybody called him because he had an unbelievably square head. Jeff Burroughs also graduated, along with Tom Blake. I used to run around with these guys and occasionally still see Tom. Both Doug and Jeff married their high school sweethearts. I could only imagine doing that. It would have been a dream of mine to marry Michele Henke. Unfortunately, that was not going to happen. She had gone to Mizzou now to be with Terry.

That basketball season had some characters. The most prominent, besides me was a guy named David Lewis. David was a transferee from Little Rock, Arkansas. He came up at the end of our freshman year. He was an unbelievable basketball player. He was one of those players that when you played with him, he just naturally made you a better player. When we made it up to McCluer, he automatically went to the varsity team. The head coach of that team was a guy named Larry Jacob. He was an old redneck coach who had that Adolph Rupp, Kentucky mentality. He never liked black people, never wanted to be around them if he had a choice. He lived in a house right behind Ferguson Junior High School. When Ed Shannon retired as Director of Athletics, the job was passed down to Larry. If you were a black athlete at McCluer, it meant that at some time or another, Larry Jacob would make an attempt to try and screw you, and let's just say he hated me more than most. He had a son named Kurt. Kurt was, in his mind, the second coming of Larry Bird. He wanted to go to Indiana State University, just like Bird did, and really believed he had the skills to do so. Reality is a cruel thing sometimes. These are the facts. Kurt had a set shot, not a jump shot. Not good! He was about six feet six, but his vertical jump pretty much only allowed him the ability to jump over a credit card, *a flat credit card*, and unfortunately for him, he caught mononucleosis his senior year and missed about half the season. None of these add up to an NCAA Division I scholarship opportunity. Let's just say that Kurt and I never really got along at all. He always had this elitist attitude, as if he was somehow better than everybody. Truth was, he was an average athlete who thought he was better than he was. He had a couple of little butt buddies that would always run around smelling his ass too. Mike Johnston and Jeff Atchison were his little cheerleaders, especially Atchison. If Kurt would have stopped on the dime, Jeff's face would have gone about two feet up Kurt's ass.

Now I will tell you why Larry really hated me. He had a real cocky asshole for a son, but then there was Kristy, his daughter. She was about three years younger than me, and man, was she beautiful. She used to baby-sit for Pete and Donna when I was a kid. Kristy and I had a short-term thing, but it was just enough to infuriate Larry Jacob. To imagine that his little princess of a daughter might be doing the horizontal cha-cha with one of the most arrogant, rule-breaking niggers in North County drove him up the wall. He would often let me know just how much it drove him crazy.

He looked for clauses in his infinite set of double standard rules to keep me and every other black athlete from participating in athletics. Once I had to attend my cousin Brian's funeral and missed the entire day of school on the same day we had a game. Well, the rule was that if you missed school on the day of a game, you were prohibited from playing that night. I made it back for the game on the same day of the funeral and was warming up when Coach Rupp—I mean, Coach Jacob—walked up to me on the court and said, "You know you are not playing tonight, right?" and I said, "Why not?"

"Because you were not in school today."

I told him, "You should check your rules if you are going to enforce them."

The rule stated that if it was an unexcused absence, I would not be allowed to play. I quickly let him know what the rule stated. His response was, "Well, I don't excuse you," and my very swift and arrogant comment was, "Last I checked you don't have the authority to excuse or not excuse me. I believe that falls on the principal."

Now I had a great relationship with Wayne Fields. He was the head principal, but he had three assistants who all pretty much hated me, but I knew if I talk to Mr. Fields, he would excuse me. We both walked over and explained both of our sides to Mr. Fields. Afterward, he rendered his verdict on the spot. He said, "I do believe we can treat a funeral as an excused absence. Get on the floor and have a good game." The look on Larry's face was as though someone had just slammed his dick in a car door. He was pissed. It made him even more pissed when, as I walked away, I said, "Tell Kristy I said hi!" That made him even madder.

Getting back to basketball, Truman Gilbert was like a boyscout. He never cussed or allowed any of us to cuss. If you did, you had to run like a dog until you were almost dead. The shitty thing is he made you do it before practice ever started. Obviously, David and I were the clowns of the program, and we were always pulling pranks. David once stole everybody's underwear while we were taking a shower. It was kind of funny to come back and find that your underwear was missing and to watch some guys just say in their minds, "Fuck it, I'm going Rambo." There was always that one guy who had no sense of humor and, on this occasion, ran and told Coach that someone had stolen his underwear. I don't know too many people who would do that because personally, if someone wanted my underwear that bad, they could have them. Coach came into the locker room half laughing and half pissed off about it. He said, "Whoever has the underwear, please give them back." David handed them back out, but with great descriptions such as "Hey, Tony, you had the white ones with the skid mark, right?"

We were always pulling stunts like that to be sure that this team never got too full of themselves. We had this thing that when we played on the road, we would always see just how much stuff we could bring back with us. I mean, if it was not nailed down, it was coming with us when we left. We would always say "The Lord giveth and the Comets taketh away." Well, anyone who has ever done this knows that when you play an away game, they always put you in a minor sports dressing room. Well, that was an open invitation for us. Once, when we played at Parkway West, not only did we win the game, but when we left, we had shoes, T-shirts, equipment, and just about anything else we wanted. That was great, except on this occasion, their athletic director called McCluer to say that some things were missing. Well, by the time practice had rolled around, it made it all the way up the chain to both Coach Gilbert and Coach Rupp, I mean Jacob. Jacob demanded that Gilbert suspend all the players who had anything to do with it, "especially those nigger kids 'cause you know all of them stole something." We were all caught, but nobody snitched on anybody. We were all called individually and asked "Did you take anything?" Our standard answer was "No, but I know who did." "Will you tell us who?" "No, I can't do that." Gilbert loved us for sticking by each other, and obviously, Jacob hated the whole scenario. Wayne Fields suspended the team from the Wentzville tournament, and it was over. Hell, we didn't want to play in the damn thing anyway.

Things were developing between Susan Walters and me. We were actually a real item, and very public. Her mother tried to be supportive, and her dad just completely hated the idea of his little princess seeing some nigger boy from the other side of the tracks. Back in the day, you had clubs for teenagers to hang out at that played great music and served no alcohol whatsoever. That was not to say we didn't drink. I drank a lot, or what I considered a lot on the weekend. I always had the cardinal rule that I never drank during football season, and that lasted all the way through my college years, but after football was over, I would drink shoe polish if it tasted good. I was what you would consider a "social drinker." I would drink one to two beers a night on the weekend and hold on to the third. I was never an alcoholic. I always believed that you are not an alcoholic until you go to the meetings and you are sitting in a room with everybody that has no last name. You know, "Hi, my name is Bob and I am an alcoholic," and everybody else in the room looks at you and says, "Hi, Bob."

We would hang out at a teenage club called Animal House, referring to the fraternity movie starring the late John Belushi. It was down on South Hanley Road, just south of Highway 40. The only way to get there was to drive the fourteen miles down Hanley Road where there were more speed traps than you could count. Susan was a beautiful girl. Tall, thin, with a very proportioned body and what you would call child-bearing hips. We would hang out with Kevin Lowell and his slew of girlfriends on Saturday night. There was never anything more than heavy petting in the beginning. We kissed a lot, but as far as having sex, well, we thought about it but never did anything until we graduated. I watched her play basketball, and she watched me. We would hang out together. I was really not welcomed or comfortable in her house, so she spent a great deal of time with me at the apartment with me and Mom.

My mom really liked her, Pete and Donna really liked her, and those were really the only validations I was looking for. She was a wonderful girl. She was very much aware of my deep feelings for Michele. Michele always insinuated that she was with me to make her jealous because they had had some kind of competition thing for Terry at one time. Not sure if that was true or it was being said to create some type of conflict in my mind. Susan didn't care about that. She loved me, and for the first time since Michele, I was really in love with someone else. People say that when you are young, you don't know what love is, but that is unfair. I have always believed that when you feel so strongly about someone that you are willing to completely lay it on the line for them, and I mean mind, body, and soul, then who is it for anybody else to say that you are not in love?

I found the year was racing by. I would also find myself looking back over the years and seasons of the past, and was thinking that this would all be over soon. We would all move on to very uncertain futures. Some to the military, some to college, some straight to the workforce. You go through your childhood, and you meet so many people, and you just assume they will be around forever. David Poenicke was one of those. David was killed one night when he was hit by a drunk driver. David was my friend, and I loved him. It is a strange thing to lose someone that close to you. Even today, I miss him very much. That, along with many others, made growing up very surreal at times. You think when you are going through those moments that life is over for you as you know it, but it is also in those moments when you really find out who you truly are and what kind of psychological foundation you really have. Little did I know that in the coming years I would be tested beyond belief, and that on numerous occasions I would come to a crossroads in my own life, not knowing whether to take the easy way or to experience the road that was less traveled.

I still had not made any decisions on my future, and the school year was half over. I was getting a bit nervous. Then one day, a man named Charlie Coe walked into my life. Charlie was the former head football coach at Normandy High School, but now, he was an assistant at Ball State University in Muncie, Indiana. It was part of the Indiana Big Four, referring to the four Division I football teams in the state: Notre Dame, Purdue, Indiana, and Ball State. Charlie showed up at school one day and was watching film on my season in Coach Ballard's office. Charlie was a black man from St. Louis. A Vashon High School graduate, his background was in baseball but he went into football also. Charlie, over the years, had and still has a great reputation as a relentless recruiter. He told me that he wanted me to fly up to Muncie and talk to the head coach. His name was Dwight Wallace. I agreed but tried to be cool about it. I was excited because there had not been much attention given to me because my name was not high enough on the all-state list. I got on the phone and told my mom immediately, and she was excited for me. I found Susan as fast as I could and told her. She jumped me and kissed me in joy. I called Michele at Mizzou and let her know. She was also very happy for me although she had her own turmoil. Her and Terry, the guy she had graduated early for to be with, had broken up. I knew, but I was never going to let her know I knew. I was never into the "I told you so" stuff, and she did not need me to throw it in her face. She was hurting, and I loved her too much to let her know I already knew about the two of them. To this day, I have never told her I knew, but I assume if she ever reads this, she will know then. The only other people I told were Pete and Donna Gallagher, who at this time had a two-year-old addition to their family by the name of Caroline Devlin Gallagher. She had flaming red hair and, even as a baby, had a certain disposition about her. Not a bad one, but one that meant she would never settle for anything less. Not sure how the red hair came into play either. We all joked that there was a redheaded mailman in the neighborhood, and he was obviously doing more that sticking it in the box, if you know what I mean. Pete and Donna were my second family who had watched me grow up. If I had a game, a problem, needed a place to stay, or anything else, I knew I could count on Pete to be there.

I flew up to Muncie. The first leg of the trip was from St. Louis to Chicago Midway Airport. Now back in the day, when you flew into Midway, the flight route always brought you in very low and across the Lake Michigan side. It was one of the scariest flights I had ever taken, but nothing compared to the second leg of the journey. When you landed at Midway, you had a two-hour layover before your next flight. The terminal was more like a cargo warehouse. I don't remember there being any heat, and this is January in Chicago. If you have the choice of having anything to survive in the dead of winter in Chicago, your first choice would have to be heat. As I said, the first leg was very frightening, but when they called for the boarding of the next leg, I would never have believed what pulled up to the terminal. It was a four-seat twin-engine prop from Britt Airways. This was nothing more than a flying casket. It also had four seats, one pilot no heat. The only thing that came to mind was I knew exactly how Buddy Holly and Richie Valens, two singers from the fifties, must have felt. This thing started up, and it had the same sound as a Sherman Tank that had not been started since the end of World War II. One of the engines actually had to be hand-started because they couldn't get a spark for the engine to start by key. By the time they got this crop duster started, I wanted to get off and take up badminton and see if I could get a scholarship in that.

Charlie Coe met me at the Muncie Municipal Airport. This airport had all the modernization of Kitty Hawk, North Carolina, in the late 1800s. I thought Orville and Wilbur would be walking by me sooner or later. Charlie picked me up and took me to Lafollette Hall where I spent the night with Dominique Galloway and Jeff Burn. Dominique went by Dom the Bomb. He was a short, fat defensive back from some little town in Ohio. He couldn't play a lick but thought he could. His roommate Jeff Burns—they called him Reality—he was a real good player.

These two took me to a party on Friday night. Now I had been to parties before, but nothing like this. First off, we didn't even leave to go until around 11:00 p.m. When we got there, there were not many people there, but by 1:00 a.m., the house was packed wall-to-wall with people. It was then that I realized that football players on the campus of Ball State University were absolute gods. I mean, when we were in the room, people would part the area to let us move where we wanted to. The other thing was that women were automatically drawn to you. I mean, if they knew you played football, you got rock-star treatment. You could get these girls to do just about anything. Dom had girls that would clean his room, wash his car, type his papers, and anything else that he wanted, and I do mean anything. They would sleep with you, and I use the term *sleep* very loosely. They were groupies that wanted nothing more than be in the cool-kids club, and the cool kids were the football players. When those guys introduced me, I became Mr. Man-About-Town instantly. Girls wanted to dance with me and find out where I was from and if I was coming to Muncie. By the end of the night, I mean, 4:00 a.m. when the party ended, I found myself drunk in a room with three women, whose only interest was to see how many times they could get me hard enough to satisfy them. I was young, dumb, and full of, well, you get what I mean.

I knew where I was going. I had visited Oklahoma the same weekend with Brian Bosworth, the infamous linebacker who turned bad actor. I also visited Michigan State with their famous running back Lorenzo White. Offers never came from either of those universities, and I really liked Muncie. It was far enough from home that I would not need to run back and forth but also close enough that if something happened, I could get home in a reasonable time if I needed to. It was the place for me to be.

I returned home after the visit with the commitment made to attend Ball State University. I had the weight of the world lifted off my shoulders. All I had to do was finish the year. Things with Susan and I were heating up big time. Basketball was going great. The only thing that was in major turmoil was my family life. My father had become threatening to my mother on a more regular basis. He would still often stalk her after work. He would often sit outside our apartment, waiting for her or me to come home just so he could be more harassing. He attacked her one time while I was in the car. He even chased us to church one morning until I turned around and drove to the police station, only to have them do nothing because at one time he was a "on the job", but at this time he was no longer a police officer, and because they had what they called a blue bond, they refused to do anything. That went on constantly for a number of years. That was also one of the reasons I chose to go to the school where he did. I didn't have much of a support system for my brothers and sister. Tony was in the army, in Korea. Felice was living in Chicago, where she had been since she graduated from college. Mike was actually living with my father, but he had his own life and was not willing to get involved in the situation with my mother and my father. In my opinion, they all pretty much stuck their heads in the sand and tried to avoid all involvement. This left me, at seventeen years old, pretty much having to deal with the entire situation myself.

It became unbelievably stressful for both me and my mother. Over a six-month period, I watched her lose almost thirty pounds because of the situation. She didn't have much of a support system either. Many of her friends were their mutual friends and also chose to avoid the situation. So it was, for the most part, her and I against the world. When I tell you that she is an extraordinary woman, I truly mean that. We all have heroes in life. My mother, Barbara, is truly my hero. She left the man whom she was married to for nearly thirty years with nothing. When I read these stories of women who are afraid to leave a bad situation because they don't know what they will do, I have very little sympathy. The fact of the matter is, if you really want to get out of the situation, you will do whatever you have to do to get out of that situation. My mother chose to do exactly that. She chose to do whatever she needed to do to be safe and to have peace of mind about her own life.

Senior year was coming to an end. In the back of my mind, I also knew that my relationship with Susan was about to go through a change also. She was going off to Bradley University. And I would be neighboring in Indiana. I was not a very good guy about the ending. In fact, I was much of a gutless prick. More so, I was very much afraid of the future at that point in time. I had no idea what lay waiting for me and what changes were in store for me in my own life. Because I didn't know, I desperately tried to hang on to the friends and relationships that I had at the time. Susan was one of those relationships. There was never really a closure to the relationship when we went to college. And I guess I wanted it that way. I wanted to be sure that there was the possibility of an open door if at some time I wanted to come back.

JOHN STEPHEN PARKER

CHAPTER NINE

The most difficult thing is the decision to act, the rest is merely tenacity. The fears are paper tigers. You can do anything you decide to do. You can act to change and control your life; and the procedure, the process is its own reward.

—Amelia Earhart

SEE YA LATER, HELLO FUTURE

THE SCHOOL YEAR wrapped up with a huge graduation party at John Crone's house. I remember drinking so much that night that I couldn't see straight. I kissed a lot of girls that night, many of which, even if you gave me $1 million today, I could not remember their names. I remember a bunch of us fooling around at the pool area when somebody broke a beer bottle on the deck of the pool. David Wilhelm fell down in the glass and cut his arm pretty bad. We took him to the hospital to get him stitched up, but sad to say, that cut was not the only diagnosis made that night. Later in the week, we found out that Dave had leukemia. It's ironic that it took something as minor as a cut to find out that he only had about nine months to live. Sometimes, life is not very fair. Time and fate actually caught up with Dave much faster than we expected. Dave died later that summer. That night was a finale that we all knew was coming.

For myself, Jimmy, Bill, and John, it was the beginning of a temporary hold on our friendships. We were all going in separate directions and probably would not have any contact for the next six months. That was going to be the strange part. We had all spent endless hours together. We shared the wins and losses, both on and off the field. We shared gains and losses in each other's love life, school life, and home life. We were full of life and had the world by the tail. We had no idea where our futures would take us. We were listening to Jackson Browne, the words from the song "Running on Empty":

> Looking out at the road I really spent my wheels. I don't know how to tell you just how crazy this life feels. I look around for the friends that I use to turn to, to pull me through. Looking into their eyes, I see them running too. Running on Empty, Running Dry, Running into the sun, but I'm running behind.

Little did we know and realize that this was the last time we would be pulling practical jokes, cruising around the local fast-food restaurants, cheering on the hockey team in the freezing Dellwood Ice Arena, or waiting with anticipation for the yearly battle with McCluer North. When the reality of all this sunk in during the summer, there were some really sad moments. I knew that Muncie, Indiana, was going to open my eyes to a completely different world. I was secure in my world in North County. I had my friends, I had Pete and Donna, and now Caroline. I had my brother Mike, and of course, I had my mom. If there was a place

JOHN STEPHEN PARKER

where I could have actually gone to college and played football, I probably would have never left, but I knew I needed to go out and somehow find out who and what I was. I would never have found any of those out if I had stayed at home. I knew that I needed new people in my life. I knew I needed to develop new relationships. I had not really experienced major loss in my life yet. Of course, not having a healthy relationship with my father was a major loss and, really, the only major loss I had experienced. I never really realized what I was missing until l really needed the help and perspective of a fatherly figure. Of course I had Pete and my mom's new friend, and I was very appreciative of both, but I have friends who had great relationships with their fathers, and I was very envious of those. Jimmy, Bill, and John all had outstanding relationships with their fathers. With me not having that, it left a huge empty feeling. I guess that is why I am so animate about my time with my son, Jordan. I want to teach him all he needs to be a man and him not to turn out like the sorry son of a bitch his grandfather, my father, was.

I went through the summer training like a madman in order to prepare myself for the world of college football. I ran more miles and lifted more weights that summer than I think I did my entire career. Mainly because I had no idea whom I would be competing for and competing against. By the end of the summer, I was in the best shape of my life. Now it was time for the going-away party. I was determined to have the blowout bash of the summer. My father, who at this time was a little bit less of an asshole, decided to let me have the house and pool for the party. We had about four hundred people show up, and me, being the future politician and the salesman that I am, invited all the neighbors so that I knew they would not be calling the police. Some of the things that happened at that party, most people would get arrested for. I remember Steve Sims and another guy had some young lady in the corner of the pool, engaging in some deviant sex act for the display of all my entire guests. By 3:00 a.m., we had gone through our fifth keg of beer, and there were still 250 people there. My own guest list became quite interesting. Not only did Susan come to the party, but Michelle actually came home from Mizzou to say good-bye. I thought there would be some tension there, but it wasn't at all. Susan left about 11:30 p.m., after which Michelle was all over me for the next two days before I left. All I can say is, it's good to be the king. After spending that time with her, she got my mind right for me. It was not about sex as Michele and I were never intimate sexually. There was something always a bit deeper between us than anything we could have experienced sexually. We could talk for hours. I left for Muncie very soon thereafter.

The drive was quiet. Mike drove me up with Mom. Back in those days, the NCAA would let teams bring in their freshman class three days earlier than the returning upperclassmen. This was done so that we can get used to the practice style before the older guys would come in and beat the shit out of us. It also gave us a chance to get to know each other and a chance for the coaches to get to know the freshman class.

Our freshman class was a group of very interesting young men. One of the ones that stand out in my mind was Avis Hines, who was a strong safety from Louisville, Kentucky. Not a real talkative guy, but Avis had the ability to knock the cowboy shit out of you. There was Tony Anderson, who was from Gary, Indiana. Obviously, we know what famous pop star is from Gary, Indiana, and Tony did his best to imitate him, all the way down to the parachute pants and jheri curl. Ricky George was from Dayton,

Ohio. Ricky may have been one of the best wide receivers that I have ever seen. He stood about six feet one at about 185 pounds, and he could run like the wind. Ricky was eventually drafted by the Dallas Cowboys, and I believe he played about two seasons in the NFL. Of course, my roommate Robert Smith. Everybody called him Dunk, although I had not known the reason why. Dunk was a short, kind of pudgy fullback who was *not* overly fast but had pretty good power when he was running the ball. The one thing you remember about Dunk was that he got a 4 on the ACT. The funny thing about that was that if you sign your name and answer *B* to every question, you will get a least a 7. My only guess was that he must have misspelled his name.

Life in Muncie was great. We arrived early, about three weeks before the rest of the student body arrived. They kept the entire team in the oldest dorm on campus before school started, and naturally, all the freshman were housed on the third floor. Did I mention that this dorm had no air-conditioning whatsoever so you naturally were going to sweat your ass off? None of us had enough sense to bring a fan, so this was total torture. Naturally, they put me and Dunk in the same room just because we were both from the same place. There were a few things I remember about staying in this place. One was the heat. The second was of the coaches trying to be friendly to the freshman players. All the other guys fell for this ploy, but I knew there was something coming down the pike that was going to change all the fluffiness that the staff was sending out. Sure enough, I was right. What was coming down was the return of the upperclassmen. When those guys got back, the freshmen became lower than whale shit.

The first practice with the upperclassmen was a complete change of pace. The first thing we had was a fitness test, which I knew I was going to pass, but I could tell that some of the rookies and a great deal of the upperclassmen were never going to be able to pass. These were some of the biggest guys I had ever seen. We had one of the largest offensive lines in college football, averaging about 310 pounds across the front. When the standards were set for the test, you could just tell who never had a chance of meeting those. The penalty for not hitting the mark was "dawn patrol" every day for a week. Dawn patrol was when Coach Wallace came to your room at 3:00 a.m. to wake you up, and he would say, "Get a jacket because it is kind of cold outside." He would then take you outside and place you in front of his car and tell you to start running, and he would slowly drive behind you. You would eventually run around the entire city of Muncie. Thank God the city was not very big. Muncie has tripled in size since I left, and I would hate to have to run around the city now. You could probably die.

I enjoyed my time at Ball State. We were the gods of the gridiron. Everywhere we went, people got out of our way. We had privileges that no other student on campus had. On the first day of class, we could walk into the bookstore, and while all the other students were basically praying and hoping that they could find the proper books for class, the books for all the football players who were on scholarship were stacked up for each individual player for each class. All we had to do was pick them up. Here is the best part: the books were ours to keep. We never had to give them back, and we could sell them if we wanted. I would always stand outside the bookstore and sell mine for a dollar less than they had them inside. Even then, I knew how to undercut the system in order to get what I needed. The other thing that I figured out was that sex was very easy to get if you were an athlete.

I lived in Lafollette Hall, which was referred to as the Ghetto. It was a high-rise coed dormitory that placed men and women on alternating floors in the dorm. This made it very easy to have contact with the girls. Once they found out that you played football, they were on you like stink on shit, and you literally had to beat them off with a stick. They would do anything for you. To this day, I have never typed a paper because I had the choice of twelve to fifteen different women who would do it for me at the drop of a hat. There were a few that I can remember that were especially unique. Dawn, from Goshen, Indiana. I don't know whatever happened to her, but she was wonderful. She would let me drive her car when I needed to run errands. She was really put together also.

Since I was in college, I have always been lucky with my attraction to women. I have never really had a bad-looking hookup. The girls that I got together with were all very attractive. Dawn, Angie (volleyball player), Christie (ended up becoming a nurse), and at least a dozen others, which I can't remember today for the life of me, were all great and great looking. Through all this, two people were always on my mind. Michele was at Mizzou, now in her second year. Everything had fizzled out between her and that asshole boyfriend of hers, and she was finally enjoying life a bit more. The relationship between Susan and I had never gotten any closure. Mainly because I was a complete horse's ass before I left for school. I took the child's way out and just stopped calling her and stopped returning her calls. I left for school and never spoke to her, mostly because I have a hard time saying good-bye to anyone, or anything, which is probably the reason why people who come into my life have a tendency to stay for a long time. To this day, Michele and I talk at least once every couple of weeks, and Susan and I call each other on our birthdays.

I called Susan that spring, and I could hear her crying on the other end of the line. She was dating a guy named Glen, she appeared to be happy, but had never gotten any closure between us either. We stayed in touch but decided it was best to just stay friends at this point. We had gone to prom together our senior year and made a statement. We were one of the first interracial couples to ever attend the prom, and that was something in 1983. We had history that not many people understood.

It was about this same time that I started wavering on Ball State, Muncie, and of all things, football in general. I had serious self-doubt going on. It didn't help that my mother was in hell at home with my father still harassing her all the time. They were finally divorced, and my mother was dating Millard Johnson. Millard was what you referred to as good people. He worked in a rock quarry for over thirty years. He was a hardworking guy who tried to always do the right things. He was a dedicated husband and father and a deacon at the church. He was not a highly educated man, sometimes naive. He had gotten taken for a ride by his first wife, whom he eventually divorced. His son, Ricky, was an army recruiter, and ironically, he got my brother Tony to sign up for the army.

When Millard came into my mother's life after thirty years of a horrible marriage, I could not be happier, but then my father became the jealous-boyfriend type. Stalking Mom and hassling her. I being away from here, knowing that all the crap that was happening made me crazy. I made a decision to go back to Missouri and be closer to her. Now I was a fairly heavily recruited football player out of high school. One school that stayed with me, even while I was at Ball State, was Missouri Valley College in Marshall, Missouri. There was also another benefit to transferring there. It was going to put me closer to Michele, who would be right down the road at Mizzou in Columbia. Little did I know I would meet a new special person who would make me feel brand new.

CHAPTER TEN

The common people have no history: persecuted by the present, they cannot think of preserving the memory of the past.

—Jean Henri Fabre

FUN AT THE VALLEY

I ARRIVED AT Missouri Valley College, and I found a school that had a grand total of 510 students, over half of which were athletes. The school itself had a very loose atmosphere. How loose, you ask? Well, let's just say I lived in MacDonald Hall on the west side of campus. The greatest thing about Mac Hall was it was coed, but with a twist. There were no resident assistants in the dorm, so you were free to run the dorm all night with women all over the building. Now let's remember, I was 6'0" tall, about 195 pounds, with about 3 percent body fat. I looked really good then, and I was in the best shape of my life. Not to mention I was new on campus, so every girl on campus wanted a piece of me, and boy, was I willing to even up the slices. Karree Karnes walked into my room one morning at about 3:00 a.m. She was a cheerleader, and I had met her the day I arrived on campus. She was a very "in shape" girl with huge breasts. I mean, like a 44 DD. When she came in my room that night, she was more than happy to let me measure those things. Funny thing was I had no ruler or tape measure.

There were many episodes like that during my first few weeks at Missouri Valley. I met Tanya Blanding during my first couple of weeks also. She was a cute little black girl who just thought the sun rose and set on my ass. She loved my sense of humor, which was usually very sarcastic. We used to laugh and hang out together all the time. Occasionally we would get together and study, which usually turned out to be us sucking face within the first hour we were together. We never really put a certified label on our relationship, and eventually, it faded.

Fall season started, and I was introduced to some strange characters. My new roommate was a guy name Charlie Henke. He was of no relation to Michele. Charlie was a career student. When I met him, he had already been in school for about three years. He would always start the semester but end up dropping his classes before the end of the semester. He was a basketball player. We had a great time. We would party all the time, except I was always the one who was a bit more responsible when it came to academics. Charlie would party but then turn around and sleep all day. We really never had any money. We would do whatever we needed to do to get money. We used to go to the blood bank in Columbia and sell the plasma from our blood for fifteen dollars a pint. That really sucked because I was paranoid of needles. Just could not stand having someone stick me every week for a few bucks, so we had to find an alternative to this moneymaking venture.

One night, Charlie came in and said, "Let's take a ride." I said no problem. We drove about twenty-five miles out of town where he had found a pretty large pot field. That was the biggest one I had ever seen. They were known to have these in random places throughout the rural areas of Missouri. We had managed to find a very large one. This was an opportunity to make a bunch of quick, easy money. We came prepared. We brought a couple of hay cycles and began chopping down as much pot as we could in a three-hour period. We had to do this in the middle of night, but it had to be done before the sun began coming up. We managed to cut down about fifty square yards of the plant. We loaded it in trash bags and in the bed of Charlie's pickup truck and hauled it back to our room.

Charlie and I had hundreds of pounds of illegal drugs on the floor of our room, and we knew that at anytime the police could knock on our door, and we would be going away for a very long time. This would not be just a possession charge. This would have been a distribution charge of the highest magnitude. We locked ourselves in our room for about four days and began stripping the leaves off the plants and bagging them up. We had Chris Ann Gonder, who was this beautiful girl who was from Marshall, bring us food. She was a great girl who was built like a brick house. We used to get together occasionally when she just wanted to screw around. We always referred to it as recreational sex. There was never any obligation to each other. She used to stop by my room sometimes when she was a bit intoxicated, and she was there for only one reason, and we both knew the reason.

Charlie and I were in that room for four straight days. By the time we were done, we had bagged up seven hundred ziplock plastic bags of pot and stored them in the drop ceiling of our room. We left them there for about a month to be sure that they were all dried up before we made them available for sale. I could not believe that. Of all the things I had done in my life that were

JOHN STEPHEN PARKER

very against the law, I had never dealt drugs. I had seen the effects of drugs on my friends and family, and I have never been a fan of drugs. I never used drugs as a kid growing up. My brothers and sister smoked pot, but I was always of the athletic mind and tried never to do anything that was going to damage my body, but when the opportunity came to make a great deal of extra cash distributing a product that we knew people were going to want, it was too easy not to do this business for a while. So we went into the sales and distribution of marijuana. The only difference between me and other drug dealers was that I knew that this was going to end, and I never was going to make a lifestyle out of this venture. When the pot ran out, I knew the business was over. So we sold it as long and as far as we could and made plenty of money to eat, party, and take a trip here and there whenever we wanted. Life was pretty good for us, and we never got caught.

When the other players reported to practice that fall, I was surprised by their abilities. At Ball State, I was surrounded by some of the finest athletes I had ever seen. When I arrived at MVC, there was a New Jersey pipeline of players headed up by Jeff Todd and Charlie Renner. There were a mess of farm kids from all over the Midwest, most of whom had no intentions of graduating but only going to school for a while before eventually going back to the family farm, regardless of how close they were to graduation. The most interesting guy I met was a guy named Tony Walker. He was king of the hill when I arrived on campus. Tony was a huge steroid monster of a running back. Most of the guys in the Tau Kappa Epsilon fraternity house were pretty much afraid of him because of his freakish size. Tony could pretty much have as much ass on campus he wanted. Problem was, he hung with some of the ugliest women I had ever seen. All except one, which I will talk about later. She was a real treat. In fact, I was crazy about her then, and pretty much still am.

Life at the Valley was pretty normal. I went to class, hung out with the other players, hooked up with a couple of chicks here and there. Everything was pretty standard college stuff, except, even with everything going well, I was feeling very empty inside. I did meet an incredibly wonderful girl name Jill Huey. She was very sweet and very nice. She was from Excelsior Springs, Missouri. We hung out all the time. She was dating a guy named Denny Marker, who was in school at Mizzou. Whenever I went down to visit Jimmy or Michele, I would give her a ride so her and Denny could spend time together. I was crazy about her but knew it would never work at that time. She was from a small town, where people would probably not understand her and me in a relationship. I would have loved it, but Jill was an angel, and there was no possible way I could prepare her for the scrutiny that she would have to endure if she were in a relationship with me. I always kept Jill in my heart and hoped that one day things might be different for both of us. She ended up marrying Denny and having a couple of kids with him. They were divorced later, and she married again and had a couple more kids. She is still living in Excelsior Springs. She is a schoolteacher now, and I bet, just knowing how she was then, that she is probably damn good at it. I always wondered if she would be happy in her life and always kept her close to my heart. In a different time, Jill could have been Mrs. John Parker. Sounds funny, but you never know what kind of game love will play with your life.

I really didn't have a lot of true friends in my life. Jimmy and Bill were at other schools. All my past flings were back in Muncie, and we had ended our relationship over the summer. John Snead was at Georgia Tech and in ROTC. I received a phone call one day, and I had gotten some disturbing news from Columbia, Missouri. Michele and I were talking about every couple of weeks, mainly to stay in touch and see what was going on in each other's lives. One evening, she called me to tell me the most crushing news ever. She told me she was engaged. His name was Dan Hearst. He was from St. Charles, Missouri. This changed my entire outlook on college, football, and life in general. Everything that I had focused my life on was now disrupted in one phone call. The person whom I had been in love with since I was fourteen years old was going to walk down the aisle with someone else. Let me explain something: I am not and have never been a very secure person. When I get attached to something, I stay that way for a very long time.

Michele and I had a great deal in common. We were both raised with very violent fathers. We both had fathers who were child molesters. We both were dying to get away from our childhood situations and both desperately looking for that one person. We always knew that eventually, we would end up together. When we separated as teenagers, we still kept in touch all the time but didn't see each other as often as we wanted. I guess at some time her thoughts of me faded, but my feelings and love were undying. Not many people have understood our relationship, and it never bothered me at all. They were not supposed to understand it. Ours was a unique relationship to say the least.

The news of her engagement shook the foundation that I lived on. I was completely lost for a time and did not know what I would do if she was not in my life, and even worse was the thought of her making love to another man. Oh yea, if I neglected to say, Michele and I had never slept together. Honestly, there had never been an opportunity for us to. I knew in my head that I had to get closer to her. I had to find a way to see her and to make myself more accessible to her. Well, I decided to transfer schools one more time. I was going to be a Missouri Tiger. I would make the transfer to the University of Missouri-Columbia and make every attempt to get her back.

CHAPTER ELEVEN

I do not feel obliged to believe that the same God who has endowed us with sense, reason, and intellect has intended us to forgo their use.

—William Falconer

SUMMER OF FUN

THAT SUMMER, I was hanging out with Steve Simms. Steve was a brother who was the lead singer of a rock band that used to play at Animal House on the weekend. He had a lot of friends in the music industry. He was dating a woman named Jennifer Beck. Well, you can probably guess where this was going. Jennifer had a friend who was single, and we all ended up going out a couple of times. Her name was Jackie Gould. They were private school girls who had attended Duchene High School in St. Charles, Missouri.

I was immediately attracted to Jackie. She was a very eclectically mixed woman. She had purple hair. This was during the era of Prince and the Revolution, who later became just the symbol. Jackie was a great girl who loved to hang out and wanted to have sex all the time. This was also the summer that my mother got remarried to Millard. I was changing schools again. I was wandering in my own self-support. I didn't really know where

I was fitting in. Jackie came into my life and kind of gave me security in a nonsecure moment. Although I was making all my plans to go to Mizzou, I still hung out with her all the time.

Jackie and I were together all summer. We spent every day and every night with each other. Her parents were also not very happy about the situation. She came from a very Catholic family. They were also very prejudiced. Jackie didn't give a shit. One thing about her, she was a free spirit. She had her own way of thinking. She was a very eclectic, nonconforming woman. She was living at home, which sometimes made it difficult on our relationship. I have no idea why I started the relationship with her. I guess I was very much in need of knowing that someone actually cared about me and would lay it on the line for me. My mother had gotten remarried, my psychotic father was seeing a real gold-digging bitch named Gloria, Mike had his own life, as did Tony and Felice. When most of my friends had very close families, I was not as lucky. Growing up we were close, but as we got older, things changed. We all had different interests. Jackie came along in my life when I had nobody, and I will always be grateful to her for that.

Jimmy and I were going to live together at Mizzou. We had another guy living with us by the name of Steve Farrier. Steve later went on to become a state trooper in Missouri and actually runs the post in St. Charles County. We made plans to move into University Place Apartments. Back in the day, these were the old Tiger Towers where most of the wild people lived. Since Jimmy and I had known each other since third grade, it made it easy. I was very excited about the idea of moving to Columbia although school was not a major factor in my thought process. Frankly, education was never a major factor in my thought process. I always knew I would graduate from college. It is really not that hard. With the exception of philosophy, school is never about what you really know. It is more about what you can remember. My memory skills have always been very good. As both a player and a coach, I have always had the ability to remember to the smallest detail of any situation. Nobody could ever beat me in a trivia contest, especially when it came to music trivia.

That was truly a summer of fun. Jimmy and I were running crazy with Steve Simms. We were running around partying all the time. When we were not hanging out, Jackie and I were enjoying each other. Although I was having more fun than one man is entitled to, I had a huge vacancy in my heart. The woman that I loved and had been in love with for a very long time, and who was in love with me, was going to marry another man. Michele and I understood each other very well. This happened mostly because we had the same upbringing. She left high school early because she had to get away from the life she was living in Ferguson. Terry was her way out. Although she probably did love him, she knew it was her way to a new life. She gave herself to him fully and found herself in a very controlling relationship. She rode it as long as she could, and I was happy for that, and for her. Although it was crushing me to know that she was with him, I knew that she was doing what she had to do for her own peace of mind.

Getting back to Michele and back in her life was my number one priority. I was willing to do whatever was necessary to do so. I kept up my workouts all the time because I knew at some point I was going back to football. I had planned to join the team at Missouri. Steve Miller and the former head football coach at Hazelwood Central High School had come on board at Mizzou, under Head Coach Warren Powers. Steve had great players at

Central: Michael Scott, Lee and Mario Johnson, and the great Tony Van Zant.

Tony was a running back and was a *Parade* Magazine all-American player of the year. He went to Missouri and was expected to be the Second Coming of Christ. They made the mistake of putting the entire weight and success of a program on the shoulders of an eighteen-year-old kid. The only thing they could not control was the injury factor. The summer prior to his arrival at Mizzou, he was the feature player in the Missouri Lions All-Star Game in Jefferson City, Missouri. On his third carry of the game, he cut right and blew out the ACL on his knee. From then, he was never the same, and his career at Mizzou was pretty much over. He never really played very much at Mizzou, and he went through a coaching change from Woody Widenhoffer to Bob Stull, neither of which was successful in Columbia. I felt bad for the kid because all he wanted to do was play college football. Instead, he ended up barely graduating. He got a chance though. He is giving back to a game that gave him an opportunity to get an education. He is a high school football coach outside the city of Detroit.

The summer was winding down. We had begun to pull everything together for the big move to Columbia. Both Jimmy and I rode up together with our mothers, and we moved into Apartment 515 in the University Place Apartments. I had no idea what I was getting into. All I knew was I was going back to be around someone that meant more to me than life. I knew the opportunity would be there again for me to try and regain something that I had lost. The only thing I didn't know was if I had the guts to actually take the bull by the horns and really go for what I really truly wanted.

JOHN STEPHEN PARKER

We started at Mizzou in August of that year. I was excited. Jimmy knew the lay of the land a bit better than me, having lived there for two years prior to my arrival. I was finally close to my soul mate, and I could not wait to see her. She was living off campus and had to make arrangements to see me.

The first time we saw each other was at her place. It was kind of awkward at first because you have to remember that she was engaged to be married, so it was important that we not necessarily cross any lines right now. We were just happy for the moment to be in each other's company. Not sure how the guy she was going to marry felt about us getting together, but neither one of us cared about that. We had been separated from each other for a very long time, and nothing else mattered but this one moment.

I never told Michele, but I was still involved in a relationship with Jackie. Although she was still in St. Louis, I would make the trip home on the weekends and see her. I started class at Mizzou but never really felt like I fit in there. I was a football player but was ineligible to play because of the transfer status. So all I could do was work out, go to class, and hang out. Although I was closer to Michele, we really didn't get much of a chance to spend time together. Jackie had started classes at Southwest Missouri State University, in Springfield, Missouri. That campus was known for having some of the most beautiful girls in the state. Guys used to say that any girl that was rated a 10 in St. Louis would be rated a 4 at SMSU. I once went down to visit Jackie, and I found the rating system to be absolutely accurate. We saw each other quite a bit, and I found that we were very much alike. We were both kind of in a limbo as far as our lives were. I knew I had the junior blues. I just was not interested in going to school anymore.

The transition to MU had not really worked out. The search to get back involved in Michele's life had definitely not worked out the way I had hoped. She was planning a wedding that was a year away, and I was disappointed that she would not just drop everything for me. It all came to a head one night when she came to my apartment. She walked in looking better than any woman had a right to. I can remember it like it was yesterday. She had on jeans, a black V-necked sweater with a white lacy shirt that was sticking out over the top. We sat on the couch and had a couple of glasses of wine and talked for a few hours. Sometime afterward, we moved to my bedroom, and as I lay on my bed while she sat next to me. I remember knowing that this was my chance to lay it all on the line and tell her everything. If I did that, the ball would be in her court to make any decisions about us. For some reason, after all the time I had been longing to be with her and wanting her back in my life, I, who has never been at a loss for words in my entire life, could not find the words to tell her that I was in love with her and wanted her to break off the engagement. Instead, I sat there and let the moment slip away. Soon she leaned over, kissed me and got up and left. I knew right then that I would probably never get another opportunity like that. I had let something, this person whom I had been in love with since I was fourteen years old and had consumed my every thought for many years, simply kiss me and walk away without any fight from me. Believe me, it was much harder for me to just let that happen as it is to now write it down. One thing is for sure, I would never have that opportunity again.

I was like a fish out of water in Columbia. Jimmy was much more comfortable because he had spent two previous years there, but I was not adjusting very well. Jackie had already quit SMSU

JOHN STEPHEN PARKER

and was heading back home. Maybe that was why we got so close. I knew I was being forced to put Michele out of my life although I knew I never really would, and Jackie was floundering the same way. All we really had was each other. During the week I was going to class and hanging out at Déjà Vu, one of the bars in Columbia where all the football players used to hang out at. Myself, Eddie Essen, Jimmy, John Clay, Santio Barbosa, and John Redd. These guys would come over to the apartment and drink beer with Jimmy and me. Then we would all head to downtown Columbia. Again, we were in the cool kids club. The sea would part when we walked into the bar. The locals all hated us, and the girls all wanted us. Jimmy and I were leaving the bar one night, and two girls flagged us down. Lisa Chrisco and Laura Mangelsdorff were part of a group of girls, which very inappropriately nicknamed themselves the Nasty Girls, taking after the song that was made popular by the girls group Vanity 6.

Lisa was from Eureka, Missouri, and she pinned me the first time we ever met. I don't know how it happened, but we became two peas in a pod immediately. We all hung out a bunch. We were constantly having parties at our apartment. Jimmy and I used to make mixed tapes to play at our parties. When we knew it was going to be a "belly rubbing" party, we would make mixed tapes with nothing but slow jams. Luther Vandross, Alexander O'Neal, and Freddie Jackson were just a few of the artists that we put on tape. People used to say that if you could not get laid while Luther Vandross was playing, then you just couldn't laid. Jimmy and I would have girls at our place, and it ended up being a free-for-all. We had separate bedrooms, and as you guessed, mine was the one with more traffic. Jackie never visited me. I would go home on the weekends and see her, but during the week, I had heavy traffic in University Place. I was having fun, and school was not on the priority list. Eventually, with Michele being out of my life and not having much interest in school, I finished the semester and made a decision to take some time off and get my head together.

I moved back to St. Louis in December and got a job at Kendall and Davis, a head-hunting firm in downtown St. Louis. I continued dating Jackie and just joined the workforce. Sometimes, you need to step away from your situation and take a real look at where you are to realize where you want to be, and where you never want to be. Over the course of the next few months, I would go through some very life-changing events that even I could not foresee coming.

I started at Kendall and Davis after the first of the year. It was truly corporate America, and I really believed that this was what my future held. To be what I have always referred to as an *execudroid,* who put on the suit and tie every day, jumped into the morning rush hour traffic, and slaved away at a nine-to-five job that provided me all the satisfaction of a peanut butter sandwich. I did this every day, believing this was my path to success.

On January 7 of that year, I received a call from my mother. She said I needed to get home to my father's house. I said why, but she just said that something had happened and I needed to get there as quickly as possible. I told my boss that I needed to go immediately but I didn't understand why. I ran out of the office and headed to my car. When I arrived at my father's house, Reverend Robert Johnson and Ronnie Satchel, an old friend of my father's, met me at the door. In the back of my head, I had a feeling of what I was headed toward but refused to think that it

JOHN STEPHEN PARKER

could be that tragic. When they met me at the door, my disbelief became a tragic reality.

My father had not shown up for work that morning. He was now working as a caseworker for the Missouri State Department of Human Services in the St. Charles office. After not showing up for work and making some of his coworkers make inquiries of his whereabouts, they contacted Ronnie and he went to the house. He walked in the house and found my father dead on the couch, with the television on and a plate of food from the night before in front of him. I had just seen him the night before. I remember stopping by to see him for a moment as I was running around Berkeley that night. One of his friends, whom I won't mention, was there also. My father had some money lying on the table in the dining room. The odd thing was, when I arrived the next day, that money was gone. Not sure if this "friend" took it, or if there was someone there after me that evening, but nonetheless, the money was gone. I saw his friend sometime afterward but never asked him about it. Funny thing is, the guy couldn't look me in the eye.

My father and I have a difficult relationship at best. When you are molested by someone who is supposed to protect you and look out for your well-being, you become a very distrustful and negative person. I had definitely become that way. My sense of humor had become very dry and sarcastic over the years. I had developed a cynical attitude about many aspects of life, including true love. When I walked in the house that day and found him sitting upright on the couch, I became a very angry person almost instantly. We were actually having conversations before his death. I mean actual, cordial conversations. I had yet to reconcile and/or forgive him for the way he had treated me, my mother, and my siblings growing up. The day I found him, I erupted in anger. I ran away from the situation for a bit. I ran to the only person I knew who could give me solace. I ran to Bill Quigley, my junior high football coach. Bill happened to be in class, but I knew he would drop everything for one of his own. That is the way he thought of all the young men who had ever played for him. We were all his sons.

I went to see him immediately, and he told me to go wait in his office. He could tell that something was drastically wrong with me. I went to the office, and when he walked in, he only asked one question: "Who died?" and I said my father. He dropped his head. Then he stood up and told me to come to him. I did, and he hugged me for what felt like was about two hours but was actually about three minutes. For some reason, I just didn't want to let go. There was always a certain security in being in the presence of Q. That was the kind of security that I always wanted in my own father but without the deviant thoughts that you knew were going to follow. From there, I went up to McCluer and found Truman Gilbert. I told him I needed a basketball because I needed to sweat out some aggression. So I went and shot some ball for about an hour.

I returned back to the house, which by now was full of people. The funeral home had not arrived to take my father's body away, so he was still sitting upright on the couch, but by now, he had been covered up with a big comforter. I walked into the living room and found my brother Michael, who has never taken death very well. He and my grandmother Mildred were born on the same day. She died on February 14, 1972. Mike took it real hard. In subsequent years, we would lose other relatives, and again, Michael would take them all very hard. When I walked in the living room, there were a large number of neighbors, many of whom watched me grow up in the neighborhood. Some of which I had always thought never gave a shit whether we lived there or not, and I actually always believed that these people never really wanted us in the neighborhood, so it was surprising to see all these people, some of whom had never set foot in our home when I was a kid, gathered to comfort us in our time of sorrow.

Mike was a bit of a mess but managed to pull himself together. Felice and Tony were out of town, in Chicago and California respectively. We got ahold of them and told them the news. I knew Tony would come running as fast as he could. I could not say the same of my sister. She got there in due time.

We all knew the upcoming days would be difficult ones at best. There were hundreds of people that needed to be contacted. Friends and family. My Aunt Jennetta, my father's younger sister, somehow became this leader in the matter of arrangements that needed to be made. This became a source of major discomfort for me. You see, I have a hard time putting up with hypocritical people. I told people for years that my father had mental problems. Whether they stemmed from the divorce from my mom or his upbringing or his excessive drinking, he was screwed up. Nobody on his side of the family would ever hear of it. He had diabetes, glaucoma, heart disease, and a broad range of other ailments that he never recognized and, for sure, never took care off. When you brought these problems to discussion with his family, they would just stick their heads in the sand. Please understand that this was the history of his family. They cooked everything in heavy grease. Nothing was ever made from a healthy standpoint. Then they would have eating contests, like "Let's see who can eat the most cake or the most pie." It is no wonder why most of them were dead before they were seventy years old. My father died when he was fifty-four years old. What a waste.

Those next few days were very tough. I had Jackie step up and stand by my side. She really got me through the next few months. We were trying to make the arrangements but were at a real loss. We needed help. Jennetta had never supported our belief in his illness, but when he died, she wanted to be the boss. It was kind of like a fire chief showing up at the fire after it had been burning for about three days, smoking a cigarette. It irritated me beyond belief. I felt like none of those people had any right to be involved in any of the planning because they never had to go through any of the pain and sacrifice of having to live and endure this man's wrath of destruction, and the kind of pain he caused many people in his life. Therefore, they had no say whatsoever on how we planned a memorial service for him. We went to the only person that we felt knew him the best and deserved to be included more than anybody. We went to my mother. She was married to this man for almost thirty years and knew almost everything there was to be known. The other person we contacted to help us was my grandmother Geneva, who only gave us advice. It was the smartest advice given. She said, "Keep it dignified, put a blue suit on him, with a striped tie." But her direct advice was even simpler. She said, "It does not have to cost a lot. Put the man in the ground, not your money."

We went to the Wade Funeral Home the next day and picked out a casket. Once in the funeral home, I could not go downstairs and help pick it. I was still very angry. I was angry with myself. I was angry with him for both living and dying. I felt like I had been cheated out of something that I deserved. What that was, I don't know. I just felt like he had more coming back to him for

JOHN STEPHEN PARKER

the way he treated me, and I was very angry that I would not get the opportunity to see him have it all come back. I was also very angry with God. I felt like I deserved better. That my mother deserved better. Eventually she did find better in Millard, but somehow in my mind, that just didn't even the score. I felt like I had more coming, and I never got it all back. I felt cheated.

Over the course of the next few days, everybody was arriving for the funeral. It was amazing that with how much of an ass this man was to me and much of his family, he was liked by thousands of people. He was Good Time Charlie. He was the life of the party, but those people never knew his alter ego, and I figured this was not the time to burst their bubble. This was their hero, and I was not going to ruin it. This was not the time or place for it. I would have come off looking like a bitter child, and even though I was bitter, and still am, I did not want to come off looking bitter. Never let them see you sweat.

As people were arriving, we made everybody feel welcome, and we welcomed their condolences. He had a close-knit group of people whom he had known for a long time that all showed up. There were the Scales brothers, Al, Burrell, Harvey, Ernest, and I think there was one other that I could not remember. Burrell owned a tavern in the city called the Circle S. It was a local black-owned watering hole in the old neighborhood. They used to all get drunk in this place on a regular basis. There was Al Ross whom everybody always called Rabbit, Emmit Vaughn, and a number of the old crew from Camp Rivercliff. This was a camp where my grandmother used to send my father and my uncle Frank to in the summer basically because she never wanted them around when they were out of school. There was one man who came, whom I always had the utmost respect for. His name was Phil Kilgore. He lived over in Cincinnati, Ohio. When I called him about my father, he and his wife made a beeline to St. Louis. Reverend Johnson had also gone to school with my father. They had attended Philander Smith College in Little Rock, Arkansas. Reverend Johnson told me that when he arrived to the school, he didn't have a place to sleep. He said my father had given him his bed so that he wouldn't have to sleep on the floor. These are the things that I don't understand. How can someone who was such a monster to his family be such a nice guy to other people?

The funeral was approaching fast. Everything was coming into place, except for the fact that I did not give myself time to do something that must happen when someone dies. I never gave myself time to grieve. I was too helping Mike with the planning and preparing for the funeral. I was still very angry about my father's death. I was angry about my aunt trying to run everything. I was irritated by the smallest things. Little did I know that several months later, my lack of grieving would all come to a head and I would end up losing all my faculties for a few days.

We were a day or so away from the funeral, but we hit a glitch. In order to be buried at the National Cemetery at Jefferson Barracks, you had to have your discharge papers from your military service. Well, here we have a glitch. We had no idea where he kept any of those papers. I, Mike, and Tony tore the house apart looking for the forms. People always ask why we didn't just get a copy from the U.S. records center. Well that's because the record center used to be located by the airport, but in 1974, the record center caught fire, and because computers were not the information centers of the day like they are today, there was never a backup for the records. When the building caught fire, 70 percent of all federal records kept at the facility were lost.

When we failed to find his DD214 discharge forms, we were in a huge bind. The night before the funeral, we were at the end of our rope. We had no idea where those papers were, and we were completely stranded. Finally, in the process of our search, something told us to look behind the picture of my father on the wall. We did and found the forms we were searching for. We all looked at each other as if Rod Serling himself had just put us in an episode of the *Twilight Zone*. We were all relieved to find those forms so that we could get on with the process and finally get some closure to this whole time.

We had the cars from the Wade Funeral Home pick us up at ten o'clock the next morning. It was a sunny January morning, but the temperature was in the mid-twenties. The owner of the funeral home, Wade Grandberry, himself attended himself. He was a longtime friend of our family. He had buried most of the people who had passed away in my family. I was still not behaving very cordially toward anybody. I was still a very angry person. For the most part, I held it together. I cried a bit at the funeral, but there were many people both in my family, and friends who were inconsolable. We got through the day as difficult as it was.

Just like most funerals, you get together afterward and people give you condolences one after another. Everybody brings food because I guess when people die, the people who have to go on living somehow lose the ability to cook for themselves. Black funerals in particular are ridiculous about this. I used to joke with my white friends about this fact: most black funerals are usually on Friday at 11:00 a.m., and this is usually at least one week after the person had died. White people bury their family members very quickly while most black people tend to wait until all their cousins, many whom are two to three times removed, show up to give their respects. And this is the other fact: if there is a Kentucky Fried Chicken within two miles of the post-funeral party, you can believe that they will be sold out of over half of their stock because every black, post-funeral gathering will include a minimum of at least ten buckets of Original Recipe.

We all managed to get through the time. The following week, I turned twenty-one years old. I was still working at Kendall and Davis, hating life even more. I took the bus to and from home to the apartment everyday. Except on this day, I walked in and found my mom, Millard, Mike, Tony, and Felice, along with Jackie, waiting for me. They had made reservations for dinner at Stuart Andersons Cattle Company Restaurant, up on Dunn Road. We all had dinner that night. We tried to laugh and have some fun in the epilogue of the funeral. It was a wonderful night, and it would be sometime before we would spend that kind of time together again.

CHAPTER TWELVE

Music doesn't lie. If there is something to be changed in this world, then it can only happen through music.

—Jimi Hendrix

WORDS AND MUSIC

THROUGHOUT ALL THIS, I have failed to recognize something that has always been a factor in the backdrop of my life. Those have been words and music. I grew up listening to the music of the sixties. It was the Temptations, the Four Tops, Smoky Robinson and the Miracles, and Diana Ross and the Supremes. I was a huge Motown fan. My brothers and I used to watch the Jackson Five when we were kids. We saw them one time on the old *Ed Sullivan Variety Show*. Very soon after that, we were practicing steps in the family room of our house. One night, we had our steps down and decided to invite the other kids in the neighborhood over. I remember the Armstrongs, the Merellos, and Chris Keenan, and the Miller kids all packed into our family room, listening to me, Mike, and Tony lip-synch to the Jacksons' third album. It had one of their first hits on it "I'll Be There." Later, Mariah Carey did it over, and it was a big hit for her in the early nineties.

It was amazing what songs really affected me when I was younger. I have always like old soul music. Kids today have no idea what I am talking about because they have this belief that rap music rules the world. I will not shortchange the fact that it has its place and that some of today's artists—and I use that term loosely—have some talent, but back in the day, it was true pageantry at its best. You have a horn section. Singers would actually sing and have their steps choreographed. There was true professionalism. They behaved with like ladies and gentlemen instead of the loudmouthed hoodlums of today.

I always had an appreciation for all kinds of music. Old soul music was my favorite. I mean, Curtis Mayfield, James Brown, Smoky Robinson were the artists that I really listened to a great deal. These guys all had stories behind their music. Stories of hard luck, drug abuse, bad marriages, and the like. I remember Al Green singing "Love and Happiness":

> Something that can make you do wrong and make you
> do right. It will make you come home early, and make
> you stay out all night.

When you hear lyrics like that, it really makes you think what is going on with a person. Johnny Taylor used to sing a song. The words were "Who's making love to your old lady, while you been out making love." Later, as I got older, I became a fan of what people now call classic rock and roll. I have always been a fan of the Beatles, the Rolling Stones, and many of the bands that were part of the "British Invasion." People thought that was kind of unusual that a black kid would prefer to listen to music that wasn't usually associated with the black community. I always said that music transcends race. It is one thing that people of every color can have an appreciation for. I have lived a life of some of the strangest experiences. Through all those experiences, there was always a backdrop of music. I can remember most of the tragedies and the music. The women I have loved and the relationships I have been involved in, and a song that always reminds me of them.

Words and music have always gotten me through some tough times. I have always been a television and movie buff. As a kid, I would go to the movie theater on Sunday afternoon all by myself and watch movies. I would watch the same movie two to three times if I could. This was before we had VCRs and DVD players. I was always a big fan of the Irwin Allen disaster movies, like the *Towering Inferno*, *Earthquake* and, my all-time favorite, *The Poseidon Adventure* starring Gene Hackman. I was also a fan of musicals. No, that does not mean that I am gay. I was always amazed by the detail that had to go into the making of a musical. Not those modern things, like *Cats* or *Rent*. I mean the older Rogers and Hammerstein musical like Oklahoma. My favorite two were always Carousel and Yankee Doodle Dandy, starring James Cagney as George M. Cohan. There is nothing that compares to Jimmy Cagney tap-dancing down the stairs of the White House after receiving the Medal of Freedom from President Roosevelt. My mom to this day still calls me whenever the movie is on because she knows my love for it.

In the early seventies, it was the music of Sly and the Family Stone. Sly Stone was a bit of a character. He once got married at Madison Square Garden during halftime of a Knicks game. I believe he did it on the old Mike Douglas talk show also. Later in life, Sly went to jail for drug usage and trafficking. In 2005, he made an appearance on the American Music Awards. It was a sad site, because I was such a fan of his, and to see where he was now in life gave me a real reality check

By this time, I had a real appreciation for all kinds of music. I have white friends and black friends. This put me in a position where I had to adapt to whatever was playing at the time. I listened to Boston, Grand Funk Railroad, and Peter Frampton when I was with my white friends and the Jacksons, Rick James, and George Clinton and the P-Funk All Stars when I was running with the brothers. Lots of my friends would ridicule me for what I listened to, but I didn't care. Music always had fitting moments for me. Whenever I hear Aerosmith sing "What It Takes," I think about Michele and our relationship. There is a line in the lyrics that goes

"Girl before I met you, I was F-I-N-E fine, but your loves made me a prisoner, yea my hearts been doing time."

I have spent my entire life being in love with someone whom I could never have. So in a way, I kept myself in a prison. She was still everything in the world to me, and I was bugged by that fact. No matter what I do or who I meet. She is always with me.

Music had a huge influence on me in my life of sports also. This is not as big a factor for women as it is for men. Guys always remember songs that got them fired up prior to a game. In high school, we could never get fired up in a football locker room without some good music. During football, it was John "Cougar" Mellencamp singing "Hurts So Good." This was also the evolution of a new era of television. It was called cable television. It enabled people to watch television twenty-four hours a day if they wanted to. You could watch some of the strangest things that you could never see on regular television. Home Box Office or HBO was one of the first movie channels. They would show movies that had recently been in the theaters nationally. Later, channels like Showtime and the Movie Channel would come along. Cinemax—or as my friends called it, *Skinamax*—came along. They would show soft-core, B-rated pornographic movies after 10:00 p.m. Also, with the creation, came something called MTV or Music Television. This was a channel dedicated to the world of music videos. The first one ever shown was ironically called "Video Killed the Radio Star." Most of the music industry's biggest stars are big because of MTV. It gave them a chance to put a story line and a face behind a song. Songs of the big stars today such as Madonna and Michael Jackson were very big because of the video age.

When I was in junior high, another new genre of music hit the airways. Some thought it was a fad that, like the Hula-Hoop, would eventually go along the way, but it has, to this day, stood the test of time and continues to be one of the most popular styles of music. It was called rap. I am not entirely sure where it started, but it became popular very fast. There were many artists who were involved with the creation of rap. Grand Master Flash and the Furious Five, Kurtis Blow to name a couple, but the original song that took the nation by storm was a song called "Rappers Delight" by the Sugarhill Gang. Rap takes real-life situations and lets you put them in a rhyme style. You would hear verses in lines like this:

> Have you ever went over a friend's house to eat and the food just is no good. I mean the macaroni is soggy, the peas are mushy, and the chicken taste like wood.

Later, the lyrics and style of rap music turned a bit more hard core, or what the industry labeled gangsta rap. It took the more realistic view of life in the neighborhoods of South Central Los Angeles and the rougher areas of New York, and created rap stars with the likes of Tupac, Dr. Dre, Snoop Dog, and the Notorious B.I.G. When this style of music started to become more popular and began moving into the communities of "white suburbia," it became something of an infestation. Then it became popular to blame the popularity of rap music for the problems that teenagers were having in society. That is completely ridiculous. Every generation has had musical influences, but to blame bad behavior on the music of the generation is completely crazy. The fifties had rock-and-roll music with Bill Haley, Elvis, Buddy Holly and the Crickets. The sixties saw the British invasion: the Beatles, the Rolling Stones, a huge four-day concert on a farm in upstate New York that featured a no-name black guitarist named Jimi Hendrix and a blues-singing white girl from Port Arthur, Texas, named Janis Joplin, and the emergence of the Motown sound with Berry Gordy, and Smokey Robinson starting a style that would live on even today.

The seventies had hard-core rock music from artists like Kiss and Black Sabbath. Later, it saw the birth of a style that started a revolution in music. It was called disco. Made famous with the movie *Saturday Night Fever*, it was the first you heard of artists like the Bee Gees and the Tramps. Disco also led to the rise of the nightclub industry. Clubs opened in almost every city in the country, with one of the more popular ones being Studio 54 in New York City. This was a club where many of the hottest stars of the day could be seen. It was also a place where just about "anything goes" was the motto of the day. Both public and private sex occurred. When I say it occurred, that means people were free

JOHN STEPHEN PARKER

to play on all their inhibitions and fetishes. Free drug use was the norm of the atmosphere. Cocaine became the drug of choice, but it was the drug of the wealthy. Of course, a cheaper, more lethal form of it ended up being made and sold in the lower-income areas of major cities. They called it crack cocaine. Of course, it targeted the black community first and was quickly exploited in the media as being a "black problem." The only problem was that black people do not own the planes they use to fly it into the country, but society needs a scapegoat with every problem, and the black community always seems to be the easiest.

I can remember certain situations I have had to live through. Whenever I hear a certain song, it makes me think about the person I was involved with or the traumatic event I was dealing with at that point. Early in high school, it was Prince, Morris Day and the Time, Vanity 6, and the rest of the sounds of the Minneapolis music scene. Later, AC/DC came out with an album titled *Back in Black*. They wrote a song that, little did we know at the time, would go on to be the rock-and-roll party anthem of all time. It was titled "You Shook Me All Night Long."

> She was a fast machine. She kept her motor clean. She was best damn woman that I ever seen.

Those few words, even today, have the ability to get the party jumping in any venue.

The relationship with Susan brings to mind the group Confunksion singing "A Penny for Your Thoughts." It went like this:

> A Penny for your thoughts, a nickel for a kiss, a dime if you tell me that you love me.

Susan and I would always give each other sixteen cents every day. Kind of like a young cheesy thing, I know, but that was popular then. I remember running around with Doug Clark, Tom Blake, and Craig Winscott. The music playing was Van Halen's "Running with Devil," the Cars singing "Just What I Needed," and Phil Collins banging out "In the Air Tonight." It was made popular on the pilot episode of the eighties' detective show *Miami Vice*. Believe me, I had the white sports jacket and the huarache sandals. Man, that was a great time to be young. Jackie is always brought to memory when I hear Foreigner sing "I Wanna Know What Love Is," seeing how I was in a very strange point in my life at that time. I was kind of lost between her and Michele. Hell, I have always been in a strange place when it came to Michele.

"Missing You" by Diana Ross always makes me think about my father and the relationship I wish I had with him. I saw my friends grow up with fathers that were supportive while mine was an abusive jerk. I have no idea why I get all teary eyed and weak when I hear that song. I can remember dancing with Jackie at a bar called Flight 99. It was a bar at the top of the Breckenridge Hotel by the Lambert International Airport. We were dancing together on the floor, and that song came on.

That was shortly after my father's death. I broke down that night right there on the dance floor. It was so embarrassing to have to walk off the dance floor crying like a little baby. I couldn't understand why I was crying. The man was gone. A man who did terrible things to me while I was young. I was actually upset that he was gone, out of my life permanently. It was a mental nightmare for me.

JOHN STEPHEN PARKER

CHAPTER THIRTEEN

Do you know the difference between education and experience? Education is when you read the fine print; experience is what you get when you don't.

—Pete Seeger

LATE SUMMER OF PAIN

THAT YEAR BEGAN with the death of my father. A moment in time that to this day still haunts me. I always refer to that moment as an unfinished business in my past, and it will always remain that way because he is gone. Just before he died, we had actually begun to have a civil conversation without me not wanting to be in the same room with him. Here I was, a grown man feeling uncomfortable being in the same room with his father. But it was a fact. It really bothered me.

There was no possible way I could return to school after that. I was so mentally drained, it would have been a significant waste of time at that point. Michele was getting married in the fall that year, Jackie had since packed up and moved to Kansas City, Mom had gotten remarried. I never felt so all alone in my life. I decided to stay home for the spring semester and get my head together. I was hanging at a new club over in Maryland Heights called TOPS, which stood for Tavern on the Plaza. It was a hip joint on the edge of West County in St. Louis. It was a popular hangout, which had more women in one spot than I had seen in a very long time. Just what I needed: more women to confuse the shit out of me. They were like a drug that had a hold on me that I could not understand. I met more women during this time than ever in my life. I had a mind-set that was simple. It was "More is better." I dated a lot at that time, and I use the term *dated* very loosely. I was also hanging at a place in Berkeley called the 94 Aero Squadron. It was a restaurant/nightclub by the airport. The name came from the fighter wing that was stationed at Lambert Field. It had all the decorations of an old airfield, old photos of pilots from the early wars as well as some local hero's. I would hang out there, and there was always a great deal of traffic, if you know what I mean.

I told myself that I would work for the spring semester and then attempt to return to school in the fall. I took a job as the manager of the Athlete's Foot. It was an athletic school store in, of all places, Frontenac, Missouri. This was probably the richest part of the St. Louis County. Most of it was really old money, but there were a number of new subdivisions that were being developed. All these homes would start in the low seven hundreds. Which meant one thing: there would be, with the exception of professional athletes from the city, no black people. I had a great time running that store, but to say the least, I was a fish out of water in that part of town. I was driving a Volkswagen Rabbit GTI. I had traded in my mom's Chevy Impala and wanted to get something small and gas efficient. It was a great little car, especially when you are driving about fifteen miles to work every day. I really loved that little car.

JOHN STEPHEN PARKER

It was also about this time that I learned how to look and act like I had more than I really did. I used to hang out at these swanky bars in Clayton, which is the business district of St. Louis County. I can remember hobnobbing with lawyers and major business owners when I did not have a pot to piss in or a window to throw it out of. I would just jump into a conversation with a group of people, most of whom had great careers, and they would never in a million years believe that I didn't even have a college degree at the time, let alone a solid career. I came to these bars with maybe twenty bucks in my pocket. I would be what you would call suited and booted, meaning I would be dressed in business attire. Black suit, white or blue shirt, unique patterned tie, shined shoes, and a conversation for business. I could have discussions about anything from the economy to politics. I positioned myself to connect with people who at the time were all so far outside of my circle of friends. I also became very attractive to older, professional women. I won't mention any names, but some of the most powerful women in St. Louis have had me in their homes. Now understand they were not as powerful then, but if I were to mention them by name in this memoir, it would probably upstage the foundation of some major companies in the St. Louis area. All the while I was leading this life, I was really only spending money on my attire. Smart guy, huh? As with all good things, just about when you are riding a wave of good luck, the bottom falls out and walls come crumbling down. That was what happened as I was leaving a club one night with a young lady.

When you are young, you have the belief that you are Superman and you can never be hurt by anything or anyone. That myth was locked into my head. I mean, I had gone through years of major sports. I had survived a violent father. I figured if God had really wanted me, he could have taken me at any time. But none of that could hold a candle to what I was about to endure.

I was driving home one time at about one o'clock in the morning. In those days, the Missouri State Highway Department passed a law that there would be no streetlights on the major highways after dark. This was unfortunate. Little did I know that a young man with a blood alcohol content of .35 had managed to turn down the exit ramp of the highway and ended up on the inside lane of the highway, going the wrong way. To add to the situation, he was traveling at about eighty miles an hour. Now just when you thought it couldn't get any worse, let me throw this into the mix: he didn't have his lights on. Now, I realize this sounds like something out of a season of reality television, but this is as accurate as it can be.

As I traveled down the highway that night, I was listening to Billy Joel. CD players were not out yet, so I was still on cassette tapes. It was his greatest hits. I was always a huge fan of his music, not to mention that at the time he was married to one of the biggest supermodels of her time Christie Brinkley. I remember fast-forwarding the tape until I found the song "Only the Good Die Young." The next thing I knew, the fire department was cutting me out of my car, and the young lady who was with me was screaming in pain as they were removing her. The oncoming car had hit us head-on. I never even saw him coming, and by the time I did, the engine block was exploding through the dashboard and crushing my right leg at the knee joint. That in addition to the fact that I detached the retina in my right eye, broke about four ribs, cracked my sternum, broke my nose and jaw. The young lady I was with suffered a compound fracture on the upper leg. I am sure she was in a great deal of pain, but at the time, I knew

JOHN STEPHEN PARKER

I was in a life-threatening situation. I heard Billy Joel singing. These were the lyrics:

> They say there's a heaven, for those who wait. Some say its better, but I say it ain't. I'd rather laugh with the sinner's, than cry with saint's. The sinner's are much more fun, you know that only the good die young.

The next thing I knew, I was living the song. It was truly a reality.

Here is where the Superman part comes in. They carted me off to the hospital, where I laid on a table for about two hours. About twenty minutes into it, my mother came in with my stepfather. I had a white shirt on, and they had cut it a bit to tend to my cuts and bruises. It was filled with blood, which made the situation look even worse. When my mother walked in and found me, I appeared to be dead, which really scared her. My face was filled with blood, as if I had just had a major prizefight and I went the distance of fifteen rounds. After about three hours in the hospital, they made the mistake of sending me home. I crawled into the back of my mom's car and went home. I returned to the hospital later, and Dr. Harlan Hunter admitted me, where I remained for quite a stretch. He was the best orthopedic surgeon in the St. Louis area. He was recognized as the team doctor for the St. Louis Cardinals football team when they were still in St. Louis prior to them moving to Arizona. He took about 150 cc of fluid off my knee and immediately scheduled me for surgery. He also agreed to fix my nose, which was under my left eye after being banged on the steering wheel. I ended up breaking the steering wheel with my face.

I had been looking forward to returning to the field that fall at Missouri Valley, and in an instant, it was all taken away. Here I was thinking I had the world by the tail and then realizing that control is nothing more than an illusion. We fool ourselves by thinking that we have control of any situation that life gives us when, in reality, none of us has any control over anything in our world. I learned this very painfully. That car accident ruined me for, what I would come to find out, the rest of my playing career.

This was one hell of a year. I had not only lost my father, but I had probably lost all ability in a sport that was arguably the most important factor in my life. That fall, I returned to the workforce as soon as I could and made preparations to try and return to school in January. I only had one more agonizing thing to go through during this year. Something that I knew I was going to have to sit through and witness, and again, it would be something that would change my life.

As I was recovering and going through rehab on my leg, a date was fast approaching. I had received an invitation to a wedding. One that I had been dreading for quite some time, but I knew it would inevitably come. It was the invitation to Michele's wedding. When I got it, I felt like I had just gotten into another car accident. Every muscle in my body hurt all over again. I called John and gave him the news. He was silent on the other end of the phone. He already knew where I was with this. His first question was "Are you all right?" He already knew the answer to his question. John Snead knew how I felt about Michele, and he was the only person who could understand where I was at that moment. He actually flew in from Atlanta and went to the wedding with me. I could always count on him, and to this day, I still can.

Michele and I had the opportunity to talk about a week or two before the wedding. At first, we didn't get into anything deep, but more just reminiscing about old times, and old stories about old friends. I fought very hard to stay away from any subject that would bring tension to what was already a tense situation. We both knew what was about to happen, and there was no stopping it. In less than two weeks, she would be walking down the aisle with someone else. The only thing was that the person she would walk with, well, she didn't really love the way you I felt you love someone if you were going them. I felt it was a marriage more for safety than for love. She had given herself totally to someone else a long time ago. She was in love with that guy, but he had failed her. That person hurt her so bad that she committed herself to never giving that much of herself again to anyone. That was the part that really scared her when it came to us. She knew that if she was ever going to give herself to anybody like that again, it would be me, and believe me, I knew it and she knew that I knew it.

The conversation turned toward our personal history, which was not what we wanted but knew it would get there eventually as it always has. We talked about our personal history, both separate and together. We laughed a bunch, and cried a bit also. It was an emotional moment because we knew that this might possibly be the end of our relationship. We had started as friends in the seventh grade. We both had much of the same background and upbringing. We connected on day one with each other. Not sure when, but we were just always close. Maybe because neither one of us really fit in with the crowds we were trying to run with. I was a black kid from Berkeley who lived in a predominately white neighborhood. This put me in a bit of a pickle because most of my friends were either black or white, but my friends didn't really associate with each other. This always put me in a bind because I was always trying to play the middle and, I guess, maybe bridge the gap between the two different cultures. That was a difficult task.

Michele had just as much trouble because she was a poor kid from a large family. Her father was the town drunk of Ferguson. She had nothing growing up, and most of the people she hung with were a bit better off. She kept up a great front and never let anyone know that she really didn't have a lot. I always knew, but I would never give her crap about it, because I didn't have anything either.

We talked for hours, never really concluding anything other than the fact that we were in love with each other and had been since we were about fifteen years old. We knew that it would be a very long time before we ever had another conversation. I was feeling all kinds of things at that moment. It was funny though. Because toward the end, one of the feelings that moved to the forefront was anger. I felt angry because the woman I had been in love with my whole life was going to marry someone else. I was angry because when I had an opportunity, I didn't fight for her. I was mad that Terry had screwed it up for anybody who could make her commit totally. Instead, it forced her to hold back her real feelings and settle for a life of convenience and for loving someone "in a certain way" instead of with everything that is within her, as I know she is capable of. She agreed to go through the rest of her life giving what she needed to give instead of giving more than she knows she is capable of. Cheating herself and her partner of all the wonderful gifts she has as a person. I was angry that she settled. I was angry that she didn't choose me, and up until

JOHN STEPHEN PARKER

the actual ceremony, I still didn't believe she would go through with. We laughed about it. We both joked that if she looked into my eyes while she was walking down the aisle, she could not go through with it. She would be all smiles, but one look at me would change her thoughts and plans, and she would not be able to say those words after looking at me. She knew this to be true so much that she asked me not to look at her as she walked down the aisle. Actually, she begged me not to because it would make her think, and she didn't want to think on her wedding day. She just wanted to go through the ceremony without any hitch, and looking at me would have definitely thrown a wrench into her plans.

As the day approached, I really tried to get my mind right for the ceremony because I knew how hard it would be to sit through. John agreed to come with me, and we would join Gary Connors and Susan Hughes, who were longtime high school sweethearts. That's a whole different story. Instead of marrying Gary, Susan went on to marry his cousin Ken and have a couple of kids with him. If you can't get the one, nothing wrong with going to the next one. How about a first cousin? That will work. It's kind of funny when you think about it. They have been married now for what must seem like a lifetime.

The day finally arrived. I was still walking around with a pretty good limp from the accident. So I was kind of using my cane, but I insisted on not using it when I went to Michele's wedding. I want to be sure I didn't show any sign of weakness going there. I had to be sure I put up every sign of strength I could because this would be a very hard day, probably the hardest one of my life. I knew it was going to rip my heart apart, and I began to get mad all over again. I again didn't believe that she would actually go through with it. How could she, knowing the truth about how she really felt about him and how she honestly felt about me. There was no way it was going to happen. I have no doubt she loved Dan, but it was not the kind of feelings we had for each other, and least that what I wanted to believe.

I arrived at the church, and John was right behind me in the Mustang. I gathered myself in the parking lot. John asked me if I was doing OK. I told him yes, but he could see pretty clearly that I wasn't. I was on the verge of a breakdown right there, but remember the Right Guard commercial that used the slogan "Never let them see you sweat"? I was not going to let anybody see me lose it. Not her, not John, not anybody else. I was going to be strong and get through this no matter what I was feeling.

I walked in and sat about midway up on the left-hand side of the church. John came in right behind me. Gary and Susan came in then and sat right in front of us. I purposely sat on the end because there was no way I was not going to look at her as she walked up that aisle. I had to look her in the face and actually see if she could walk down the aisle and marry someone else, full well knowing that I was in love with her.

Even with the writing on the wall, I still didn't believe she could go through with it. I was fixed on the fact that we had something that nobody could ever understand. We had been in love with each other since we were kids. Our friendship and love had survived life and death. It had survived people who hated the fact that we were friends at all. Many of the people we knew never really got behind us. They tolerated the relationship because they thought it was a passing fancy. Little did they know that this relationship would last for the next thirty years and, hopefully, beyond.

JOHN STEPHEN PARKER

The ceremony began, and here came Michele's loudmouthed college roommate coming down the aisle. Debbie was her name, and she had all the tact of a warthog at a feeding trough. She was one of those women that you could dress up, but you don't dare take her anywhere. Kind of like putting an outhouse in the middle of the Augusta National Golf Course in Georgia. You never knew what was going to come out of her mouth. The four of us once went to McDonalds one day. I say four because the other person was Lisa McCarthy. Lisa was a friend of ours from high school. She managed to get pregnant during our sophomore year. John Breedenkamp was the lucky guy. I will never forget the day Lisa brought the baby to school. She was about two years old. She came running down the aisle of the cafeteria screaming "Daddy, Daddy." That made for a great scene. Tough break!

Anyway, getting back to my McDonald's story. There happened to be a heavyset girl and a few of her friends sitting next to us eat. Okay, let me back up. I said heavyset, but in reality, this girl was nothing more than *fat*. I mean, she was a biscuit away from three bills from a weight standpoint. She was swollen up like a big M&M, just sitting there stuffing her face like winter was coming, and she would be hibernating. Well, Debbie, being the tactful person that she was, began laughing at the girl and looking away. The only thing the girl believed was that the black guy sitting with these three white girls was making fun of her, and she immediately wanted to kick my ass. When she and her friends left, they drove around the parking lot to our window, and she was more than happy to flip me off, which really made Michele, Lisa, and Debbie fall out laughing. Not to mention Lisa and I had got into a little spat right before, and she did something that not only shocked me, but Michele also. I said something, and Lisa took it upon herself to reach out and slap the living shit out of me. Obviously, that was not something I would appreciate. It was a great combination: Me getting slapped. Me getting slapped in public. Me getting slapped by a woman. Me getting slapped by a woman who had all the tact of a trailer park chick you would meet in a bowling alley. And finally, me getting slapped in public by a woman, by Lisa McCarthy, in front of the woman I have been in love with since all my life, with her college roommate sitting next to her. Now you can imagine my anger, but apparently, the look on my face was more than priceless. Michele and Debbie were almost on the floor laughing.

Not sure who was next, but soon, Michele's sister Jamie was coming down. Funny thing about the Henke family, all the kids pretty much look alike, so when Jamie came down the aisle, it was kind of a warm-up to who was coming next. I put my head down because the music started playing. When I looked up, the old man was coming down the aisle with Michele on his arm. My stomach about fell out of my body. John, Susan, and Gary were standing within arm's reach of me. As soon as the procession started, I had that feeling that you get when someone dies. Like you are never going to see them again. Well, it was just like that. I was never going to see Michele again. At least not in the same way. She was going down that aisle in one way and coming back in another.

My friends could see where I was at that moment. They could see the anguish on my face and that my heart was breaking with every step she took. I could feel all the eyes of everyone that had known about our relationship staring at me, waiting to see if I would actually cause a scene. When I saw her, I could tell she was trying not to make eye contact with me. I was staring at her as

JOHN STEPHEN PARKER

intensely as possible, as if to telepathically communicate to her that I was looking at her, and that more importantly, she should look at me. She finally could not help it anymore and looked up. She looked right at me, and even with a fixated smile on her face, I could tell that she was a little sad inside. Here she was on what was supposed to be the happiest day of her life, and she was happy for all that were there, but inside, she had a slight sadness because the guy that I felt she was really deeply in love with was watching her start a new life with another man.

They started a typical Catholic wedding. You know what I mean. A whole bunch of standing up and sitting down. I sat there with John and died a slow death. Occasionally, he would ask me if I was OK. I appreciated it very much, but there was nothing he or anybody else could do for me. I was miserable, and the only person who could get me through this moment of misery was me. It came to the part when the priest asks the question of who objects to this union. It was all I could do not to shout to the heavens my extreme objection to this whole thing. I guess at that moment, I realized that she has a right to be happy, and that if she was happy with that guy, then I need to get around to the fact that she was going to be one with him, and me hanging on to the dream, or better yet, the illusion that she would come back to me, was just ridiculous. In the next fifteen minutes, my illusion would be over. I never would take a shit. I remained on the proverbial pot. I did not have the guts to fight for what I really wanted, and now, it was going to be over.

The moment finally came, and she said "I do." I fought back my tears and did a pretty good job of it, if I say so myself. When she started back up the aisle as a married woman, she chose this time not look at me. At that moment, this feeling of anger slowly came over me, and when I say slowly, I mean that I was OK through the first part of the reception, but at some point in time, I lost all recollection of time. Now I know what you are thinking. Maybe ol' JP had a bit too much to drink and passed out or blacked out, but that was not the case. In fact, I purposely didn't drink anything because I was afraid I would say something or do something that I would regret later. So I did not partake at all. All I knew was at some point in time I became very fed up with the evening and left. Not to mention that angry feeling was still growing inside me, and I could not help it. I jumped in my car and got out of there as fast as I could. That was the last time Michele and I spoke for a long time.

I returned to Missouri Valley College in January. I limped in, still banged up from the car accident. They stuck me right in the Tau Kappa Epsilon fraternity house. I was originally by myself, but then I got a roommate named Rod Williams. Somewhere halfway through January, I got a phone call. Back then, there was only a pay phone on the floor before we had the conveniences of cell phones. Somebody yelled that the phone was for me. I went out and answered it. I heard a soft-spoken voice say "Hello."

Now just about the moment that I had a grip on my anger, she called. I said hello in kind of a way that she would know that I was still not happy at what had happened. She said, "How are you?" and I responded with "How the hell should I be? You just walked down the aisle with somebody else, full well knowing how you and I felt about each other. Now I am supposed to be OK with all of this. Well, that is not how it works. We don't need to talk for a while."

That was the last time Michele and I talked for about three years. That was a huge mistake on my part. I let my personal feelings stand in the way of a friendship I had with someone since I was a kid. I could not believe I was acting this way toward her, but I could not stop myself. I was angry. I had been in love with her since I couldn't remember, and I still was and could not do anything about it. I was mad and helpless, and I needed to lash out. She was my world, and my world had been destroyed, and all I could do was watch it from a church pew. How helpless was that? In my head, I heard Chicago playing "Hard Habit to Break." It was very fitting.

CHAPTER FOURTEEN

Life must be understood backwards; but . . . it must be lived forward.

— Soren Kierkegaard

BACK IN STRIDE AGAIN

I WENT BACK to Missouri Valley and very quickly hit my stride. I remember lying in my room one night. A few of the guys who were there during my first time around were still there. Gary Barnes, Kurt Harris, Rich Willard just to name a few. I came in during winter intersession. Got back into my groove slowly. When all the students arrived, I was living upstairs in the TKE house. I was lying around one night, talking with Rich Willard, and I heard this young lady coming down the hall, and believe me, I use the term *lady* very loosely. She came around the corner, and she had on a big flannel shirt, jeans and, of all things, a fishing hat. Her name was Carrie Garvey. She was from Lake Latawana, Missouri. The only way I can describe Carrie is that she was a blond female version of John Parker. We thought alike, spoke the same language, and had many of the same beliefs. That was uncanny. We used to hang out a lot. I will not go into the depth of the relationship in the pages of this compilation because there is no way to clearly make people understand just what Carrie and I meant then and still mean to each other. We have both grown up and have careers and families and a broad range of responsibilities. I will only say that Carrie Garvey is one of my best friends on the face of the planet, and there is nothing I wouldn't do for her. Jill was back in my life also, but things had changed for her also. She was now married to Denny Marker, and she was the resident director on the Alpha Sigma Phi house on campus. She was also pregnant. My, how things have changed for both of us.

Classes started back, and I was back at it like the past fourteen months had not happen. I had one thing in mind: I wanted to graduate and get on with my life. I went back to playing football at Missouri Valley. I was happy to get back on the field. Ken Gibler was happy to get me back also. I had no idea that he wouldn't be around very much longer either. Little did we know that he had cancer, and it was ravaging his body. He would only live a couple more years. That would be the end of a true era of college football and, definitely, the conclusion of an era in the history of Missouri Valley College. I was just happy that I had the opportunity to play for such a good coach and an even better man.

My time at MVC was moving fast. As with most seniors, I had some idea of what I was going to do but no direct plan of action. I was dating, and again I use the term loosely, about five different girls. I was having fun and finishing school. About this time, I decided that I wanted to go to grad school but had no idea what I wanted to study. I figured with as many injuries as I had over the years, I might try going into medicine. I knew with my grades, I would never get into Harvard, so I chose a different route. There was a new graduate school for sports medicine that had just opened up in Daphne, Alabama, called the United States

Sports Academy. It offered graduate degrees in sports medicine. I figured this was it. Let's just stay in school for another eighteen months and finish the master's degree while I am still in full student mode. I will get it over with.

I finished school without a hitch. My time in Missouri Valley was more than just college. It was a developmental change in my life that I really needed to go through to help me grow as a man. I met some great people there and established some relationships that, even to this day, are a rich part of my life and my future.

Around the first of August, after graduation, I left Missouri for the adventure of Baldwin County, Alabama. Wow, this was like the land that time forgot. I moved to the town of Bay Minnette. Now make no bones about it. I was naive about the South. I was what folks in the South would call an uppity nigger. I was even more of the enemy because unlike most of the black people in Baldwin County, I was educated, and in the South, even today, an educated black man is still considered a very dangerous man.

I was going to class at the academy. I had no money to speak of. Unlike the other students at the school, I did not have a trust fund or some rich parents who were willing to pay for grad school, so I was forced to work for a living. I found a job, among all things, coaching football at Baldwin County High School in Bay Minnette. My head coach was a man named R. L. Watson. The R. L. stood for nothing. That was really his name. He was an old redneck boy who had just taken the job at BCHS. He came over from Alba High School in the city of Bayou La Batrie. It was down on the gulf coast and famous for the shrimp boats. When I first arrived there, I could hardly speak the language. It was a form of English that I had never heard before. It slowed down the pronunciation of the words but sped up the conjugation of

JOHN STEPHEN PARKER

a sentence. I didn't say anything for the first couple of days of practice because I couldn't understand anybody.

The people were good-hearted but still very ignorant of the progress of society. All the black people in town were all subjected to living on one side of town, which naturally was on the "other side of the tracks." I suppose I made some major waves when I decided that under no circumstances was I going to live in that neighborhood. I had grown up in Berkeley, Missouri, in the late sixties and had already been through the "I can live anywhere I want to" stage. So me living in the area of dirt roads and random indoor plumbing was never going to happen and if that meant that I would have to make a few waves in a small Southern town, then so be it. My family has never been one to do things quietly, so why would I change now? Let's not forget, I have a family history of a unique member who had made a huge splash when it came to getting attention in the local law enforcement.

Bay Minette, Alabama, was a town that had its own history. I was your typical old Southern town. It had a town square that rolled up at five o'clock every evening. There was nothing for the kids to do but get together in parking lots around town and drink beer in their big trucks. Most of them had gun racks in the back window. Funny that the local high schools would allow kids to come to school with actual guns in the windows of their cars.

I was living in a small apartment close to the United States Sports Academy. That drive from Daphne to Bay Minette was not only costly, but traveling those back roads was a bit dangerous for a young educated black kid from Missouri. Not to mention I was traveling in a 1986 black-and-gold Trans Am. Oh, that made me even more of the "uppity nigger," which people in the South are still very paranoid of. The problem was I had a unique personality. I was outgoing, articulate, intelligent, and very well versed. Just like today, I had the ability to talk to anybody, about any subject, at any time. This put me in two dilemmas. I was a threat to most of the white men in the area, and I was a very sexy, attractive man to the white women of the community. This combination in the South can be very dangerous and, in some cases, *will* get you killed. I was very much aware of where I was living. Five years previous to my arrival in the area, the Ku Klux Klan had kidnapped a young black man from this same county. They beat him and then hung him from a tree on Airport Road, which is the main street that runs through the city of Mobile. The year was 1984. It is hard to believe that this behavior still exist, but looking back over the last twenty-five years, the South really has not changed all that much. Many of the high schools still have a black prom and a white prom. Much of the culture is still very segregated. The living conditions can still be labeled by the race that has been educated to believe that this is where "we" belong. Black people living in the "bottoms" where there are dirt roads and the occasional outhouse. White people living the country-club lifestyle on "snob hill." Many still have minorities working as servants or domestics, which, in my opinion, is about one step above slavery.

Getting back to Bay Minnette, it was a nice town but very backward in its thought process. R. L. was a little older, but he was a good coach. He had age-old beliefs. We rode to Selma one time for a track meet. He had an inquiring mind and genuinely wanted to know about me. We were talking about marriage and relationships, and he made it clear to me that he was not an interracial relationship fan. In fact, he made it clear that and he actually stated that blacks should stay with blacks and whites should stay with whites. That really surprised me because I thought this man was more liberal in his thinking. Come to find out that, even though he was a good football coach, he was still a racist person. That was disappointing to me but par the course in the South.

I met a lot of wonderful people in Bay Minnette. One person in particular was a woman named Donna Watts. She was married, and her husband's name was Bill. He was the pastor at the Baptist church. She had four kids. Christy was her oldest, Rick was a junior at BCHS. Mandy was a cheerleader in junior high, and Matt was a neat little grade school kid. Donna befriended me right away. Now don't get me wrong. Donna Watts was a beautiful woman and very well put together. We got to be very close and would talk pretty much every day. Bill was a good guy and a great father, but it was clear that he was putting her feet to sleep. Donna and I became the best of friends and spent a great deal of time together. Every time you turned around, someone was asking if we were having an affair because you know that would have been the scandal to beat all scandals. Imagine, a young black man from the North, swooping in and having some torrid love affair with the wife of the local Baptist preacher. Not only would that be enough to get her run out of town on a rail, but for me they would be reenacting a scene from *Mississippi Burning*, and I don't mean any of the funny parts, if there were any. I mean the part where they find the three civil rights workers buried in a landfill.

I guess you could say we were having an affair in a way. We were both at unique times in our individual lives. She was unhappy in her marriage and searching for something. It wasn't another person but more of something within her as both a woman and a wife. She was a great woman, and nobody would ever assume that she was in need of anything, but even with everything she had in her life, something was missing. Laughter, excitement, a little of the unknown was what I believed she was seeking. Any type of relationship with me was going to bring all those elements. I was just what she needed in her life at that time.

As for me, I was lonely for someone to actually give a shit about what was going on in my life. I was living in racist hell. I was paranoid of everybody around me at the time, not knowing who to trust and who to let trust me. I was single at this point. Susan was out of my life, just based on distance. It was difficult to carry on a great relationship when one person is thirteen hours away. So I let it just go away. She was pretty much moving on with her life also. She had moved to Chicago and was back in the fold of her old friends. She had moved past me. So spending time with Donna was perfect for me. There was nothing romantic involved in this. Donna was an extremely beautiful woman, and we used to flirt with each other all the time. Although everybody in town wanted to believe we were sleeping together, we were not. It was never on the agenda. We would eat lunch together when I could get away from school, or I would have dinner at the house with her family. They really took care of me while I was living there, and she was the best thing in the world for me then.

I didn't know how long I would be there, but I knew I would not last more than a year. I was way too liberal for these people. They had a real problem with anybody from the North. They still had a real problem with black people and any type of association with the two races. They had a black prom and a white prom. They had a black homecoming and a white homecoming. It was hard to believe that in 1989 this was still happening. I remember hearing the stories and partially living this as I was growing up in St. Louis, but this was right in my face every day. It was like living in a time warp.

I have a personality that is way too outgoing. I talk to everybody. I always have and I always will. That was not a good mix with the closed mindedness of the South. They were desegregated in the laws of the South, but they were still separated in their minds, and make no bones about it. Ol' JP has always attracted attention. Whether it is good or bad, that has been the rap on me. When I am around, things are usually not quiet. This attitude was something that I had no use for, so I knew at the end of the school year, I would be moving back to Missouri.

I went to the beach with a bunch of students for spring break as a chaperone. There were a bunch of parents, and because I was so low on funds, they asked me if I would like to watch over a group of them. I was more than happy. Me in a condo at Gulf Shores, with a group of fun kids and parents for a week. Oh yea, I was definitely in with that plan. I had never been there before, but everybody said it was a great place. It was perfect timing for me. The year was wearing on me. Between BCHS, attending the Academy, and the attitudes of the environment I was living in, I was stressing pretty bad. That was a week for me to do nothing but have a couple of cocktails at a beach house and relax. The parents that I was with were a great bunch of folks to hang around with. Most of them knew that I like to have a good time, and they were more than willing to show this single black man some true southern hospitality kids. The funny thing was some of their daughters were unbelievably gorgeous. They would hit on me and even be significantly more forward about things. I actually had one that used to leave her underwear on my car every night. When you are twenty-three years old, you're not that far removed from being a high school student. So the temptation was always there, but you'd have to be very, very stupid to follow through with it, because everybody knew that would be professional suicide to have a relationship with a student at the school. Regardless of the fact that most of them were already eighteen years old. But oh my god, they were fun to look at. I knew my days at Baldwin County High School were quickly coming to a close. I had met some really, really nice people, but the undertone of the entire situation did not fit my lifestyle. It was now time for me to leave.

CHAPTER FIFTEEN

Everything that is new or uncommon raises a pleasure in the imagination, because it fills the soul with an agreeable surprise, gratifies its curiosity, and gives it an idea of which it was not before possessed.

—Joseph Addison

BACK TO THE SHOW-ME STATE

WHEN THE SCHOOL year ended I was set to load up the car and head back to Missouri. Not really knowing where I was going to be brought some serious anxiety. So I decided, along with the decision-making process involving my mother, to come back home and seek out a couple of jobs. I'm was very interested in doing in coaching college football still. It had now become a serious passion of mine. Bill Quigley once told me that when you get bitten by the coaching bug, you will know it. You will stay in it for a very long time. And then one day, when it's not fun to you anymore, you will get out and you will find something else to do. I never knew just how correct this statement would be.

When I returned to Missouri, I sought out coaching positions at a number of local high schools. I was a pretty good athlete in high school, and everybody in the area was very familiar with me. I didn't think it would be very difficult to find a coach in the area that would not want me to be on his staff. Unfortunately, I could not have been more inaccurate about that. There were still a bunch of old-school coaches at most of the programs in the St. Louis area. The old-school staffs who had been together for many years and who were unwilling to infuse any new ideas and, how do I put this, "younger" ideas. It was going to be a difficult search, but I knew eventually I would find one. I looked in the paper, in the classified section, and found an available position for a defensive coordinator at, of all places, Rosary High School.

Rosary was a small Catholic high school in North County of St. Louis. Tuition was about five thousand dollars a year. They had Mass once a week on Wednesday and then again on every single Holy-Mary-Mother-of-God holy day there was, and as a Catholic kid from North County, let me tell you, there are a bunch of them. Tuck Boston was the head football coach. Tuck and I went back a few years. He was the former head football coach at Aquinas High School. Aquinas had the record for the worst loss in Missouri state high school football history. They were beaten by Hickman High School, 99-0. Every third time Hickman touched the football, they scored. I watched the game that night. I had never seen anything like it and still have not to this day.

Tuck was a good guy, but he had a boatload of trouble. He drank a lot, and when he did, he would get a bit out of control. He had a wife who was always strung out on some type of narcotic. Not sure what, but it was ridiculous how that situation would keep him and I from getting our jobs done. I remember when she was supposedly in the hospital. It was game night, and right in the middle of warm-up, there came Debbie Boston staggering out on the field in some kind of drunken, high, intoxicated stupor. I thought I was going to have to coach the entire team that night by myself. He managed to do whatever he did to get her off the field, but I can tell you, he sat on the edge of his seat all the time when it came to her.

The one thing I can remember about coaching at Rosary High School was my extraordinary very-difficult-to-deal-with principal. Her name was Sister Karl Mary Winkelman. She was a real piece of work. There were many incidents and run-ins that we had, but the one that sticks out in my mind the most prominently is that time I put in many long hours during the summer. We were responsible for the maintenance and upkeep of both the playing field and practice area. During the summer, I spent my own time and funds trying to keep the game field in some kind of playing shape. This meant you had to water the field regularly, and you had to seed and fertilize it. Obviously, there was no budget for this kind of work, so I took much of my own money—what little I had—and bought seeds and fertilizer for the field.

I distinctly remember that summer. It was well over one hundred degrees outside every day for nearly a month and a half. The heat was unbearable, but we didn't have much of a choice. The field was being taken care of, and the soccer coach had no interest at all in helping us do this although he would reap many of the benefits of our hard work. So all day after day, I would be on the tractor cutting grass, spreading fertilizer, and dragging what were unbelievably heavy hoses all over the field, trying to be sure that the field was taken care of.

Finally, when the first game rolled around, the night before our first game, the soccer team had a game. All of a sudden, while we were on the practice field on that Thursday afternoon, one of the custodians came out driving a tractor. He decided that the grass was too high to play soccer on, so he and Sister Karl Mary made a decision to cut the grass down so that the soccer ball would roll better. Naturally, that sent me into a rage of uncontrollable anger. I ran off the practice field and made a beeline to the principal's office. She then told me that the soccer coach had complained that the grass was too high and that he needed it cut. My argument was at no point in time during the summer did the soccer coach put forth any effort or give any input as to how the field should be cut, seeded, watered, or maintained.

She came back at me with this statement: "Rosary High School is a soccer school, and will always be a soccer school. We only have football for the people who do not want to play soccer. That is the only reason we have football." She ended that with "Is that clear to you?" and I actually came back, in true John Parker form, with "You can go to hell! Is it not clear to you?"

Now one might say that on that day I took the hell express, which is what happened when I went there with her, and I would disagree with those people. I would say that she was able to make her point and ask if it was clear to me, so all I did was make my point and I asserted myself so that I was clear to her. Again I knew my days at Rosary High School were probably going to be numbered, but I figured this position was not the be-all and end-all. My ambitions were significantly higher than this little high school, this little small parochial high school that had no ambition of its own to be great. It was at this time that I also began thinking about my destiny and what exactly it truly was. I know I was meant to coach football, but it was significantly deeper than that. I knew I had the ability and the capability to change the lives of the people I meet and the young men I coach.

I need to be on the college level, but I also realized how difficult it was getting to that level in this profession. I traveled around the country and visited with staffs, worked at camps, sat in the front row of clinics, and soaked up the knowledge that I knew I would need to reach my own personal goals.

At many of these clinics that I attended, I met and became good friends with a gentleman named Larry Kindbom. Larry had just recently moved to St. Louis from Ohio. He had taken over as the new football head coach at Washington University in St. Louis. We would run into each other quite frequently at camps and clinics in St. Louis. Then he also invited me to work at his camp in the summertime.

The following fall, the season at Rosary High School began with a bang, but I could sense that the principal wanted me out of the high school. And I can sense something coming down the pike. The evening before the third game, I was called to the principal's office, where I was accused of having an inappropriate relationship with a student. I figured that if they were beginning to trump up charges this ridiculous in nature, then it was best that I try and move on.

The very next morning, I went to see Larry. I gave him the scenario of the situation, and he told me to get my ass down where he was and go to work. That was my welcome to college football. It was not the greatest of situations, but something told me that if I worked hard for Larry, he would help me move up in this business. Besides, I got a great feeling working for him. Larry was as sincere and upfront as any person I had met. He honestly wanted me to be great in this business.

Working for Larry was a great experience for me. Although I was not getting paid a great deal, I was at the office on regular hours, and Larry gave me a position to handle. That was my introduction to coaching quarterbacks, specifically the freshmen quarterbacks. That was also where I developed my frank and down-to-earth approach to coaching this game and my spirit of seeing a task through, not accepting anything in victory that I would not address in defeat.

It was nice being back in St. Louis. Although I was living in the basement at Mom's house, I was comfortable being back in familiar surroundings. I was running with the homeboys again on the weekends and working odd and end jobs during the day and making the ends meet. I truly had found my calling, but like any young coach in this business, I had to pay my dues, and that meant hard work, low pay, and go where the job was. Jimmy and I were together again, and in fact, we decided to get a small apartment in Ferguson. Ironically, it was in the same complex where my mother and I lived when she divorced my father, when I was back in high school.

Jimmy was working at Ralston-Purina. It was a good move, and boy, did we have some fun. That place was party central. We would have people over, and let me correct that. We would have women running through our place all hours of the night and getting up and going to work the next day. We were running hard as hell, and when the weekend came, we ran even harder. Back in those days, Jack Daniels, Cuervo, Segrams 7, and the like were on a constant flow. I was not in any kind of a steady relationship at this time, so I was playing the field, and believe me, it was a big field to play in. It was an era that was made for me. Jimmy and I were hanging out in the clubs and getting more ass than a toilet seat, and really enjoying life. There was a couple that lived under us in an apartment, and they used to say that sounds coming from

JOHN STEPHEN PARKER

the ceiling were like a high-class pornographic movie, if there was such a thing. It was a great time.

I distinctly remember one New Year's Eve. The weather was not the greatest in the world. The streets were actually pretty icy, but we were determined to get out and have some fun. We made it to our regular joint, the 94 Aero Squadron Restaurant and Bar. It It had a small dance area, but it was very popular. We made it there and ran into the weekly crew that was always there. We hung out there all night and rung in the New Year. It was a great night, and man, did we get full of holiday cheer that night. When we were leaving, we were laughing and clowning around in the parking lot. We started walking toward the car, and I forgot about the ice in the parking lot. Well, I am a pretty smooth guy, but nothing was smoother than when I tried to hit a James Brown routine in the parking lot and failed at my attempt. The next thing you saw was a pair of size 11 Stacy Adams shoes up in the air and me on my way to hitting my ass on the ground pretty hard. It hurt like hell, and I looked over at Jimmy, and he was damn near in tears laughing as I was rolling around on the ice. I managed to try and contain my embarrassment to get back on my feet, but as soon as I did, what happened next was completely unbelievable. I managed to walk about four steps before, bam, my feet were back in the air, and I was flat on my back again. Now it became even more hilarious. There I was, dressed to the nines, looking cleaner than the Board of Health, and I couldn't walk ten feet without falling on my ass. It wasn't very cool, but that was not a time to be cool. I started laughing while I was lying there flat on my back, and it was a very cool moment. Not because I was lying in the street, but because me and my best friend were laughing our asses off at what had to be the funniest thing we both had ever seen.

We got through the winter, and shortly after the New Year, Larry managed to help me get an interview to be the offensive coordinator at Mac Murray College in Jacksonville, Illinois. It was a small river town about ninety miles north of St. Louis. The position required me to live in the dorm as a resident director. Luckily for me, it was the academic dorm, so the kids living there were a bit smarter and a little calmer. I was working for a guy named Mike Hensley. He was the most arrogant asshole of a person you could ever work for. I guess I may have gotten spoiled working for Larry, but this guy was just bad. I arrived there in February, and I knew it was not going to be long, but I also knew I was going to have as much fun as I absolutely could in the short period I was going to be there. Jimmy used to come up, and I would always make my way back to St. Louis. Because it was only about an hour-and-a-half drive, this made my access to things very convenient.

My counterpart in this job was a guy named Bob Frey. Bob was a crazy guy, married with a daughter living in the dorm behind me. Bob and I used to have a truckload of fun, but Bob was a lot crazier than I was. Whenever Bob and I would go on the road and stay in hotels, if I stepped out of the room for a moment, he would take off his underwear and bare-ass all the pillows on our bed. He would not tell you until it was time for you to crash out in bed. He would then inform you that he had, at some time when you were not looking, taken your pillows and wiped his ass with it. The fun part was calling housekeeping and trying to get them to bring you two or three pillows to your room, and then trying to explain the reason why you need them. That was the embarrassing part.

JOHN STEPHEN PARKER

As I was saying, Hensley was a nightmare to work for. I remember my first day there. He told me I was not his first choice for the position, nor was I even in the top five, but because the position was also as a resident director, I was interviewed with a broad range of people on campus, including the president. I impressed all those people, but Mike Hensley was above impression when it came to me. I am sure he had someone in mind, not to mention I have no doubt he did not want a cocky young black guy coaching any position on his football team, let alone being his offensive coordinator. He was your typical bullheaded football coach, angry at the world because he never made it to the level he thought he should have been coaching at. He would always give me the shitty jobs to do. He previously had a guy in my position that had a drug problem. He actually went recruiting in Chicago once, where he got caught up in a drug sting. The vehicle he was driving was impounded by the Chicago police and sat in the impound yard for nearly a month. Myself, along with Bob and the two graduate assistant coaches, went to Chicago on a recruiting trip. I was assigned to go to the Stoney Island Impound Yard on the south side of Chicago at 9:00 p.m. and pick up this vehicle.

Now for anybody who has never been to Chicago, the south side is known as one of the most dangerous and violent areas of the city. I am not one of the faint at heart, but that is definitely not where I would ever choose to go after dark. Of course, Hensley would send the black coach to pick up this vehicle, assuming that I would naturally relate to whatever type of criminal element might be lurking in that part of town since, clearly, all black people will understand and be able to communicate with each other. At least that was his thought process on the whole thing.

I got to the impound yard and gave them the appropriate paperwork to retrieve the car. You have to also remember that football recruiting in the dead of winter and in the city of Chicago can be worse than any other place on the face of the planet. So there I was, prowling around the impound yard at night, in the Chicago cold, in February. I swore to God that if I got out of there, I would never set foot on the south side of Chicago after dark as long as I stayed black. Not to mention that when I finally located the car, it was a complete mess. I got in the car and got the hell out of there as fast as I could. Susan had called and asked me to come to her as soon as I arrived in Chicago. We had been talking again and decided to hang out a bit while I was in town. I had no idea if it was going to go anywhere, but it didn't matter. I always felt comfortable with her, and it was our time to catch up.

I still had to get this vehicle back to campus, and I had a feeling there was still a huge adventure ahead of me. God, I hate it when I am right. After four days of freezing my ass off in Chicago, I now had to drive this heap of shit Ford Escort all the way back to Jacksonville, Illinois, in the dead of winter. Well, the trek started, and I got about two hours down the road, and wouldn't you know I was about to experience Murphy's Law. The back end of the car began to wobble, and I immediately knew what was wrong. I had a flat tire.

Now if you can picture that, you have got to be laughing your ass off. Here is a young black man on the side of Highway 55, in about five-degrees-above-zero weather, in the middle of flat-farm-country Illinois. I mean flat like "you can watch your dog run away for, like, three weeks" type flat. I am standing beside this shitty Ford Escort with a flat tire, and people are driving by me at seventy miles an hour and aren't even thinking about stopping to

JOHN STEPHEN PARKER

give me any assistance. I forgot to state that I am also dressed to the nines. I mean suit, tie, shined shoes, topcoat, leather gloves. The whole freaking thing.

Naturally, nobody would help me do anything, let alone help me change a tire. I managed to get it all done myself and get my ass back to Jacksonville and the warmth of my cozy apartment. I was done with the trek from hell, but I was not done with Mike Hensley. He was going to hear about this shit, and so was the director of athletics and the vice president for student affairs. I was so fucking pissed, and I really had nobody to blame but myself.

Summer rolled around, and I got a unique opportunity from out of the blue. It was the opportunity that I had been waiting for since I arrived at Mac Murray College. I got a call from Bernie Anderson, the head football Coach at Michigan Tech University in Houghton, Michigan. It was an NCAA Division II institution. I had no knowledge of the state of Michigan at all, but I knew how to read a map. I broke out the atlas, and I found Houghton Lake. It was in the middle of the state, but I had no idea that Michigan was divided into two parts, respectively called the Upper and Lower Peninsula, being divided by the Mackinaw Bridge in the center, which was a five-hour drive from each end of the state. Little did I realize that Houghton, Michigan, the home of Michigan Tech University, was in the upper half of the state. I found it on the map, and it scared me when I saw the location. It was located approximately four-and-a-half hours north of Green Bay, Wisconsin. The only thing I could think of was how goddamned cold it could actually be in a place like that.

I agreed to take the interview. They had some type of minority hiring program that had been approved by the university. Because they were so far north, the chances of luring more minority faces to the university was difficult, so they created this hiring program. I didn't care anything about the program. I just wanted to get out of Mac Murray College as fast as possible.

I took the flight. This was an expedition that I would not soon forget. Leg number one was from St. Louis to Chicago. After that, there were three legs on an eight-seat puddle jumper that finally ended in Marquette, Michigan. Now let's remember, when I left St. Louis in July, it was in the one-hundred-degree range, with about 100 percent humidity. I was about to experience a huge change in the weather. When I landed in Marquette, I noticed that the flags were blowing in the wind pretty hard. I just figured that the wind was just blowing. I had no idea that in the month of July, there would be a significant change in temperature. When I exited the plane, the temperature was forty-five degrees. In July, forty-five degrees is colder than a well-digger's ass. To top it off, I saw people standing at the airport in shorts and T-shirts, as if there was some kind of heat wave going on, and all I was doing was looking for Bernie, the car, and the knob to the car heater. That was also when I found out that we still had a one-hundred-mile drive in front of us, and to top it all off, Bernie also brought his mother with him, who was something right out of the movie *Fargo*. She had the accent that was full of "aaas" and "yaaas." Every sentence was "Are you having a good day, AA?" Or "Yaaa, today it was a bit nippy." It was worse than the foreign language I heard when I first arrived in Alabama, but this was the total mispronunciation of the English language. I had no idea in the world how she was speaking. It was a combination of slowing it down and adding breaks in the words. Whatever it was, it was a total butchery of the language.

So we began this excursion up to Houghton. Now I have to remind everybody I have an extreme allergy to mosquitoes. If I get bitten once or twice, it will be OK, but if there are any more than that, I will get pretty ill, so I have to be very careful that I don't get bitten too many times. That was definitely going to be an issue in the UP because it was nothing but trees, woods, and water, and the temperature never got up high enough for the mosquito nests to die, so every day was an epic in survival for me.

I arrive at MTU. It was a beautiful setting. The school sat right on the Portage Canal, which was a tributary river off Lake Superior. It was an unbelievable setting. I knew that if I was offered the position, I would no doubt accept it. We had dinner and got to know each other a bit. It was a fun place. There was one very noticeable thing about this place: there was nobody that looked like me anywhere around, and I mean anywhere. This was so far north that most people didn't even know where it was, and for sure, black people didn't have a clue as to where this place might be.

Bernie and I had a great visit, and the next day, he offered the job to me at a salary of twenty-four thousand dollars a year. It was more money than I had ever made in my life, and I accepted immediately. The only issue with the position was the fact that I had to be there in about three to four days. I had to get back and resign from my position at Mac Murray College, which I could do in god speed. I had been dying to get out of that place and get away from Mike Hensley as fast as possible. I hustled back and told Larry Kindbom where I was headed. He just laughed his head off. A black man actually choosing to move to the UP. This was quite unusual to say the least.

I managed to get everything packed into one of those Rider trucks where you pack your own things in and move yourself. I decided to split the trip into two days. I drove from Jacksonville to Chicago and spent the night with Susan. Our relationship was over from a romantic standpoint, but we were still the best of friends, and she invited me to come to her before I made it to the UP. I had no problem at all responding to her request with a big yes, and an even bigger smile on my face.

JOHN STEPHEN PARKER

CHAPTER SIXTEEN

Any change, even a change for the better, is always accompanied by drawbacks and discomforts.

—Arnold Bennett

COLORING UP THE NEIGHBORHOOD

I MADE THE eleven-hour trek to Houghton, Michigan. After driving about four hours north of Green Bay, Wisconsin, through what was mostly woods, I came upon a sign that I thought was for real, but it was a joke posted by a number of the students at Michigan Tech University. The sign read "The End of the Earth—2 miles, Houghton, Michigan—4 Miles."

Although it was a joke as I have always thought, there is some truth to every joke. This truly was the end of the earth, but at the same time, it was the beginning of August and it was truly a beautiful time of year in the area. More trees than I had ever seen in my life. One thing that did amaze me was the wildlife. I was coming into Houghton, and I slowed down and came to a complete stop at one point. I saw what could only be described as a "herd" of deer in the middle of the road. When I say *herd*, I mean anywhere between twenty to forty deer just standing in the road. These were not your usual average-size deer. I was a hunter for many years with my brothers and my uncle. I have shot and killed many deer in my time, but nothing like the ones I was looking at. They were all on the side of 200 to 250 pounds tops. There were both doe's and big bucks. Most of the bucks had antler racks on their heads, which resembled a chandelier in some rich guy's house. I mean to tell you, that you better have a cannon if you have intentions of bringing one of these things to the ground.

I drove into Houghton and found the university and went straight to the football office and found Bernie. He was excited to see me. I met a couple of the other guys. The offensive coordinator was a guy named Kurt Huffmaster. He was a graduate of Northern Michigan University. He was a gruff kind of guy with the personality of a brick. He was a great coach who could motivate the offensive side of football. We were a Wing-T team offensively. It was an outdated archaic offense. It was not very exciting at all because we hardly ever threw the football, but we averaged about four hundred yards of offense a game, and when we didn't step all over ourselves, we had the potential to be a pretty good football team.

I didn't know anybody at all when I arrived. Kurt and I had dinner a couple of times. Randy More was the defensive coordinator. Randy and I were the same age and had been to a couple of other places, and we knew what was going on fairly well. We also had much of the same personality. He introduced me to a woman named Mary Kaminski. She was the associate athletic director and also the head volleyball coach. Mary was a nice lady but a bit of a strange bird. Mary had dated a number of guys in town and had also been married to Roy Britz. He was a deputy sheriff in Houghton County, who also doubled as the assistant equipment manager in the Athletic Department.

JOHN STEPHEN PARKER

Randy and I decided one day to go have drinks on the patio deck at a bar called the Downtowner. It was one of the local hangouts in town that got a lot of traffic. When we arrived, we sat at a table with Mary, who invited us to sit with her. Lo and behold, there came Roy to join us. I could already tell that Mary was uncomfortable. She and Roy had a very vivid marriage by all accounts of the people I had talked to, and she was not happy with his arrival.

Well, her nature of discomfort was about to get worse because we were about to be joined by Mary's current boyfriend. His name was Craig. I didn't really know much about him other than the fact that he was significantly younger than she was. He and Roy didn't seem to have any issues. I think Roy was actually happy that Craig was in her life and that someone else could endure her misery. But there was still one piece of the volatile puzzle left, and it was coming around the corner. His name was Jim Courtright. He was the owner of a bar called the Library. I had already met Jim because Kurt and I had gone into the Library a few times when I first arrived. I was then made aware that Jim and Mary had just ended their relationship, and it was also a bad breakup. I believe Jim really liked Mary, but Mary had moved on, and Jim was not happy about that or the fact she was not involved with a very young kid in comparison to him.

So here we are. Randy and I, Mary, Jim, Roy, Craig, all sitting at the same table. This is when the fun starts. Mary is sitting here with her current boyfriend on one side of her, her recent ex-boyfriend on the other side of her, her ex-husband right in front of her and two innocent bystanders in Randy and me. It gets even more interesting when Jim starts blowing snide remarks at Craig, not really realizing that Craig has neither the age nor intelligence factor to understand any of the remarks. While this is going on, you have Roy sitting across the table just fanning the flames with the hopes that the other two will get into a physical altercation of some kind.

I finally got up for a bathroom break. Roy came in right behind me, and he was absolutely laughing his head off. He said to me, "I realize we just met, but let me fill you in on what is exactly going on out there." I told him I already knew, and we had a good laugh about it.

I was getting settled in at Daniel Heights Apartments. It was nothing spectacular. A simple two-bedroom, one-bathroom place. The people on campus called it Chinatown because of all the Asian students that lived there, and they were always cooking rice or noodles or something. It always smelled of cooking something very un-American. Practice was starting for me very soon, and I didn't really care. I was about to be very busy and wasn't going to be home anyway. They told me who our first game was against, and I almost fell out of my chair laughing. We were going to play the University of Missouri at Rolla. They were an engineering school in southwest Missouri, which I was very familiar with. Evidently, their president and ours were good friends, so they decided it would be a good idea if we played each other. It is always funny when administrators begin making decisions for people when they really have no clue as to how things really operate. If they had any clue, they would have realized that Rolla was on a nineteen-game losing streak, and we were pretty good, but the streak, combined with the fact that we were bringing a bunch of kids from the UP down to Missouri in the raging heat of August, was not a good combination. When I say heat, I mean picture two fully grown rats fucking in a wool sock. It was going

JOHN STEPHEN PARKER

to be so hot that these wimpy-ass Michigan kids were not going to be able to stand it. I was very familiar with it already, having been raised in the Midwest, but these folks didn't have a clue. This was even more evident when we began making travel plans. Bernie was a pretty nice guy, but he had never traveled outside of the UP in his life. So when he started making travel plans, it was almost comical. We had a staff meeting, and the first thing he said was he will allow the players to wear shorts. I almost fell out of my chair laughing. His reason was because he didn't want those guys to have anything hot on their legs. As if pants had just become sweltering pieces of the standard wardrobe of a man. Not to mention these were college kids, which meant this: if you don't give them a basic set of rules and regulations to discipline them by, then you are opening Pandora's box for just about anything you could imagine. The staff knew this, but Bernie was not the sharpest tool in the shed. We were to bus down to Marquette and fly from there to St. Louis via Chicago, but he was under the impression that buses don't have air-conditioning, as if we were living in the fifties and innovations such as air-cooling systems had not hit the busing industry. So he didn't make any of the players wear pants. We looked pretty ridiculous as a team. In Marquette it was OK, but when we landed in Chicago, we looked like a clown show. All the coaches were in coat and tie, and the players all looked like a bunch of homeless people. I was never so embarrassed in my professional career. All this was because our head coach was a really nice guy but didn't really have a clue about things like this.

We arrive in Rolla, and as I expected, it was ninety-seven degrees outside, and the first thing I heard were both players and coaches complaining about the heat. Not me, I was already prepared having grown up in this region. We got to the hotel and got the rooming assignments. Well, obviously, I drew the short straw because I had to room with Bernie. This was a goddamned nightmare. Nobody told me he didn't sleep before a game and would sit up all damn night watching television. It also just so happened that the U.S. Open tennis matches were being played in Flushing Meadows, New York. I had no idea that he would also sit up all damn night watching match after match while I was trying to sleep. What a freaking night that was. Not to mention we were getting ready to play a game against a team that was on a long losing streak, which can only have one of two results. If we win, then we are supposed to win, but if we lose, we end up on a Trivial Pursuit card somewhere. Either of these would be of no benefit to me as an individual or to the program as a whole.

We played the game, and just as I had feared, everything that could go wrong did go wrong. It came down to the last play of the game, which was a pass into the corner of the end zone, which was dropped, and we were beaten 21-19. UMR had broken their losing streak, and we had a long trip back to the UP. The most outrageous thing I saw was at the end of the game. Kurt Huffmaster was a great coach but had the personality of a brick and could never have a conversation with anybody, let alone Bernie. What was worse was the fact that Bernie would allow him to talk to him in any way he liked without much respect for his authority as the head football coach. Huff would cuss at him, tell him that his ideas were "fucking stupid," and a broad range of stuff like that. It had gotten out of control, and what I witnessed at the end of the game was a surprise to me but a regular day for everybody else.

JOHN STEPHEN PARKER

When the clock ticked off at the end of the game, Huff took off his headphones, and while Bernie was walking down the sidelines away from him, he threw them like a pitcher in the ninth inning of a play-off game. It was a strike, and they hit Bernie square in the back. Bernie turned around and looked at Huff but never made a move to confront him about it. Randy and I were in the box and witnessed the entire thing. I didn't know whether to laugh or be pissed at the lack of respect for the head coach, but in any matter, I assumed we would have a new offensive coordinator on Monday. Not only was I wrong, but I was completely off base with my assumption.

We had our staff meeting on Monday, and not only did he not fire Huff, but he blamed the entire loss on the defensive side of the ball. I was a bit pissed about that, but that would all be gone soon because of the team meeting we would have later in the day. You have to understand that Bernie was truly a good guy. He was a bit ignorant about the rest of the world and naive to some things about life, but you could not blame him for it. He was raised in the land that time forgot about and had no interest in catching up to. One of the things he had a bad habit of doing was speaking before he had a few minutes to think things through. This lack of preparation always made him come off as if he was not very intelligent. I have always believed that you can be stupid and quiet and nobody will know how stupid you really are, but if you are not prepared and you open your mouth and speak, you will leave no doubt. Well, Bernie left no doubt on that day.

The entire team gathered for the team meeting. During these meetings, the staff members usually stood in the back of the room while Bernie talked. Bernie walked in the room, stood there for a moment before he began speaking. We were all hoping he was thinking about what he was about to say, but such was not the case. He began speaking, and what he said first was the beginning of the most ridiculous speech I had ever heard. He said, "Gentlemen, I have three words for you. THIS WILL NEVER HAPPEN AGAIN." Clearly, anyone who could count knew that this was more than three words. We had forty members of our football team who had 4.0 grade point averages. They were all sitting on the front row with their hands out, counting their fingers. Meanwhile, when this sentence came out of Bernie's mouth, the coaching staff went running out of the back of the room because we were laughing so hard, it would have been even more embarrassing to Bernie. We got outside in the hall and had a great laugh, and even though we had lost the game to a team we had no business losing to, that one moment got me right past it and I was ready to get my ass back to work. The season went on, and we had our wins and our losses. The nice thing was that there was more wins than losses.

On our trip to Duluth, a few of the coaches would always go out and have a cocktail the night before the game. Huff and a couple of the guys always wanted to go eat ice cream. That was their vice. I could not do it. I needed a cocktail before the game, not freakin' ice cream. I and Keith Willis managed to find a place called Mothers in downtown Duluth. It was your typical college dance bar. Lots of women and lots of drunken guys trying to show off for them. Keith and I happened to be having a drink at the bar when this woman in a black-and-white houndstooth skirt walked over to us. I figured this was Duluth, Minnesota, and there was no way a white woman this far north is coming over to speak with me. Clearly, she was coming to talk to Keith. Boy, was I wrong.

Her name was Amy. She was in town visiting a few of her friends and happened to be out. She didn't appear to be drunk, but later, I found out she was pretty hammered that night. I was not sure if I was just lonely or just amazed by the fact that some woman would find me attractive enough to come over to me in the bar, but I found myself infatuated with her. She was younger than me and a bit naive about the realities of life, but she was fun. The relationship between Amy and I would go on for a couple of years, and would be as volatile as any I had ever had in my adult life. She moved in with me at one time, but she wanted to be married, and after I got to know her and her personality, there was no way in hell I was going to marry her. She was way too needy, and I was not mature enough to be married to anybody. I was still playing the field, living on the edge, and rolling the dice in my life. This was part of the compartmentalization ability that I had. I was Superman in my personal life. Completely bulletproof, with nothing being able to get to me. I enjoyed life to the fullest, and I was having a great time.

CHAPTER SEVENTEEN

All love shifts and changes. I don't know if you can be wholeheartedly in love all the time.

—Julie Andrews

ROMANCE IN THE U.P.

LATER IN THE season, they have something called Hobo Days at Michigan Tech. It is basically self-explanatory. You dress up as a hobo and go out and party. I had gotten to be pretty close with the basketball staff and their head coach Geoff Kottila. He was an MTU alumni who had played basketball and was all-everything while he attended school there. KO, as everybody called him, was a single guy but had more women than you could shake a stick at. He lived out on the Portage Canal in a big house. It was a party house, and there was always something going on out there whether it was a party or an orgy of some kind. KO's place was always the place to be.

One of the things KO had a problem with was keeping his cock in his pants when it came to the students. He had dated a number of students, some of whom were women's basketball players. This was not unheard of. Kevin Borseth, who was the women's basketball coach, was dating one of his players and eventually married her. He moved on and is currently the head women's basketball coach at the University of Michigan.

KO and I were out at this bar in town during Hobo Days. The name of the bar was JD's Boathouse. It was downtown on the Portage Canal. You could actually drive your boat down the canal and dock right behind the bars. KO and I, along with a few others, were always doing this kind of stuff. We were in the Boathouse, and all the crazies were out. They were dressed as if Houghton had just become the homeless capital of the North. KO and I were standing at the bar when a group of girls came up to us. One of them was dressed in army fatigues. She had her hair up and playing cards hanging from her ears as earrings. Her name was Laura. She was in her final year at MTU as a biology major. Her younger brother Mark played tight end for us on the football team. She was dressed like a complete bum, but there was something about her that gave me a moment of pause. There was only one problem. Her and KO had some type of relationship at the time, and I did not want to get involved in that situation. Besides, I knew it would not last because KO had women all over town and he was getting more ass than a rental car. So I decided not to pursue this right now, but I also knew in the back of my mind that this was not going to go away. Not to mention I still had a good bunch of playboy left in me. I was in good shape, and I was some sort of an anomaly in the U.P. because there were not very many people that looked like me.

I got through the season and went home to St. Louis for the Thanksgiving holiday. Managed to hook up with Bill and Jimmy. These two were now living together in a town house over in Hazelwood. Whenever we got together now, it turned into a drinking fest because we didn't see each other that often. I had also just bought a new car. It was an Eagle Talon TSI AWD. A red sports car that was faster than greased lightning. I could drive it in the snow because it had an all-wheel drive. Mine was a five-speed stick. KO had a similar one that was an automatic, and his was black.

I managed to drive it home and had the boys out one night while I was there. We went to one of our old reliable hangouts. A bar in the Westport area called Senior Frogs. It was a dance club, which was more of a meat market. Behind it was another bar called Mike Talania's New York Club. It was more of an older club with an older crowd. Many of the women there were what you would call cougars by today's standards. They were older but were always looking for a younger guy to play with, and I and the boys were just the playthings they were in need of.

I decided, while we were in Frogs, that I would take a stroll over to the other place and see what was going on. In my walk over, I passed a woman in the parking lot between the two clubs. She was wearing green denim jeans, which were, of course, painted on, boots, and a black leather jacket. Her name was Angie. She had dark curly permed hair and was fine as hell. We stopped and had a short conversation in the parking lot and then went back in the bar where the boys were. I introduced her to Bill and Jimmy, and they were a bit amazed that in the short time that I had been there, I had managed to get picked up by a gorgeous woman. We had a drink, and then she said to me, "Can we get out of here, I want to get you naked." Well, who was I to argue with a request like that. Of course we got out of there with god speed and went right across the street to the Red Roof Inn, where we got a room and made love all night long and again early the next morning. She did reveal a bit of information that I did not know the night before. Angie was married and had a son named John. Her husband was a guy named Jim. I never met the guy, but because of the affair, we would eventually cross paths. Angie and I would keep up a relationship for quite some time, but eventually, it would fade into the distance. Ironically, she ended up marrying Bill, which is funny because she hated him when she and I were together. I mean, she used to talk about him and Jimmy both like they had tails and shit in the woods, but somehow managed to bag him with the gold digger role that she was always meant to play. Bill never comes around us anymore and never brings her around at all. We have all moved on, but he was always the type of guy that could never let anything go. The only thing I could do was wish them luck. She was never the type of girl that I was going to bring home to Mom, but I could definitely bring her home to an aunt or an uncle. They are married now and have a daughter. I have never laid eyes on her, but life is too short to hold grudges, and I have moved on. Bill and I have been friends since the second grade, and to let some woman, especially one that had more miles on her than my tires come between us, was pretty stupid.

I was on the road recruiting and made it back to Houghton. Amy was living with me, but that was about to end. I was feeling cornered, and I was not in any mind-set to be married to anyone yet. I asked her to move out. I felt bad about it because she had moved to Houghton to be with me and had basically turned her back on her family, who were a bunch of rednecks from rural Minnesota. They were a bit backward, with her mom and dad living in the fifties still, where the only black people they knew were the lawn jockeys that they had in the front lawn. It was probably inevitable that she would leave there. Amy was everything that they were not. More than anything, her mind was open to the world and trying to figure out where she fit into it. I knew this, and although my treatment of her was probably a bit cold and cruel by some standards, I did what I felt like I needed to do because she was never going to grow being involved with me. She said she was pregnant when she was leaving Houghton, and her mom would help her handle it. She told me that it was mine, but I knew that was not the case. She had "dated" a couple of guys, so I knew that if she was with child, it was not mine. Many years later, she called me and told me that she was only trying to hurt me by saying that to me at the time. She was never pregnant, but she couldn't figure out any other way to do it. She did, however, actually get pregnant by a guy in Houghton. He had the hots for her while we were together, but she would not give him the time of day. After I was out of the picture, he swooped in like a vulture. He got her pregnant and then didn't want anything to do with her. I guess everybody wants to go to heaven, but nobody wants to die. She is a nurse now, living in Ohio with her daughter.

One of the reasons I was not real interested in Amy was because of the young lady I had met in the bar during Hobo Days. I was so infatuated with her, but I had not seen her in a very long time. I wondered if she was still involved with KO or if she even knew who I was. I would frequent the Boathouse with the hopes of running into her. Whenever I did, I would make every attempt to get her attention. I thought she was great, but my attention span was short. There were a bunch of women in the game at this point, and although I was playing the field, I knew even then that it was all going to come back to Laura someday. She had

JOHN STEPHEN PARKER

something that none of the others had. Not sure whether it was the ability to keep me grounded or the fact that she had a true appreciation of me, or at least, the "me" I really wanted to be. She would eventually be the focal point, but first, I needed to grow up, sow my oats a bit, and continue playing the field. This would more than a few times get me into trouble with Laura, among others, but looking back now, that trouble was exactly what I needed to help me grow up as a person and realize what was really important. A few years later, I would come to find out what a cavalier attitude about life would actually do for you and that pretty much every action has a consequence, but for now, I was going to grab with gusto all that life had to offer, and keep myself one town in front of the posse.

I did experience some things in Houghton that were not on the happier side of life, but it woke me up to the fact that no matter how far north you go, you could never escape racism in this world. Many people say that racism is based on fear. Most of the racism I experienced in Houghton was based on ignorance. The fact that there were very few people of color living in the U.P. made many of the residents ignorant to the social climate of the rest of the world. They didn't know how to speak to people of color in anyway. Simply, they didn't realize that I was no different than them, but they would make racial comments and laugh, believing it was OK but having no clue to the fact that things like that were horrible to say.

I guess I have to say I perpetuated the situation at times. I was the first black coach at Michigan Tech University, and don't think I didn't play that card many times. I remember one time there was video equipment missing from the office. Bernie had left the door open, and someone had walked in and removed the blow-up projector for the office. He tried to find blame with someone, but there was nothing he could do. Well, I had gotten a keg of beer, and I needed a trash can to put it in, so I went to the office in broad daylight and got one from the maintenance department and took it out of the side door. Mind you, this was with their permissions. Well, I got called about an hour later, and I was accused of stealing equipment from the building. I was brought into Bernie's office, where Rick Yoe, the absentminded Director of Athletics, was waiting with him to interrogate me on the issue. Instead of just coming out and asking me if I had stolen anything, they decided to make a futile attempt to be politically correct. Dancing around the question, like it was a hot tin roof in the summer. Finally, I just put their feet to the fire on the subject. I said, "Are you trying to accuse me of stealing from the building, because if you are, I need to make it clear that regardless of what you may have seen on the news about crime in the inner city, or how the media has portrayed us, or how you have seen things in the movies, all black people don't steal! Now is there something in particular you want to ask me, or can I go?" On that note, I excused myself from the room. Their ignorance to the outside world and their inability and lack of knowledge on cultures that were different than theirs kept them from dealing with me or any person of color.

That same year, a new guy joined our staff. His name was Karl Borree, and man, was he a character. Karl was from Appleton, Wisconsin. Karl was a free-spirited guy who lived life in a very nonrestricted way. He could sleep anywhere. He was never a fashion-conscious person, and he smoked a great deal of pot. I mean like he would spend afternoons on end getting baked in his apartment. Karl and I became very close friends and pretty much did everything together. We worked together very well. When we traveled, we always took my car while the rest of the team rode the bus. It gave us a great deal of freedom when we got to where we were going. The other coaches wanted to go eat ice cream on Friday night before a game. Karl and I were more interested in going somewhere where we could get a few cocktails and gaze at some scenery. The biggest reason we always took my car was because usually, the night before we left, we were in Nuttini's Bar in Hancock until well after closing, drinking Jack Daniels like it was going out of style. We used to do some crazy things, with most of it centering on drinking in some way. It made living bearable in what was probably the most secluded place on the face of the earth. Not to mention Karl was one of the few people in Houghton that didn't make off-color jokes and then laugh at them as if they were funny. Sure, he and I had spats. What friends don't have them every once in a while, but he and I were on the same page about things other than football. Things in life that mattered, and I know that he always had my back.

I really enjoyed my time there in Houghton. I met a lot of very nice people. Julie Foster, who was the secretary in the hockey office, got to be a really close friend of mine. She was a single mom, working hard and keeping her head above water. Every time there was a position open that I was interested in, I would call Julie and she would take care of my résumés and cover letters. She was also much more to me than an office aide. Julie was an objective voice of reason to me, and like a true friend, she would call me out when she thought I was screwing up. She was one of the things I knew I would really miss when I left Houghton, which I knew was coming soon. I was wearing out my welcome because I did not fit into the stereotypical mold that the people up there had seen on the news or read about in some news magazine. I didn't speak with a "yo, baby" lingo, or wear big "bling" jewelry, or stay within the African American culture when it came to relationships and dating. I have never seen color when it came to whom I was attracted to. Once again, my open-minded beliefs didn't fit into the culture of my surroundings, and it was inevitable that I would soon be departing. Only this time I would be taking more with me than just my belongings.

In March of 1994, I was downstate in Michigan. By this time, Laura and I had been living together, sharing bills, and really taking care of each other. Sometimes, you never know which way God is going to take you, but I decided to just let go and he would take me wherever he wanted to. We were attending her parents' wedding anniversary party, and it hit me. I was really in love with this woman, and I really needed to make the next step. I was not sure why. Like most people, I guess I felt like it was the next step. After her mom and dad said and renewed their vows, I decided to embarrass myself and propose. Obviously, anybody who knows me knows that I am not a very subtle person, and I never do anything major without some grand production.

I told her sister Beth I was going to do it, but she had to be part of it. My knees were not the best in the world, and I didn't want to be the guy who had fallen and couldn't get up, so I had Beth run and get a pillow from one of the rooms in the hotel. While the music was playing and I was sitting there with Laura, I gave a wink to the DJ to kill the music. I stood up, snapped my finger, and Beth threw a pillow at me to kneel down on. I threw it on the floor, and right there in front of about two hundred of her relatives and friends, none of whom resembled me in any way, I got down on one knee and asked this woman to marry me. Now mind you, I didn't have a ring yet, so I was sure that some of those folks were looking at me like I was a cheap son of a bitch with absolutely no etiquette, but I didn't care. All I knew is that I was asking this woman to spend the rest of her life with me, and to be honest, the words were coming out of my mouth, but I felt like I was standing outside myself, watching as this crazy man was committing to something that he had no idea of how it was going to work out. Then I thought, *What if she does not accept my proposal? Then I am really screwed here.*

That is the story of my life. Leaping into something, not knowing how it was going to work out, taking lump after lump along the way, and hoping that another window of opportunity would open up for me to go in another direction. You would think I would learn, but I have always been lucky enough not to really hit rock bottom. People say life is a bowl of cherries, and I can say that at times, I have found the pits, but have always been able to crawl out of them. Well, she said yes, luckily, and I knew that I had found someone who was tremendously patient because as most people know, I am no picnic at the beach to deal with.

CHAPTER EIGHTEEN

The world hates change, yet it is the only thing that has brought progress.

—Charles Kettering

CHANGE OF SCENERY

SPRING HAD COME to Houghton, and clearly, I had worn out my welcome. I was not coming back as a football coach to Michigan Tech University. I had created too many enemies, and my lifestyle was a conflict to what they saw as a normal black person. That meant I was different from the criminals and drug dealers they saw on the nightly news.

I remember one of my evaluations. They gave me credit for attending the funeral of Dan Dopp, one of my players who was killed in a traffic accident. What kind of Athletic Department evaluates you on the attendance of a funeral? I always thought that was just simple human compassion for another person and their family. When they gave me credit on an evaluation for this, I knew right then and there it was time to leave, not to mention I was sick of the people there. They were so phony and inbred, and I could no longer stand it. I coached track in the spring, handled the banquet, and left in peace. I began interviewing for jobs that spring also. I was all over the country. I finally got a call from Pat

Behrns. Pat was the new head football coach at the University of Nebraska at Omaha.

The UNO program was in a shambles, and they hired Pat to turn it around. He was putting together a staff that later on I would find are some of the greatest guys I ever had the pleasure of knowing and working with. There was Jeff Jamrog. Jeff was an Omaha product who was an overachieving high school player who earned a scholarship to the University of Nebraska, and played for the legendary coach Tom Osborne. Jeff's ultimate goal was to someday get back there. He got his wish and is currently an assistant coach for the Huskers. Lance Liepold was a great quarterback at the University of Wisconsin—Whitewater. A small Division III program. Lance, like Jeff, had a dream of going back to UW-W someday, and like Jeff, his dream came to life. Lance is the head football coach there now and is coming off two play-off appearances, with both ending in a national championship.

Mike Westefer was the offensive line coach from the University of Pacific in California. The most interesting thing about Mike was his crazy-as-nuts wife, Kathleen. She was just a controlling bitch who ruled Mike like he was a freaking German shepherd. I once asked her if she was still pissed about the house falling on her sister (from the *Wizard of Oz*), and she looked at me like the next words out of her mouth were gonna be "I'll get you, my pretty, and your little dog too."

Dennis Vokolek was one of our graduate assistants, along with Chris Crutchfield. It was a unique staff of personalities. One thing we all had in common was that we all agreed that Pat Behrns worked us to the bone. Sometimes he worked us way past the productive point. That first year was a rough one. We had to change the culture of the whole program.

Laura and I packed up and left Houghton in May and moved to Omaha. It was her, I, and Chelsea, our Calico cat. We loaded up the Ryder truck and put my little red sports car on the back trailer and headed to Omaha. We moved into an apartment in West Omaha at 144th and Dodge, right by the mall. It had a great sports bar called Champs. I saw many a great sporting contests in that bar. I also was in there the day one of my childhood heroes was part of one of the slowest police car chases in history, where he rode in the back of a white Ford Bronco while his best friend drove him. That was the beginning of what would be a year to remember for both me and for Orenthal James Simpson. By comparison, mine would be much less pressurized as I would not end up on trial for what was one of the most publicized and brutal murders in history. I was on trial though, and my judge was Pat Behrnes, and he was worse than any judge. He would work you until you were so tired you couldn't stand up, or until it got to a point that if any person said anything to you in a sideways matter, you were on the verge of ripping their head off and taking a crap down their neck.

Pat was a guy who had moved up the career ladder. He had risen to be an offensive coordinator at the Division I level, and I am sure that by the time he had taken the job at the University of Nebraska at Omaha, an NCAA Division II institution, he thought he would be head coach at a major Division I program like Nebraska. We always felt like he was pissed because he wasn't, and he took it out on the staff. I mean, Pat was so tough that he would barely give us time to attend church services, stating that "God wants us to win, therefore, God wants us to work." We once went and played the University of North Dakota in Grand Forks, North Dakota. The ironic thing about this was that Pat was the former head football coach at UND. He had made a couple of play-off appearances, but eventually, the powers that be ran him off. Obviously, this did not make for a great scenario. When we arrived, they made us dress in the Gino Gasperini ice area. He was the famous retired hockey coach who had won a couple of national championships. It was freezing in the arena, but you really couldn't tell because it was only about twenty-five degrees outside. It was colder than a witch's tit, but what happened next was even more surreal. Once we were dressed, they made us walk to the field, but they made us walk through the tailgate party. Mind you, these were all fans that were there when Pat was the head coach, and were probably the same ones who ran him off. All I knew was that when we began walking through the tailgate, we were hit by flying liquids of all kinds. Some of those were beer and soda. Some of those had the aroma of urine, which was accompanied by being called names most of which even made me blush.

Well, we were not very good that year, and that was putting it mildly. In all reality, we stunk, but working for Pat was an experience, and I learned a lot about the game, about coaching, about myself, and how much of a capacity for bullshit I had. I also managed to meet some great guys in the profession, many of whom are still my friends to this day. We did manage to win one game that year. The University of Northern Colorado was sixteenth in the country when they came into Omaha that year. Pretty cocky, and they had a right to be. Their head coach was a guy named Joe Glenn. Little did I know that he and I would become the best of friends, all because one of the worst football teams in the country was about to knock off a ranked opponent. Well, we did knock them off that night, and Joe and I have been friends ever since.

That year may have been the worst year of my life, but it was also one of the best years of my life. Working for Pat was crazy. Laura and I were together and trying to make a life, and in the midst of all this craziness, we were trying to plan a wedding. She figured it out one time that I was working about 105 hours a week while we were at UNO. All I remember was that I was always tired all the time. We got through recruiting and moved into spring football. The big day was fast approaching. I remember going to get measured for my tuxedo, and I weighed about two hundred pounds. Somehow, between January and June, I managed to gain about fifty pounds, except the tux was still the same size. I looked like ten pounds of shit stuffed into a five-pound bag, with the seams were crying to be free. I went around the office and personally handed the wedding invitations to our staff. When we had our staff meeting the next morning, Pat came right out and said none of the staff would be able to attend because the staff golf tournament was the same weekend, and the guys would have to work it. I was really pissed, but there was nothing I could do. Pat was good at pulling crap like this to fit his needs, or mostly just to be sure he got under the skin of the rest of us. Luckily, as usual, I always made friends with the boosters and supporters of the program and, in particular, a guy by the name of David Socol. David was the CEO of California Energy, and he sat on the Board of Directors of a number of different companies. His wife, Peggy, called me one day and told me and Laura to stop by the house. When we got there, Peggy offered something to us that we could not believe. She offered to throw a pre-wedding party for us at their home since the staff couldn't come to the wedding in St. Louis. We thought it was a very generous offer and gladly accepted. Not only did they do this, but they also brought our families in for it.

Now you have to understand that this was not just some ordinary home that they lived in. It was the Witherspoon mansion. It had a wine cellar, nine bedrooms, a bowling alley, both indoor and outdoor pools, both with spas, and an unbelievable eighteen bathrooms. Their children didn't even live there as they were away at boarding school for most of the year. There were two people living in this huge house, one of whom was traveling about half the year. It didn't make much sense to me, but different strokes for different folks. It was none of my business. All I knew was that Peggy had offered to give us this party and wanted to plan the whole deal. It was going to be a sit-down dinner for about sixty-five people. Beef fillets would be on the menu. She ordered music from a jazz combo.

It was a great evening. All the booster club members showed up with gifts, many of which we never even opened. You had to remember that we were in Omaha, so the first guy in the door at the party was a little, short older white guy with gray hair. Now I was not a very cultured person as of yet and had no idea who this guy was. He walked right up to me and said, "Congratulations, John! I had no idea who he was at the time. Remember I was a poor black kid from Berkeley, Missouri. I barely had a pot to piss in, let alone a window to throw it out of. I had no idea in the world who this guy was and what the hell he was doing at our wedding party.

I remember asking someone as he was walking away, and they said he was one of the richest men in the United States, and one of the richest in the world. When he walked in, he handed Laura a neatly wrapped box from Tiffany's. We could not wait to unwrap it. It was a very expensive vase. The first thing I said to Laura was "Don't drop it. We may need to hock it someday."

It was a great evening, and we had a lot of fun. The only thing different about the evening was Pat sitting and stewing because he was not the center of attention. He really could not believe that our largest booster had circumvented his authority and had a party for one of his assistants. Especially when he was working us to the bone. Because of him, I almost didn't even get married. He gave me some ridiculous project to do the same day I was supposed to leave for St. Louis and told me that I needed to finish it before I go get married. I guess he was trying to get me to quit, and believe me, I almost did a couple of times, but I would never give him the satisfaction of knowing that he broke me. I did his crazy project, and Laura and I made it to St. Louis on Wednesday. It was essential that this happen on this day because in the state of Missouri, if your marriage license is not on file by five o'clock three days before your wedding, then it is not legal and binding. We made it to the St. Louis County Court House at 4:45 p.m. on Wednesday. Ran up the stairs to the records office to get the license. We were burned out from the drive and the stress of the affair. We walked into the office, where we found this little old woman standing there. Now let's remember that Laura is nearly six feet tall, white, and Polish. I am a black kid from St. Louis. The first question out of the woman's mouth was "You two are not of relation, are you?" We nearly fell to the floor laughing, but it was just what we needed after the turmoil we had to endure for the past two weeks.

JOHN STEPHEN PARKER

CHAPTER NINETEEN

Every tomorrow has two handles. We can take hold of it
with the handle of anxiety or the handle of faith.
—Henry Ward Beecher

BEGINNING A NEW LIFE

OUR WEDDING WAS about forty-eight hours away.
One thing about weddings, it brings out the good and
the bad in people. One suggestion to anybody reading this, and if
you are not married: when you are planning it, give your parents
projects because it will keep them out of your hair. So we decided
to give my mom the church. That was her project, and she could
run crazy with it. We gave Laura's mom the reception hall, and I
knew that it would be taken care of with great detail. The other
thing nobody knew was that the rehearsal dinner would be the
first time that we would have our families in the same room.
Kind of a remake of "Guess who's coming to dinner." I didn't
think there would be any craziness or bad behavior. People who
know me know that when it comes to functions such as these, I
am pretty focused and serious about them, and obviously because
this was our wedding, my ass was a bit tighter than it usually is.

We got through the rehearsal dinner, and the boys and I were
off for a night of carousing on the town. I don't mind having a

good time, and believe me, I like to have a drink or two, but I was determined not to let myself get out of control, which would have been easy for me to do. I wanted to just hang out and get myself mentally prepared for the event. By the time we got back to the hotel, it was about 2:00 a.m. Jimmy and I sat up until about 5:00 a.m. just talking about nothing. The next day, we ran around and made sure everything was taken care of for the wedding. I was determined not to go crazy and not to let anybody make me crazy. The day was really not even mine. It was going to be Laura's day, and it had to come off without a hitch.

I woke up early the next day and went to work out first. I knew I was OK, but a good workout would relax me a bit more. Gave my car to Bill and told him he was in charge of the ushers. He was not happy about it because he wanted to hang with Jimmy and me a little more, but I needed him to take care of that. He did get to do one lucky thing that day. He was going to walk my mother down the aisle to her seat. He was pretty proud to do that for me. Her husband was on a cane and was not moving too well, so we just kind of put him in the seat up front where he could see the entire ceremony.

I really was not nervous. This was kind of a long time coming. Laura had pretty much sacrificed her entire future to be with me. She had wanted to be a pharmacist but put that on hold to stay in Houghton to be with me, so not only did I really want to marry her, I really owed her a life because she had given up hers for me. Also, I have to admit that I was not always the greatest person and not the smartest person at times. I put this woman through hell at times. I can honestly say I was running pretty hard at times and putting myself in some very compromising situations, some that you don't recover from unless you had some strong support.

If it was not for her, I would probably have either killed myself or been killed by somebody by now. She had the ability to keep me somewhat grounded at a time when I needed that assistance.

As the ceremony started, all the groomsmen came out from the back. As the bridesmaids came down the aisle, a little bit of tension started to build, but then I saw her, and most of it disappeared pretty fast. Rev. Wayne Lawrence did the ceremony, and he had told us he would make a short pause after he asked the question "Is there anyone here that objects to this union? Let him speak now, or forever hold your peace." Because this was the first time our families had ever met, that pause felt like it had taken an entire hour when, in reality, it had taken about one second.

When the ceremony was over, we jumped in the limos and took off. Made it to the reception after taking a few detours, walked in, and let the party begin. Most of my friends were sitting in the back, and later, I found out they were all taking bets on just how long it would last. Not cool, but given my past, I understood. I was a player who liked to have fun, and God, I had fun, but Bill Quigley told me one time that when a man grows up, he puts away the childish games. That was just what I intended to do. Sometimes it worked out that way, and sometimes, it was just too hard to not, but either way, there I was, Married, working, building a future. Oh my god! I had just cloaked myself in a brand-new garment; The garment of responsibility. Not sure how that was going to fit, but I would try it on for a while. If it was like a Nike shoe, you can wear it out and take it back and get a brand-new pair.

We managed to get through the day. Nobody told me this about my wedding day, which I want to point out to everyone who reads this and is contemplating on tying the knot: you will have no time to eat or drink at your reception because everyone will want a piece of your time. The other thing is this: take some kind of painkiller before the reception because if you are as happy as you should be on that day, your face will be aching from smiling so much. One other thing is all that wedding night bliss that everybody talks about. Well, here was our blissful evening: We got upstairs to the penthouse suite of the Hilton Hotel by the St. Louis Airport. We were so tired and hungry—and how do I say it, "too pooped to pop"—so we got an extra large Imo's pizza and took the money out of the wishing well and counted it. The next day, we had a small party at my old house on Packard where I used to live but was now where my brother Mike and his bitch of a wife were living.

The next day, we were off to Chicago for a short honeymoon of three days or so, and then to Michigan for another reception for her family members who were unable to make it to St. Louis. It was a short trip because I was working for a crazy nut of a head coach in Omaha, and he wanted us in the office pretty much all summer. I had prayed that maybe some program would call me and offer me a new opportunity, and I never dreamed that it would happen. Well, they say if you just pray, relax, and let God handle it, it will work out the way it was supposed to.

We arrived back in Omaha on a Sunday, and I was in the office immediately at eight in the morning in the dead period of summer. At about 8:45 a.m., my phone rang. It was a guy named Mike Caven. He was the head football coach at East Tennessee State University, in Johnson City, Tennessee. He said, "John, you have come highly recommended by a lot of guys, and I wondered if you would like to be the defensive secondary coach and recruiting coordinator at East Tennessee State University?"

I was so stunned by the offer that I went silent. I said, "Coach, I would like to come down and see the place," and he said, "There is a plane ticket waiting for you at the Omaha Airport."

I knew Pat would go crazy on me if this all came to fruition. He was already a bit paranoid about shit when it came to staff concerns and if you looked at another opportunity. I quickly told Mike that I needed him to call my head coach as soon as possible and make him aware of the situation as soon as possible. I also wanted to be assured that if I come down and talk with him that the position would be mine to turn down. I had to put myself in that position because I knew if I went and interviewed for that position, Pat, being the egomaniac that he was at the time, would fire me in a heartbeat if I went and interviewed for another job. Mike did call him, and just as I thought, he went nuts. It probably didn't help matters that he was on vacation in California. He called me immediately after Mike called him, and I could already hear the disdain in his voice for me and the entire situation. Pat was a guy whom I believe thought he was going to be a Division I Head Coach by this time in his career, and because he wasn't, he was a bit pissed or jealous or whatever. All I knew was that there was animosity on the other end of the line, and it was about to all come crashing down on my head.

When I answered the phone, he began to hammer me on how unprofessional I was about the situation. All I did was sit there and just take it because I knew I would not have to endure it much longer. He asked me, "Why didn't Mike Caven call me first?" and my only response was "Because I guess he didn't want to hire you." That did nothing but throw gas on what was already a raging fire. He stated to me, "That if that job is offered to you, before you turn it down, we will need to have a long conversation." Well, that was an indication to me that I was no longer needed around UNO and I had better find a new position. Before I even hung up the phone, I knew I was going to East Tennessee State University and it would be good riddance to UNO and Pat Behrns.

When I returned from the interview, I had the job in hand. In fact, because we had just gotten back from our honeymoon, we had not even unpacked the car yet. I told Laura to just leave the car packed. I went to the office and was talking with the other guys, and sat down in my office for not longer than a minute when Pat came down the hall. He stuck his head in my door and said, "Mr. Big Time, come down here and let's talk." When I walked in, I sat down and was more than gracious to him. I thanked him for the opportunity to come there. I asked him what the exit process was for leaving the university. What I heard next was unbelievable but, at the same time, pretty expected because of the source. Pat looked me right in the face and said, "Here is the exit process. Leave the keys, and leave the coat, and get the fuck out. I want that office clear in forty-eight hours!" I was pretty floored. I knew he was pissed and a bit of a tyrant, but never did I think I would get that from him after all the hell the guy put me and the rest of the staff through. That did nothing but heighten my desire to get the hell out of there and away from the guy.

Although working there was a nightmare at times, I did appreciate the guys I worked with, and two of them went on to be head coaches. As I said before, Lance Leipold went on to the University of Wisconsin—Whitewater and won a couple of National Championships. Jeff Jamrog went through the same exit I did a year later and was just as blown away as I was. He left and went to New Mexico State, became the head coach at Mankato State University in Minnesota, and eventually landed back at the University of Nebraska as the director of football operations. Dennis Vokelek was a graduate assistant coach who moved around and got a few full-time gigs. Presently he is at Missouri State University. Fred Reed was probably the guy I least expected to move a bunch. Fred left Omaha a couple of years later and came to the University of Minnesota—Morris under Head Coach—wait for it—John Parker. Left there and went to work where? At Michigan Tech University, then back to Omaha as the defensive coordinator. He moved on to Ohio University, the Detroit Lions, and the Buffalo Bills, and then to the University of Buffalo under then head coach Turner Gill.

Those were some of the greatest guys in the world to work with. One thing about working with those guys was, we would never let up on each other, so you had to be aware of everything you did, your mannerisms, your wardrobe, whom you were dating. Anything that they could possibly find to give shit about, they would find, therefore, self-awareness was of the utmost importance.

CHAPTER TWENTY

Don't aim for success if you want it; just do what you love and believe in, and it will come naturally.

—David Frost

EAST TENNESSEE, OMG!

WE LOADED UP the car, except this time, we had accumulated so much stuff that we had no choice but to hire a mover, and the university would pay for it. Never had that done yet. We made the move to East Tennessee State University.

Now Johnson City was not what I expected on the surface. It was actually a fairly nice-size metropolis of stores, malls, and restaurant chains. It was not much different than living in the suburbs, except for one thing. I was now married to a six-feet-tall white Polish woman in East Tennessee. This was the South, and although many people think it has changed, I can assure you it has not changed all that much. I realized that when I got there.

Mike Caven was born and bred a Georgia boy. He played football at the University of Georgia for Coach Vince Dooley. He later went to work as an assistant coach at Georgia for Coach Dooley. His claim to fame is that he recruited a running back named Herschel Walker to play football at the University of Georgia. One thing about Mike Caven, he had a thought process that all black people should be kept in their place and corrected if they ever stepped outside of that place. He was an old Southern guy who wanted to come across as being progressive, but in fact, he had old Southern beliefs that had been instilled in him by his segregated upbringing. He probably was never in favor of the South changing, and no question, he would have protested during the civil rights era to keep little black kids from going to school with little white kids. He limited the number of black coaches to two. There was me, who was a shit disturber from day one. I bucked the system because I wanted it to be a better program. When you are coming off a four-win season, I think you change things, but when the suggestions for those changes come from a person of color and, in particular, and rebel like me, you can best believe it fell on deaf ears.

The other black coach was Darryl Mason. Darryl was coaching wide receivers and was an excellent coach. He was from Little Rock, Arkansas, and played at the University of Arkansas for Lou Holtz. Mike didn't come down on Darryl as much as he did on me. Maybe because Darryl was on the offensive side of the ball. Maybe it was because Darryl didn't have much to say, and he kept his head down, and the bullets never really hit him. Either way, Cavan had a much-better relationship with Darryl than he did with me. The other guys on staff were all white, and all had the same mentality as Mike Caven. Simply put, black coaches, and, for that matter, black people were "necessary evils." If we were not around, there would be no politically correct pictures, and they would not win any games without those black players because they were all the best players on the team.

It was awkward working there because of the racial climate, but what added to the awkwardness of the situation was that there was something else going on that had engulfed the entire country, and would bring light to the racial lines that many people had wanted to believe were long ago covered up by the times. I am clearly referring to the murder trial of Orenthal James Simpson, "the Juice." That was the trial of the century, with a full cast of unusual characters. Looking back on it, this trial woke up racial relations in the United States and struck a nerve in the country. The murder of a white woman and her male friend. The accused was her ex-husband, who was a black man, and probably the very first black athlete that was accepted by white America. O. J. Simpson was a Heisman trophy winner and a member of the NFL Hall of Fame. He was the endorsement face of many products and even acted in some very bad movies. He was one of the first professional athletes of the modern era to diversify his talents. With this diversification came acceptance. This guy did not fit the stereotypical black reputation that most people found on their local evening news. He was young, good looking, athletic, an actor, and very articulate. White America loved O. J. Simpson. They were open to inviting him into their white world because he didn't fit their mold. His marrying of the young, sexy, and white Nicole Simpson, especially after being married to a black woman prior to this, would be totally accepted by them.

In the black community, his acceptance was a bit different. Black people in America felt as though O. J. was a sellout to his own race. They felt like he had the opportunity to influence, by his own popularity, young black men in this country, who were becoming statistics on a daily basis. They were either going to the armed forces, going to jail, or dying, many more times than not, by the hands of another black man. Many referred to him as an Uncle Tom who turned his back on the black community for the upward step of acceptance in white America. I heard one time that "O. J. had not been black since he won the Heisman trophy."

In many ways, I felt like O. J. Whether I was playing sports or in the working world, I always wanted to be the best, but I wanted to also be the best in the eyes of people who didn't look like me. This would, in turn, piss off my black friends sometimes, who had labeled me already as an Uncle Tom and gotten mad at me because I was "trying to be white." Truthfully, it was never about "trying to be White," it was more about doing the things that I needed to do and playing the game by the rules that were set down in their rule book. I knew that if I did that, and I was really good at what I did, it would be difficult to keep me out of their world, and their world was where everything would happen for me. East Tennessee State was definitely their world.

I spent six months in Johnson City, Tennessee. Some days it felt like a lifetime. I learned a great deal through working there. I learned that racism was alive, well, and living in the South. Here I was, married to a six-feet-tall white Polish woman, living in a small Southern city. I was risking my life every day. I knew I was on the outs with the staff and the other wives when we took our first trip as a team. We went to the University of Tulsa to play a game and chartered a flight. The other wives were typical Southern belles. There were concerns about their excess. Their excessive homes, theirs excessive hair and nails, and their excessive weight. It was all pomp and circumstance.

When we boarded the plane, it was clear that we did not fit in with this crowd because not a single one of those women even spoke to Laura. Not only that, but they treated her like a leper. We never did get close to those people. They were living in a totally different world than us. It was a world they were truly accustomed to as their parents and their parents before them were brought up in. They believed that interracial relationships were the worst kinds of relationships. I did feel bad about putting Laura through all that. That was not what she had signed up for. She was smart but, at the same time, very naive about the world. We once went to a cookout there, right after we arrived in town. She took a bunch of our wedding photos that we had just gotten back. She was so proud and wanted to show the photos to everyone there. Nobody asked or even wanted to look at them. I think right then she got an idea of how life in the South was going to be if we were going to stay in Johnson City.

I, on the other hand, had to work with these guys, which really was no fun at all. There was so much favoritism among the staff. If your ideas didn't flow through certain staff members, it fell on deaf ears. If any ideas came from Darryl or me, you can best believe you heard crickets in the room. As I said, we were necessary evils, and when the verdict of the trial of the century came down, that made it even more difficult on us.

I remember where I was on that day. Many people can remember where they were on important dates in history: the death of a president, the beginning of a war, a national momentous event, or a devastating tragedy. Most people can remember. I can remember that I was in the football office, sitting with Darryl Mason, surrounded by all those very Southern Caucasian people who were all hoping that not only would Simpson be found guilty, but that they would take him immediately to the gas chamber and gas him twice. When they began to read the verdict, I remember my stomach tightening up, like I was watching a horror movie, waiting for the bloody villain to step out from behind the door with a butcher knife.

When the jury foreman said the words "not guilty," I let out a celebratory but fairly low-key "Yessss." Darryl gave me a little nudge as if to say "Shut up, before you get us lynched." What was amazing to me was, after they read the verdict, there were many people, most of whom didn't look like me, in the office in tears. They were trying to figure out how the judicial system had committed such a travesty of justice by not convicting him and sentencing him to death. I was asked later during the day by a reporter how I felt about the verdict. I didn't really want to comment but felt it was necessary. I told her that it was a perfect example that the judicial system was not truly about the law but more about money and popularity. O. J. Simpson had enough money to hire Robert Shapiro, Robert Kardashian, F. L. Bailey, and the great Johnnie Cochran. That hourly bill was somewhere in the neighborhood of forty-five hundred to five thousand dollars an hour. Also, this trial was held in Southern California, which was to his benefit. A former player at USC, one of the most storied programs in all college athletics. This whole thing started off in his favor. I mean, really, what the hell is a "low-speed chase" where you have the ability to pick where the police pulls you over and arrests you?

I also told them this: We live in a system of laws. The overwhelming majority of those laws were all created by people that do not look like O. J. Simpson. What most of white America was most disturbed by was, they considered this an open-and-shut case from the beginning. It struck at the foundation of racism in this country. It was a beautiful white woman who was allegedly murdered by the black ex-husband. She was the beautiful white princess who was enamored by the black beast that was supposedly tamed by the domestication of white America, but never got his animal instinct out of his system and finally attacked his keeper. Typical *Beauty and the Beast* story line, except this was real life, and he was a human being, not a savage beast.

They were expecting this to be so easy a case. The problem was that the cast of characters were never going to make it easy. Many people referred to the verdict as "reverse racism" or "reverse discrimination." My comment to them was that in 1964, the bodies of three civil rights activists were found in a construction landfill in Neshoba County, Mississippi. In the search for those three workers, they had to drag the rivers in the area and found the remains of thirteen black men who had been lynched or shot. Many of them were castrated. Does anyone have any idea who these men were because there was never any news story or spectacle made of their murders? And yes, they were murdered. My point is that the history of white America has always majorly accepted the destruction of other races, but when any race—be it black, Native American, Asian, etc.—attacked back or is seen as attacking back and white America is portrayed as a victim, it gets labels such as reverse racism or discrimination. Reverse anything is when you are doing something and then you change your direction or, in this case, the way you think. These people are getting reverse racism or discrimination confused with another thing called karma, or as they say on the street, "Payback is a real bitch." These laws or rules of the game were created by people who don't look like O. J. Simpson. He had enough money and enough popularity to play by the rules of a game that was not set up by him. So I guess the old-school adage is true in this competition: "Don't hate the player, hate the game."

CHAPTER TWENTY-ONE

Civilization is unbearable, but it is less unbearable at the top.

—Timothy Leary

TIME TO MOVE ON

THAT SEASON WAS straining at best. Cavan had pissed off the former director of athletics, so she scheduled our first five games of the season on the road, which included two nationally ranked 1-AA teams and two Division 1-A teams. Nobody in the history of college football ever had an opening schedule like this. The thing I liked about the program and about any program I have ever been affiliated with is the players themselves. There was one in particular whom I was really impressed with. His name was Donnie Abraham. Donnie was from Orangeburg, South Carolina. How Coach Willie Jefferies, who was the head football coach at South Carolina State University at the time, ever let this young man get out of the state is beyond me. Donnie was one of the fastest players I have ever coached. Mike Cavan called him a pussy one day in a staff meeting. I almost came unglued because he had no real clue as to who Donnie was as a player or as a person. Donnie had more talent than Mike Cavan could ever imagine. You just had to know how to get it out of him.

I once saw Donnie chase down a wide receiver ninety yards from the other side of the field. That wide receiver went on to a great career in the NFL. It was Terrell Owens. That was also where I met a guy who would become not only a mentor of influence, but a really good friend to me. Harold Lewis was the president/owner of National Studios, a photography company he started in his twenties, but he was a part-time sports agent. He helped guys with their contracts. I tried to get Harold to talk with Donnie, but he passed on it because at the time Donnie really was not a highly touted player. Once he tested, though, that all changed. Although I give Harold trouble about that all the time, I admire what he has done in his career and, of course, the money that he has made. And although Harold didn't handle Donnie, Donnie did go on to be a third-round draft choice in the NFL and got an eleven-year career, including a couple of Pro Bowl selections.

As the year wound down, I decided it was time for me to strike out on my own. Since I left Washington University in St. Louis, I hadn't really trusted anybody I had worked for. That was even more apparent now I was working at ETSU. I needed to get my own program. I was young, and probably a bit impatient about my future, but I had never worked with anybody that I knew was a rising star, or at least one I knew would rise and take me with them. I began to look around for a head coaching position. I knew it would not be easy. I was thirty years old, and the outlook for head coaching opportunities for black coaches was absolutely terrible. There were 116 Division 1A football programs at that time, and only about four of them had black head coaches. There were even more programs at the 1AA and Division II levels, and Division III looked like a Mississippi lunch counter in the early 1950s. I knew that I would have to probably take a head coaching position at some place that was in terrible condition. I had no idea that I would have to go through what I was about to go through.

The position of head football coach opened up at the University of Minnesota—Morris. I had been out there a couple of times while I was coaching at Michigan Tech. It was about three hours west of Minneapolis, which, if you have ever been that way, you know that there is not much civilization three hours west of Minneapolis. The only thing that far out there is a clear abundance of is corn. I don't mean that "knee high to a farmer" type corn. I mean that really high stuff, like "If you build it, he will come" type stuff. I used to think that "Shoeless" Joe Jackson was going to come walking out of those fields someday. I put in for the position, never really expecting to get it. I really wanted the interview though. I had been interviewed many times before this for head coaching positions but had finished second every time. It was always to a less-qualified white applicant, so I didn't think this one was going to happen either. Somehow, when you have been through this as many times as I had, there really was not a reason to be optimistic.

I was called by Mark Fohl, the Director of Athletics, to come out and interview for the position. I accepted the interview. That was where the epic begins. I flew from Johnson City, Tennessee, into Minneapolis, where I had to rent a car. When I landed in Minneapolis, it was four degrees above zero, and snowing. I rented the car and headed out on Interstate 94 north toward Fargo. I could tell that this trip was not going to go well for me. The snow began to come down harder every minute I was on the road. Unbeknownst to me, they had closed the highway while I was on it. I finally got to Route 28, which was my turnoff to the town of Morris. When I came off the exit, the gates were closed, so I had to actually drive off the road to go around the gate and get back on the road. I got back on the road and headed down Route 28, doing about twenty-five miles an hour. Not real speedy if you expect to get anywhere, but it was more important to me to make it there than how fast I was moving. Little did I know that speed was not going to matter.

By this time, I was in a complete whiteout, and I mean I could not see anything in front of me at all. The road was disappearing quickly, and I had no idea what I was going to do if it did. Finally, at twenty-five miles an hour, I ran smack-ass right into a snowdrift that stopped me dead in my tracks. Now there I was, stuck in a snowdrift in the midst of a snowstorm in the middle of Bum Fuck, Minnesota. My first thought was that I was going to die out there. I could not believe that I was going to die in a snowstorm. After those years in the Upper Peninsula of Michigan, where it snows every day for over half the year, I would travel the United States and die in a Minnesota snowstorm. Ain't this a bitch! Lo and behold, I saw some headlights coming up behind me in this storm. Now I only hoped that he would see me and not run over me.

Well, he did see me, and stopped. He came up to the window and asked me where I was headed. I told him I was headed to Morris. His only response was "You are not going to make it there tonight." Now I, being the not-so-trusting person I was, first took that as he was going to shoot me in the head. After all, here is a black man in the middle of a country road in Who Gives a Shit, Minnesota. You think anybody would ever find my ass if that was what he had planned to do. But the next thing he said really surprised me. The guy said, "I'll pull you out. When I do,

JOHN STEPHEN PARKER

just follow me back to the house. You can stay with me and my family tonight. Otherwise, you will die out here."

That blew me away. I would have never thought that in the middle of nowhere, a Good Samaritan would rescue me from a snowstorm that was on the way to shutting down an entire state. I gladly followed him to his home, which was about a mile away. I wish I could tell you that this story is over, but we have just gotten to the good part.

When I arrived at his farmhouse, it truly was something right out of The Waltons, including six kids, all under the age of five, all of which were very vocal and had never, outside of television, seen a black person up close. Man, was I on display. The only thing I could compare it to was the scene in the movie *Rainman* when Dustin Hoffman had to watch Judge Walpner on "The People's Court" and he knocked on the door of the woman with all the kids. I mean, there were only six kids, but it seemed that they were multiplying by the minute, and they were all making more noise than a busted chain saw. His wife was very surprised when I walked in the door. It was like her husband went out for milk at the grocery store and came home with a very cute puppy. She was very nice. We sat down at the dinner table and had one of the best-tasting roasts I have ever eaten. After dinner, the kids began to wind down, which was the "Sound of Silence." I needed to be up and on the road again by six in the morning, so they made up a bed for me on the couch, and I crashed out. The next morning, I was up at five thirty, got dressed, and headed out. He got up also and led me back to the main road and waved good-bye to me. To this day, even with my memory, I cannot remember his name, but I will never forget the fact that this guy and his family saved my life in the middle of a raging snowstorm. They didn't have to do this, but they chose to, and I will be truly grateful for the rest of my life.

I made it to Morris that morning. I went straight to the hotel they had booked for me the night before so I could get cleaned up for the interview. When I showed up at the Athletic Department offices, I walked into Mark Fohl's office. The first words out of his mouth were "What are you doing here?" I said, "I am here for the interview." He asked, "How did you get in here? The roads are all closed, and the university is closed also. I am not sure I can even get the committee together." I said to him, "Does that mean I get the position, because I am here, and ready to go." He just laughed, but in my head, I was thinking that if I could make it here in the midst of a snowstorm, there was nothing that was going to keep me from getting this job.

Now I had done my research on Mark Fohl. He had been a graduate assistant coach at the University of North Dakota for another guy in my past, Pat Behrns. Mark was a football guy, or so I thought he was. Later, I found him to be a very lazy administrator who really wanted to pinch every penny he could to stay within budget, even if it meant that the athletes would suffer. I also did my research on the football program at Minnesota—Morris. They had the current longest losing streak in Division II football at twenty-nine games. They were operating in a fully funded conference. Meaning, the conference schools had and were able to offer scholarships. The only problem with this was that Minnesota—Morris was the only institution in the conference that did not offer any athletic scholarships whatsoever, which automatically put them at a disadvantage. Lots of my friends who knew I was having an interview there were calling me all day and telling me that "If this is going to be your first head coaching opportunity, you didn't want this to be your first head coaching opportunity." I went through the interview, got offered the position, and yes, I did accept it. Funny thing is that because this was my first time at the helm of my own program, I sure as hell didn't ask enough questions about the university. I didn't realize that this institution was in turmoil over, of all things, a racial incident. Only two months prior to my hiring, they had an incident that made national news. I mean, it was on *60 Minutes*. It was in *U.S. News and World Report* and a vast number of national publications.

On Halloween night, the assistant wrestling coach and two white wrestlers decided to play a joke on two black members of the wrestling team. They blindfolded them and took these two kids out in the woods. That was where the joke turned very real. They took off the blindfolds to find themselves standing in front of a burning cross. Now anybody who has any recollection of American history knows what this is the symbol of. How anyone would think that this could be found humorous in any way is beyond me. This clearly made me think of the insensitivity and complete ignorance of the individuals involved. This enraged the small but vocal persons of color on the campus, which it should have. Obviously, the university was sued by the families of the two young men. They settled out of court for about seventy-five thousand dollars apiece, which is very low in my opinion. Seventy-five thousand dollars for violation of civil rights in the 1990s, with no admission of guilt, is nothing. If this had been my child, it would have ended with an eight-figure settlement or at least a six-figure deal, and they would have had to name the stadium after me. That is the only way to make people understand that you cannot treat people like that, and if you choose to do so, you will be held accountable. Soon, you will read about how

I handled a racial discrimination suit and what happened to me, but for now, more about Morris.

The president of the university was a guy named David Johnson. He was your typical academician. He had very little interest in college athletics. His only focus was how the science center was going to get built. He also was out of touch with how the world had progressed in racial relations and, at the same time, how much the world had not progressed. We had dinner when I first arrived on campus, and Dr. Johnson looked me right in the face and told me why I was hired. He said it had nothing to do with my coaching ability. He looked me right in the face and said, "I hired you because you were black, and I need another face of color with some visual authority on this campus. I don't expect or care if you win a single game." I was completely floored by this fact. I guess in all my naivety, I actually thought that someone had hired me because of my coaching ability and my strong desire to turn this program around and build it into something of national stature. Instead, I was actually nothing more than a black babysitter to control the ruckus the football players could probably start problems on campus if they didn't have some type of supervision. I have never understood that. If all students on campus are college students first, why is it that when a young man gets into trouble, the first question out of anybody's mouth is "Doesn't he play football?" I mean, really, shouldn't the first question be "Is he a college student?" Why is it that on every college campus, when a member of the general campus body gets into trouble, you never hear about it, but the second some athlete has any kind of run-in with the law, it ends up on the national news, ESPN, *USA Today*, and every other wire service in the known world?

Dave had just looked me in the face and told me I was hired to keep order, and I was not feeling that at all. I had my own ambitions, and I realized right there that I was going to be on my own for my duration at Morris. Fohl was not going to help me. My only hope at this point was that neither one of those lazy idiots would get in the way of me doing what I needed to do to get this program where I thought it should be. I had two full-time staff guys. The first guy was Steve Barrows. He was a good guy at heart, but I knew from day one that it was not going to work. I knew what I wanted in an assistant and, actually, exactly who I wanted. I wanted Bob Ramsey. Bob and I had been friends since college, and we had the same ideas on where we wanted to take a program. He was on the staff of Southeast Missouri State University and was looking to be a coordinator, I knew what he would run offensively, and we would be on the same page. He was in competition for the position with a guy I did not know named Ken Crandall. I knew nothing about Kenny at all. He was from Kansas but had been coaching on the East Coast at Maine Maritime University. Now unlike most head coaches in the country, I did not have the opportunity to choose my staff members. The administration got together and picked my staff for me. I had never even heard of something like that, but it was happening to me. That was also an indication that I was probably not going to be there very long. I mean, really. They were dropping scholarships as I was making plans for the season, and now they were picking my staff for me. I did not have a prayer of building this program the way I wanted because these people were already stacking the deck against me. I figured that I would just keep my head down, set my own direction and, damn the torpedoes, just do it the way I wanted to do it and disregard what the administration wanted. I also knew that if I was going to put myself in Maverick mode, I had better be sure and walk the line. I would push the rules, as I always do, but I had to be sure that when I did, I had my own ducks in a row so they wouldn't have anything to hold over my head.

JOHN STEPHEN PARKER

CHAPTER TWENTY-TWO

Man becomes man only by his intelligence, but he is man only by his heart.

—Henri Frederic Amiel

THE HELL THAT WAS MORRIS, MINNESOTA

I MADE IT through the summer. I was trying to get everything prepared. The general public truly has no idea what goes into preparing a program for a season. Housing plans, meal plans, eligibility issues, and a broad range of issues all had to be dealt with, and I can tell you, on the campus of UMM, nothing ever moved quickly. There was more red tape than I have ever imagined, and even more for me because I was not a very patient person. I was anxious to get on with the business of trying to win football games and not the ridiculous details of administrative shit. I had one friend in the financial aid office. When you are dealing with need-based financial aid programs, this is definitely the most important. Pam Engebretson was the associate director of Financial Aid, and I can tell you that she was unbelievable. Pam was one of those people that truly care about students. She was great to talk with, and I would regularly vent at her whenever Mark Fohl would go into his usual useless mode and not want to get off his fat ass and work. I would get so unbelievably pissed off that I could not speak, and I would go to Pam, and we would just sit, and I would calm down. She was the sounding board for a lot of my great ideas and for a few of my harebrained schemes.

That first season at UMM was a learning experience. I learned not only did the administration not care, but I got a true understanding of just how much they truly could have given a shit about it. The first road game, they wanted me to get double rooms and put four to five players in each room. I mean, a player would go out and represent the institution, mind you, without any type of athletic financial aid of any kind, and he would have to share a bed with another player the night before the game. That was absolutely ridiculous, and I was never going to stomach that. Mark Fohl would not allow them to send equipment out for reconditioning. Instead, with the objective of saving money, he would have Doug Reese (the idiot equipment manager and head coach for the women's wrestling team. YES, I did say womens wrestling!) take all the padding out of the shoulder pads and just wash it in the industrial washer. Understand that when equipment goes out for reconditioning, it is thoroughly checked and rechecked for defects. If any part of it is defective, it is automatically replaced and then recertified. So if you understand this, not only were you keeping the kids safe, but you were also keeping yourself clear of any liability issues. I understand wanting to be conservative when it comes to budgetary matters, but when you compromise the comfort and safety of a student-athlete, I will always draw a line in the sand. Nothing in this world makes me angrier than to see an eighteen or nineteen year old kid getting screwed for the convenience of an athletic department.

The one thing I always get excited about is the players. Seeing them when they come back, all pumped up with optimism for a great season, is the most energizing thing to see. This group of guys were also quite unbelievable. It was a makeup of Midwest, small-town kids, and West Coast streetwise kids. The chemistry was very odd, but it worked. We didn't have many kids, only about fifty. I knew that would make it hard to compete, but I have always believed that if you can stay calm about a situation, then the people around you will remain calm. If you panic as a leader, then you are guaranteed that the people you are leading will definitely panic. Once, we went to play Northwestern College in Orange, Iowa. We rolled into town with about forty players. We had a few guys who were too injured to play, and we were forced to leave them back. I remember, when getting off the bus to go warm up, their coach Orv Otten came right up to me and said, "You have a nice-looking group of guys. Is there another bus coming?" I almost fell out laughing. It was funny trying to explain to him that this was our entire team. Not only did he start laughing at the situation, I could sense that he felt that this one was probably going to be a laugh of a game. He had absolutely every reason to believe that, considering we had forty players dressed on the sidelines. Once we got going, I think he realized that these guys were going to give him every bit of a game that a one-hundred-member team would. That was one moment that I realized the true joy of coaching and the high I got out of competition. To be able to take a group of players, many of whom were less than talented but all of whom had a big heart and would work very hard. To be able to teach them not only about football but about life and, no matter what the odds are against you, that you don't ever give up and don't ever give in, is a real honor and privilege. That night in Iowa really showed me that I might be all right in this business. We gave Northwestern College all we had that night with forty kids and came up a little short (34-28), but our kids played very hard and never gave in.

That year went like that all the time, going winless. We were able to go out and recruit some players and had a number of transfer players join us in the off-season. The only thing that didn't change was the administration. Mark Fohl was still there as the Director of Athletics. I had gone through an entire summer with him doing nothing to help the program and, in fact, doing more to stand in the way of progress. I believe that his thought process was if we were to put a successful program on the field, he would have to work harder, and that would upset his evolutionary process. This was a guy that came in at nine in the morning, and at four thirty, if you were standing in front of his 1985 Chrysler K station wagon, you would get run over. He was always more interested in saving a buck than supporting a kid. Once, we played a game in the Metrodome in Minneapolis. I had the food service cater the food for the postgame meal. After the game was over, as the team was coming into the locker room, the food was already prepared and laid out. But before any of the players could get in line, there was Mark Fohl, with his big fat bubble head (and body), stuffing his face with sandwiches and chips, which should have been for the players and staff first. Any other person would have had enough respect for the athletes, who had been out there sweating, trying to represent the university, but not this guy. Believe me, I have a hundred stories like this about him. He was truly a joy to work under. In the spring during practice, I found myself on a collision course with the administration.

They had a plan on where they wanted to keep the program, and I had hopes and dreams on where I wanted to take it, and those plans were not even close to being on the same page. I made public my desires to build a quality program, and I also made public that I didn't care what the plans of the administration were. I have to admit that this probably was not the smartest thing I could have done. If you are going to be a Maverick in your career, it probably is not the popular thing to piss off the brass, but I knew that this was not going to last long. Those people asked me to come there under false pretenses. They assumed they were getting a "good nigger" whom they could and would control. They picked my staff for me and dictated how they wanted the program run, but they had a complacent attitude toward athletics and, more specifically, football in general.

Because of my renegade attitude, the administration felt like it was important for me to get some counsel. I thought they were talking about psychological counseling at first because at this point, I know that pretty much everybody at the university thought I was crazy, but they felt like I needed to talk to someone who could get me to settle down and, I guess, come around to their life of complacency. Who they sent me to made me even more discontent with the administration. McKinley Boston was the vice president for Student Services and Athletics for the entire University of Minnesota system, but what made this even more insulting was that he was black. Their mind-set was that they could not talk to this "angry black male," so it was better that they get one of his "own kind" to try and talk to him in his "native language." Mack and I had met back in the summer. I was trying to get new game uniforms from the Gophers, and their athletic director was giving me a little grief about me acquiring those uniforms, so as I always do, I go over the head of someone if they are standing in my way. This time it worked, and Mack made those uniforms accessible to me.

Mack and I met for lunch and got to know each other a bit. He had a great legacy, being one of the first black athletic directors in the country when that position was deeply rooted in the "good ole boy" network. I told him about myself and my background, and I told him my plans for the development of the program. As soon as he heard my plans, he stopped me and said, "I can see right now that you have a clear direction on where you want to go, and that direction is in complete conflict with the direction of the university. Therefore, at some point in time, probably in the very near future, the two entities are probably going to have to part company." I had no idea how accurate he was at the time.

CHAPTER TWENTY-THREE

Action and reaction, ebb and flow, trial and error, change—this is the rhythm of living. Out of our over-confidence, fear; out of our fear, clearer vision, fresh hope. And out of hope, progress.

—Bruce Barton

SHADOWS OF CHANGE

I KNEW I would start that second season under a cloud of conflict. I had a large group of returning players whom I hoped had developed over the past year, and recruiting had been better, but you never expect a freshman to come in and play an active role in winning. This, on top of the fact that I had a major conflict with the administration, made this year crucial. I also joined an organization that, at the time, I believed would be for the betterment of my career and for the promotion of black coaches across the country. The organization was called the Black Coaches Association. At this point in time, it was headed up by Rudy Washington, a former basketball coach at a number of different universities. I was very naive about my career and the direction it would be going. You see, when I first got into coaching, I believed that I would work hard, keep my head down, and keep rising in my career. I had no idea that I would have to deal with racism holding me back. The fact that even though I was smart, demonstrated a great knowledge of the game, and had proven myself as a coordinator on both sides of the football, there was no reason I could not be a head coach at the Division I level. Unfortunately, the system would not allow black coaches to move into that position, which I never really understood. I guess it was me living in a world where I knew that racism was everywhere, but on the athletic field, I had not really ever seen it rear his ugly head. But I guess when you get interviewed for fourteen different head-coaching positions and you finish second on thirteen out of fourteen opportunities to someone you are clearly more qualified than, then there probably is not much hope in thinking that someday you are going to be the head coach at Florida State.

When I took this position, I wanted to change the world, win every game, graduate every player, and raise as much money as any coach ever has. By the beginning of the second season, I was already fixed on getting out of Minnesota. You can believe this. Mark Fohl didn't make life any easier. He tried to do everything possible to make life for me even harder. He even got some female to file a ridiculous harassment charge against me so that he could begin to mount his case against me. His plan was to create enough bad publicity for me that I would either get fired or have to quit. Let me say this. The guy pulled out all the stops. He even got the school newspaper involved. It's amazing how much change really truly scares some people. When individuals go through their daily lives with their daily routines and looking at the same people, then all of a sudden, they invite someone into their lives but then realize that this person is very different than whom they thought he or she was, then you get into a mind-set that this person must be dangerous because they are different. The only difference there, between me and them, was that I could not sit back and watch an eighteen or nineteen year old kid getting the shaft because a teacher, a coach, an adult does not want to get off his ass and put forth a little extra effort to be sure that a kids has not only more opportunities, but also the best advantages that were possible. Not the ones that they want because they have no vision, but the ones that are absolutely possible, if you make a decision to think outside the box and keep in mind why we truly do what we do. God knows how many times I thought about the millions of dollars that some coaches make in the business, and had the hope that someday I would have the opportunity to join that financial fraternity. I realize that I got into this twenty-five years ago because there is nothing in the world like the feeling of accomplishing something special, something great, and truly something that nobody expected and most people said was impossible. I have done this, and I wanted to be sure that if a young person wanted to participate, then I would do all I could to give them an opportunity to experience those moments.

The first thing we needed to do was accomplish a win. Morris had the longest losing streak in the country, and we really needed to get the monkey off the back of those kids. Something happens to a team that has lost for a very long time. Mind-sets are different, and when it rolls over into a game situation, the first time you face adversity, you begin looking for the door, and you quit. Not only that, but the people around you begin to give up on you very easily. So when you go to change the mind-set, you have to not only change that of the players and coaches, but you also have to address the mind-set of the fans, supporters and, most importantly, the administration because they control the purse strings. Well, we did address the first issue by defeating Northwestern College and, therefore, breaking the "longest losing streak" at the NCAA Division II level at thirty-seven games. Prairie View A&M University had the longest losing streak in the country at seventy-something games, so naturally, it became national news.

As we kept progressing through the season, it became more and more evident that this would be my last season at Morris. Every week became progressively worse, and I knew I could not work under those circumstances much longer. Going into the last game, I met with Fohl the day before. I told him that after the game on Monday morning I would submit my resignation. I requested that we not make it public until about four that afternoon so that I would have the opportunity to speak to the team at the meeting at three o'clock. I was composing my thoughts after the meeting with Mark. I wanted to tell these guys how much I loved them and cared about them. Although we were not the most successful team in the school's history, we did come there and make something better. I left it in better shape than I found it. I wanted to make it clear that I was not leaving because of them. I was leaving because the success of the program would always be limited because of the philosophy of the administration. Those people had no vision for what could be, and I refused to have my career handcuffed by the situation. The players needed to know that. I have always been honest with my teams because I always asked them to be open and honest with me. I don't know why, but when I decided to step down and went to have the conversation with Fohl, I made the mistake of believing that he would honor the agreement to wait so I could tell the team myself. People wonder why I don't have a big trusting soul; well, it's because of administrators like Mark Fohl. We met at nine o'clock that Monday morning. The meeting lasted ten minutes. I returned to my office, and at approximately ten o'clock, I turned on the radio. The first thing I heard was our radio announcer Brian Curtis on the radio, making the announcement about my resignation over the air. Not only did Fohl break the agreement we had made only forty-five minutes prior to this, he embarrassed me and disrupted my afternoon team meeting by making that announcement. I was immediately enraged by this and went flying into his office to let him know how pissed off I was about it.

He was in a meeting, but I was not interested in who he was talking to. I opened the door and said, "Thanks very much for opening your stupid, fucking mouth. This is a perfect example that you don't give a shit about the players at all. They deserve better than that, and so do I." I had the meeting that afternoon with the team and apologized to them for the way they found out. I told them that I wanted to tell them, but "their idiotic athletic director" felt like he had to take one more opportunity to try and screw me and the program. How sad this was because Mark used to be a football coach. You would think that he would get it, but clearly, he didn't. The old adage of "Once a coach, always a coach" did not apply to him. It was clear that the athletes, being priority, was not on his radar screen. What a shame because as I have said, there is no joy in the world better than seeing a young person accomplish something that they have worked very hard to accomplish. That's really too bad.

I met with the team. Explained the situation and told them that Kenny would be taking over for me. There would also be no search for my replacement as they had always planned for him to take over when I left. That was the whole plan when they hired him for my staff. Kenny and I got to be friends. Truthfully, he was a great assistant coach for me because I could walk away from the offense and feel assured that it would be in great hands. I knew he would be a great head coach when he got the opportunity. I walked away from my position, which is the dumbest thing to do, especially when you don't have a new position to go into. It was hiring season across the country, and I was going to the convention and make the all-lobby team. That's when you stand in the lobby of the hotel with all the other unemployed guys with a stack of résumés in their hands. Truthfully, that never works, but it does give you a chance to meet new guys in the business.

I went through the winter that year pretty much jobless. I was still teaching at the University, but that was only for a couple of hours a day. Jappy Oliver and Kevin Sumlin are calling me from the patio at some bar in Miami, Florida. They were on the road recruiting, and since I was lying on my couch, freezing my fucking ass off in Bum-Fuck, Minnesota, they figured it would be cool to call me up and give me shit. I had a number of interviews that winter, but no takers. I earned a place on the Board of Directors of the Black Coaches Association, and since I was unemployed, I buried myself in the organization's objectives of trying to give more black coaches opportunities to become head coaches. I had interviews, and made hundreds of phone calls, and put myself out there for every opportunity I could. In January, I received some news that not only made me crazy happy, but also gave me even more incentive to find a new position and find it fast.

JOHN STEPHEN PARKER

CHAPTER TWENTY-FOUR

Everything that is new or uncommon raises a pleasure in the imagination, because it fills the soul with an agreeable surprise, gratifies its curiosity, and gives it an idea of which it was not before possessed.

—Joseph Addison

NEW ADDITIONS AND NEW EDITIONS

LIFE IS FUNNY. Right about the time you think you have hit your low point, it raises you up and hits you right in the face. I had gone to the convention in January and come back to Minnesota. A few weeks later, I was awakened at about six thirty in the morning by Laura, who was wrestling around in bed. I woke up and asked what was wrong. She said, "I am late." In all my stupidity and not really realizing what she talking about, I said, "Well, you better call in and let them know you won't be there on time." She just laid there, laughed, and said, "Not that kind of late!"

Well, let me tell you that it wakes you up very quickly when you receive that kind of news that early in the morning. I didn't react well at first because I didn't know we were trying. I was under the impression that precautions were being taken and that would not be happening, especially since I was currently unemployed.

Little did I know that someone else was on another agenda. In my mind, this became an emergency situation, so me, being the overreacting guy I am, told her to get dressed, and we went to the emergency room at the hospital. I know this seems a bit drastic, but I was not thinking straight and wanted to find out as soon as I could. The doctor came into the examination room and gave us the news. I was frozen in my chair when I heard the words "You guys are going to have a baby." My jaw dropped at first, but the feeling very quickly became joy and amazement.

I was going to be a father. Just the mere thought of that was both terrifying and brought more joy to me than I had ever known. I had gone through my life up to this point, and my accomplishments were all based on the physical aspects of my talents. I had scored touchdowns, hit home runs, and made baskets. I had moved my career from that of a small-time high school coach to running my own program at the collegiate level. I had truly made a name for myself in the business, but it paled in comparison to this moment. I was part of the creation of a life. A part of me that would carry my essence. You become so filled up with joy that you just want to tell the world, which was exactly what I did. September would be the month of expectancy, and deep down inside, just as any father would, I wanted a boy for my first, and even though we had two ultrasounds, we were happy when it was determined to be a girl.

I went about telling everybody whom I could. I realize that you are not supposed to do that until after the first trimester, but I was excited. The only other priority I had at the time was that I had to find another position. I must have applied for a hundred positions. Finally, I was lying in bed one night, and I received a phone call from a man named Dr. W. Clinton Pettus. He was the

JOHN STEPHEN PARKER

president of Cheyney University of Pennsylvania. I didn't know who this man was or where the hell Cheyney University was. As he began speaking to me, I was almost ashamed that I didn't know about Cheyney. It is the oldest, historically, black university in the country. It was created in 1837 by Quaker farmers who wanted to educate Negroes. It was a stop on the Underground Railroad, which Negroes used to travel from the South to the North. There was even a dormitory on campus named after Harriet Tubman.

Dr. Pettus began speaking, and mind you, it was late. I would imagine that it was about eleven thirty that night. He said, "I have a position available, and you have come highly recommended." I said, "Thank you, but can you please call me back in the morning? I am extremely tired and can't really give you the due concentration which this conversation deserves." Now I know that that was a risky move, but if I was that "highly recommended," I assumed he would not mind. I was correct. He called me back in the morning, and like me, he got right to the point. He said, "You just broke the longest losing streak in Division II, and by doing so, you have given us that dubious distinction. We now have the longest losing streak in the country, and I was curious if you would be interested in breaking the longest streak in the country again?" I told him to let me have a few hours, and I would return his call.

Now here I was unemployed, with a child on the way, and it's funny now, but considering that I was almost rolling the dice with a job offer was stupid. All I had to do was just say yes, but I knew that if I took my time on this, I would maximize any offer that I might be getting. I called him back, and I told him that I needed to come out and see the place and meet some people on campus. He then turned it all over to a guy named

Harold Johnson. Harold was the acting director of athletics, but he was really a jack-of-all-trades on campus. He was the sports information director, financial aid counselor, admissions, special assistant to the president, and a broad range of different hats. He was a former football coach, so he understood the game and the commitment level needed to get this done.

Looking back, it was Harold that was one of my motivations for eventually coming there. As the president said, Harold took over the situation and contacted me right away. I told him that I was interested in coming out to see the place and that they should arrange both a plane ticket and a hotel room for me. He said he would call me back shortly. I was not sure if I was stepping over the boundary line of request or not, but I knew I needed to be treated with dignity and respect. He called me back and asked me if I would go ahead and buy the plane ticket, and the university would reimburse me for it. Well, that should have sent up a red flag about the position. I mean, if the place could not afford to book your flight and accommodations, were they in any position to pay you what you need? I came back very quickly with "No no no! That is not the way it works. If I am interviewing for a position that you have interest in me for, then it is your responsibility to cover the expenses." I think this may have taken him back a bit. I am not a person that settles for less than professionalism.

Well, the reservations were made, and I began the preparation for the interview. Anyone that knows me knows that I am well prepared for any interview that I go to. I do more than adequate research on the people at the university as well as the program. That was even more important this time because I knew nothing about the university, and because I was currently out of work with my first child on the way. It was imperative that I knew what I was talking about. Dr. White, who was vice president for student affairs, called me a couple of days before I was supposed to leave to tell me that the plane reservation still was not secure. Evidently, the itinerary they sent me was a bit premature, and they had not secured the plane flight. Again I was asked to go ahead and purchase the plane ticket, and they would reimburse me when I arrived. Well, I knew in my mind that was not going to happen because I do understand how the purchase order process goes at an institution, and there was no way they could have that processed in three days. Besides, a plane ticket from Minneapolis to Philadelphia on three days' notice was going to cost about fifteen hundred dollars, and what if they didn't hire me? Now I would be left on the hook for that money. I told him, "Dr. White, I live three hours from the airport. In three days, I am going to drive to the airport and check in at the U.S. Air ticket counter. If there is a first-class plane ticket waiting for me, I will get on the plane and come for the interview. I can also promise you this. If there is no plane ticket waiting for me, I will get in my car and drive the three hours back to my home, and I will forget I ever heard from Cheyney University, and you people can forget about me." I know that is pretty direct, and the question is how can I be so secure that I could be that direct. I guess it was because I have faith and a strong belief that something good was going to happen for me. I mean, God was about to bless me with my first child. I knew he would take care of me on this also. In addition, it went back to being treated correctly, with some professionalism.

The travel day rolled around, and when I arrived at the airport, there was a first-class plane ticket waiting for me. I was really relieved because truthfully, I was beginning to panic a bit about my employment. I made the trip, and Harold picked me up and took me to the Ramada Inn by Philadelphia. I was unbelievably hungry when I arrived and thought he might take me to dinner, but that never did happen. I was exhausted from the three-hour trip to the airport in addition to the three-hour flight. By the time I got to my room, I had just enough time to look over notes for tomorrow and call home before bed. I knew Harold would be picking me up at seven thirty the next morning, and I wanted to be up and rolling by six.

The alarm went off after what felt like a few minutes. It was still dark outside, but it was kind of a big day. Got up and went through my usual routine of water, shower, and ESPN before I ran downstairs to grab a piece of fruit in the lobby. I met Harold in the lobby at seven thirty, and we were off to the university. When I arrived on campus, I met with the people in admissions and financial aid. In my first observation, I found them to be very lazy and without much motivation. Over the course of the next five years, I would find this statement about my first observation to be a complete understatement. I stood there in the lobby of the Office of Admissions and Financial Aid and listened to the phone ring constantly for about fifteen minutes with nobody answering, and there were plenty of people there to answer it. I was amazed by that fact.

Next on the list was a tour of the main administration building and the office of the president, where I would meet Dr. W. Clinton Pettus. He had three secretaries outside his office, who all appeared to be competent. As I met with the president, he came across as a person who was very intelligent but not very savvy on the ways or operations of athletics. Nevertheless, he was the HNIC (Head Nigga in Charge) of this place. He did make the formal offer to me in the meeting and even agreed to pay my moving expenses if I accepted the job. I told him that I had some other meetings on campus, and when I left to go back, I would need a few days to ponder it over. That meeting took about ninety minutes. He acted as though he really wanted me to handle the program, and I felt good about him as both the president and the person he was.

It was getting to be around the lunch hour, and I knew I would be meeting with the selection committee soon, so I figured I would be eating lunch with Harold and/or a couple of committee members. Well, my assumptions were completely off. We went into the gym area where there were two players waiting for me. Pierre Campbell and Nate Floyd-Ingram were two guys who were upperclassmen and, in their tenure at Cheyney, had never been a part of a victory. This program was moving toward a five-year stretch without ever winning a game. You could see in their eyes that they were excited about a change in the program, and really wanted to win. I also knew that these guys, in addition to all the other guys, had no idea what it would truly take to be successful. I briefly talked with the two of them about some defensive strategies since I have always believed that you will always ultimately win ball games if you play good defense. They appeared to understand what I was saying and gave me their endorsement. I then went to a large boardroom where the search committee was waiting for me to answer questions. The head of the committee was a guy named Darryl Coats. He was an alum and claimed to be a huge supporter of the university. I have always understood fan support at small universities. You have people who are chickens, and you have people who are pigs. And if you think about it in relation to breakfast, chickens are animals that "support" breakfast. They get to sit, lay the eggs, and have the eggs cultivated for the meal. Then they get to wake up and do it all over again tomorrow. That, to me, is a pretty easy life. Those who are supporters from a university standpoint are the alums that show up to homecoming, buy the T-shirt, sit in the bleachers at the game, and dog cuss the coach for not winning enough games, but they never really make any real contribution in terms of money to the program. Now the animal that is truly committed to the breakfast meal is the pig because the pig understands that he is going to die for the meal to be complete. There truly is no tomorrow for the pig, and you can't be more committed than that. Those are the type of people I wanted around the program. People who were committed to making the program the best it could possibly be because it was the right thing to do.

I went through the committee gauntlet and came out unscathed. By that time, it was almost three o'clock in the afternoon, and I had a five o'clock flight back to Minneapolis. The other thing in the midst of the whole day that I realized was, these cheap-ass bastards never gave me a meal, and I mean they never even offered me a meal. Although I could see that this was a sea of confusion and that they were lacking true organization and any sign of professionalism, I saw something else in this place. I saw a program that needed me to help them. Here was a group of young men who had been thoroughly screwed by coaches and an administration who could really care less about them being successful on the field. You would think that they would want to be a bit more attentive. Cheyney was a school that, in the sixties and seventies, thrived. Because of segregation in the fifties and a good chunk of the sixties, black kids could not and would not go to Villanova, Temple, Drexel, Penn, and a number of the "white" schools in the Philadelphia area. Cheyney was thriving because it was the only institution of higher education that black kids would go. The school had about six thousand students then. As times supposedly changed and the barriers of segregation were lifted, many of the mainstream school not only opened their doors, but if they met certain "quotas," they were rewarded by the U.S. government. When things began changing and black kids began selecting other universities to attend that had previously been closed to them, Cheyney either didn't want to change or didn't know how to change how they did business. I do not believe in reverse discrimination, but I do believe that because of the system that many black Americans were raised in, they tend to sometimes segregate themselves for reasons of comfort. The administration and faculty at Cheyney were so dead set on keeping the school "all black" that they refused to change their thought process, their recruiting methods, and the fact that they needed to begin to not only open their doors to white students, but also begin to actively recruit people that didn't look like them. I knew what I was going to do to change this atmosphere, and I also knew it would not be very well received. This place was so set in its ways of complacency that there was no telling how this would go.

CHAPTER TWENTY-FIVE

Never tell people how to do things. Tell them what to do and they will surprise you with their ingenuity.
—General George C. Patton

PHILADELPHIA, THE CITY THAT SLAPS YOU BACK

I WENT BACK to Minnesota and prepared for my move. I had to get some things in order, and I had to formally resign from Morris, which would be a very easy task. I couldn't wait to get away from those people. I had worn out whatever welcome I had. Not to mention I needed to get to a city where there was true civilization, different restaurants, and a nightlife where all the guys didn't put on their best T-shirt to go out and have the same redneck philosophy on life of "my woman, my beer, my truck," and not necessarily in that order. It was again time to move on.

As I prepared to move on, I didn't realize that I would be leaving behind some people. My favorite was Pam Engebretson, who was now the director of financial aid and had become one of my true friends and truly the only person on campus I could really trust. We had lunch together, as we frequently did, on my last day there. It was a very surreal moment because I knew that when I walked away, I probably was not going to see her again, which, to this day, I have not seen her. We have talked and laughed a few times over the phone, but that's about it. She, just like a lot of friendships I have, is in compartments in my life.

I always pack only what I am going to initially going to need when I get there. I was leaving a pregnant woman to fend for herself while I went and got this thing moving in Philly. I drove first to St. Louis because I need to see my mom and her husband. He was now on kidney dialysis because of his system shutting down, and he was going through the procedure about three times a week. It was important that I get there because in my mind, I knew that someday, probably soon, I would be getting that call in the middle of the night that nobody wants but everybody knows is coming sometime. I headed south first and then east to Philly. I didn't have a place to live yet, so the university decided to put me up for about a month until I found a place. Spring practice was scheduled to start soon, and I had a great deal of work I needed to get done, with the first being to get the staff in order. That alone would prove to be a trying situation because at the center of the sea of complacency was an undriven staff of lazy coaches.

I arrived on campus on a Sunday night, and Dr. White met me. I don't know what his thought process was, but he had come up with a glorious idea that I should be staying on the sixth floor of a dormitory where a large number of my players were living. We went up there, and when the elevator door opened, there was this unbelievable stench that was only outdone by the volume level of the rap music, which was blaring. I went through this little process to appease him, but I had no intentions of staying there. That was completely inappropriate. That was another clear indication that the thought process of the administration was not geared to athletics in the least. The idea of not keeping separation between a head coach of any sport and his team is not even a concept to me. I immediately spoke up and told him that this was not going to work. It was inappropriate for me to be living among them. The players, although they were under my supervision, still had a right to their privacy, and I had a right to mine. I told him that we needed to find an alternative, and we needed to find it right now. He reluctantly agreed but had no idea what solutions he had available. Although he was living on the first floor of another dormitory that was what you call off-line, meaning there was nobody living in it. The water and electricity was working in the building, but was uninhabited by any students. I suggested that I just move into the same dormitory that he was in, just on one of the higher floors temporarily. Again, he reluctantly agreed. So I moved into Young Hall on the fifth floor. It was a complete pigpen. Evidently, the Jamaican track and field team had come for a visit and completely left the place a mess. There were spills that were not cleaned up, and there was still garbage in the trash cans that had not been thrown out. It was pretty disgusting. I told him I would clean it up enough for me to stay here, but this situation needed to be rectified or they could start their search for a new Head Football Coach all over again.

The next day, I went to the office for the first time. I arrived at about seven o'clock, which for me was late. When I arrived, I really expected to find the other coaches waiting to greet me, and we could get started working on the things we needed to accomplish in preparation for spring practice. When I arrived, there was nobody to be found. This not only irritated me, but also let me know where their commitment level was. If I was at a university and wished to remain on the staff, I would be there before the new boss comes in and do everything I could to get him adjusted to his new surroundings. These guys did nothing but just show me that they were not that concerned and that they will get there whenever they choose to. So it was right at that moment I decided to fire all of them. I would do all I could to get through spring practice with them, but under no circumstances would I allow such complacency to be a part of my program. I informed both Harold, who was the acting director of athletics, and the president of my plans but told them to keep the plan confidential at this time.

We managed to get through a good chunk of practice, and I realized that we were lacking a few key ingredients that you had to have for a successful program. We needed support, facilities, players and, most of all, the almighty dollar, all of which were going to be hard to find. We also had to establish an order of discipline that the players were going to abide by. I have never made a great deal of rules for my football teams. I have always believed that in this day and time, if you make ten rules, then you better have at least a hundred more to address the loopholes in all those rules, and that would be an entirely different set of problems that I really did not want to have. I gave the players just three rules that they had to abide by. They were simply this:

1. Do what you are supposed to do.
2. Be where you are supposed to be.
3. Be there on time.

Those were my only guidelines for the operation of the program, but I was absolutely adamant that those guidelines be followed. Those guidelines left very little gray area to fall into.

One day, during spring practice, a young man decided he did not want to do what he was supposed to do. I had no mercy on him, for if I would have, the other players' belief and respect would have been gone in an instant. When the young man refused to do what he was asked, I took his helmet and shoulder pads right there in front of the entire team and told him to go inside and leave the pants (with the pads in them) outside my office door. That got the attention of the rest of the team immediately, and they understood I was not going to put up with any stupid stuff or disrespectful attitudes of any kind. Most of them got on board pretty fast, but of course, there would be a number of players who, over the next few years, would attempt to challenge me and my position. What they didn't understand was that I would win all wars of attrition regarding this program. It was not that I was trying to be a real hard-ass about running the program, but I guess I have always believed that young men want discipline in their lives. It's just that many of them don't know how to get out of the way of themselves and just accept it. That was also a way of finding out exactly what kind of hand I had been dealt, and let me tell you this, once it was revealed, it was a clear indication that it was an even worse hand than the one that had been dealt to me in Minnesota. What these guys lacked in intelligence, they more than made up for with their lack of both speed and size.

There was one day though. We were in the stadium during spring practice, going through running drills, and I saw the kid working out, on his own. That was the finest-looking kid I had seen on campus. I asked the players who that was, and all they could say was "That's Big Keith." Well, they were correct. This young man's name was Keith Jackson, and oh my god, was he big. He was six-feet-five-inches tall and weighed just over 310 pounds. He was bigger, stronger, and faster than anything I had seen on campus or in the past. The only problem was that Keith was on his way to transferring out of Cheyney University. The problem with that was, Keith was a great kid, but he was really naive about how the business of college athletics operated and that sometimes it operated in a very dirty manner. Keith was transferring to Tuskegee University in Alabama.

Keith Higdon, who was on staff there, had formerly been on the staff at Cheyney. When he took a new position, he tried to get players—mainly Keith, who was the best—to transfer. That was not only unethical, but violates NCAA rules. They even went as far as to send Keith a high school letter of intent to make it appear official, which was a major violation with the NCAA. The head coach at Tuskegee at the time was Rick Comegies. Rick was also a former head coach at Cheyney University who had moved on to greener pastures. Rick was one of those coaches who had a habit of manipulating the rules to fit the circumstances he was in. I knew that this was his reputation, so this was of no surprise to me.

Now I knew it would not look good if one, I let Rick get away with this ridiculous plan, and two, if I let a kid like Keith get away from me. I knew if we could keep him, we would have a chance to at least slow some people down. The first thing I did was call Rick and appeal to his sense of judgment. He didn't understand that I had not just fallen off a turnip truck. I knew what he was doing. I just had never gone down that road in my profession. Rick was angry about the accusation and hung up the phone on me the first time I called. I did call him back and made a second appeal, but this time, my appeal had an addendum to it. I told him that if he didn't believe that this was illegal, then maybe I should have one of the compliance investigators from the NCAA give him a call. This time, he told me he would call me back. In the meantime, I had to talk to Keith and explain to him what was going on, and also try and re-recruit him. Keith was the type of kid that had the ability to make a difference on your football team, and also because of the way he looked. It would not bode well to let him transfer. He was a Native American kid from West Philadelphia, and he had no idea how much of a culture shock he was going to realize going to Alabama. He would not have the freedom that he had in Philly nor would he have any of the lifestyle he was used to.

I managed to talk with Keith and persuade him that transferring was not the best course of action. I also wanted him to give me a chance and let me show him that things can be different. I knew that despite all the odds against me, I could get this program turned around. People were calling me from all over the country, telling me I was crazy. There were even alums of the university contacting me. They were telling me I was crazy for taking this, but they would support me. In my mind, I hoped they would not support me the way they supported my predecessors. If they did, I was doomed to failure.

With Keith on board and the remainder of the team willing to get on the same page, we departed on what would become probably the most interesting season of my coaching career.

CHAPTER TWENTY-SIX

Every man is a damn fool for at least five minutes every day; wisdom consists in not exceeding the limit.
—Elbert Hubbard

DR. GREGORY K. P. SMITH AND OTHER NEW ARRIVALS

WE MANAGED TO get through spring practice. I had to also find a place to live. My family was still in Minnesota, and I needed to get them where I was, find a doctor, and get them settled. I managed to get my new staff hired. I had to fire the other guys before I did that. Most of those guys were OK with leaving. I always try and help guys find new positions, but this time, I didn't feel comfortable doing that. Those guys were bad coaches. They did not have the players' best interest, and worst of all, they were lazy guys who were never going to go the extra mile for the program. Therefore, they had to go.

I hired a few new guys and began working on the summer workout programs. The summer would be interesting to say the least. The university was continuing their search for a new director of athletics. Harold, having been only an interim supervisor, was moving into another position as NCAA Compliance Officer. I had no idea what kind of person they were even looking for this position. I went on with my usual summer plans of finishing up my recruiting and eligibility issues. We had players who had to go to summer school and get all their problems cleared up before the season began, and they reported to campus. I don't think they had ever had anyone like me in the Athletic Department. I had a form and a procedure for everything. I just believe that everything would go smoother if there was simple order. Not to mention I had very little help with equipment and things like that. Our equipment manager was pretty useless, and that was the only place I ever heard of that the equipment manager was an "hourly" employee. This, on top of the fact that I had very little patience at the time for laziness, did not make for a good combination.

I did finally get Laura moved out to the area, and because I didn't have a bunch of time to look—well, let me rephrase that: I didn't *take* a bunch of time to look. I was so focused on trying to get this program back on track that housing was not a real priority. I settled on a condo in Media, Pennsylvania, which was the center of the county. I got Laura moved out. We found a doctor and prepared for the birth of our first child. We had not settled on a name, but I was leaning toward Andrea. We were still a few months away since she was not due until September. After I got her there, I went on with the business of the program.

I received a called from Dr. Pettus, and he told me we had hired a new director of athletics. I told him great but asked, "Were any of the coaches consulted at all on this decision?" He said no, and that troubled me, but I was willing to give him a chance. I had witnessed my share of bad ADs, and I knew what I was looking for. What I got was nothing close to what I expected nor what I and every coach in the department knew we needed.

JOHN STEPHEN PARKER

His name was Dr. Gregory K. P. Smith. He had received his doctorate from Temple University in Philadelphia. He had never played or coached anything in his entire life. He had recently been fired by another HBCU in Virginia somewhere, and this was the best we could do. I was clearly disappointed in the choice and the fact that none of the coaches had any input in the decision, but I was willing to again trust Dr. Pettus and his decision. He had been upfront with me up to this point, and I just believed somehow that he knew what he was doing. When we had the first staff meeting that summer, I realized that Dr. Pettus had made a crucial mistake. This guy had no clue what had to be done, but I tried to help him, AT FIRST! I decided I would be constructive and take him around to meet my equipment vendors and a few other people that I felt could help us over time. The first guy I took him to see, he basically insulted right off the bat. He walked in and started demanding things. He was so embarrassing and as unprofessional as he could be. I decided that I was not burning any contacts on this guy. He had no idea how to cultivate business relationships, and I was not about to burn mine by trying to teach him. That guy was an idiot.

There were a couple of other things I came to find out about him. He was actually a certified agent with the NBA Players Association. That was clearly a major violation of ethics in all of college athletics. As soon as I found that out, I quickly made the decision to distance myself. He knew I had this information, and instead of playing nice with me, I knew he made a conscious decision to not play nice with me. What he didn't realize is that I can be a great guy, but if you squeeze me, I can be a rude bastard who can make your life tremendously miserable.

I was summoned to the vice president's office to discuss the recruiting of a player. This young man was a transfer student, and evidently, the young man's father was a friend of Dr. Smith's. I remember that this kid was a big kid who played defensive line. I told the kid and his father that, because of the situation we were in, if he came to school here and wanted to play football, we would probably be moving him to offensive line since we had a real shortage at that position. I never lied to the kid or his father. I was upfront because I didn't want the kid to come here and have to play a position that he was not happy with. Well, evidently, the father was not happy about this, and called Smith. He, in turn, had me called to the office of the VP for Student Services. He then began to try and tell me how I should recruit, whom I should recruit, and where I should have them playing. I was so taken back, not only by the fact that this person, who had never played, coached, or recruited anybody in his life was trying to tell me how to do my job, but also the fact that the VP of Student Services was sitting here allowing it to happen.

Well, I gathered myself after listening to this crap. I first explained to him that playing college football was not a requirement but more of a privilege. Second, I didn't recruit this kid. He was a transfer from another school, and clearly, he wasn't getting his way because he decided to leave. He was a freebie. Third, because of that, he comes to us and plays where we need him, not where he wants to play, and if he doesn't understand that, then there are six hundred other schools in the country that might be interested, although I don't think so because he chose us, and there were many better situations than ours that he could have chosen. My belief was that the father had worked out some kind of previous arrangement, except he didn't figure I would be

JOHN STEPHEN PARKER

a fly in the ointment. He told me "We need this young man," and I agreed with that, but I told him if he comes here, this is where he is playing. If he was not happy with this, then let him pick another school. He said to me, "I want this young man on the team," and on that note, I stood up and just told him, "I decide who plays football around here. Don't ever call me to a meeting to discuss any bullshit like this ever again." Clearly, with that statement, I drew a line in the sand. Sides were taken, and I began to encapsulate my program. He, on the other hand, began his attacks on my character, my program, my family, my philosophy of coaching, and me in general.

We had a director of media relations for the university. Her name was Mary Walter. She and Harold were my support system on the campus, and we pretty much did everything together. They were well aware of the lines that had been drawn. Harold would always say "Just do what you do, and ignore him," but that would be difficult to do when the person was your direct supervisor, but I made every attempt. It was important that my focus be on important things such as my program, and the upcoming birth of my daughter. I kept up my preparations for the season, which was now beginning. With the first game approaching, there was much to do and very little time to get it done. You can believe that Dr. Smith was making every attempt to create as much turmoil in not only the Athletic Department as a whole but, in particular, the football program.

We played our first game that season against Bowie State, and as I suspected, we were not very good, and it was going to be tough to get this program off the losing skid it was on. Not only did we lose, but Bowie attempted to run up the score on us at the end of the game. I was not happy about that at all. I was trying to get my guys to do things correctly, and running up the score on someone when it's not needed and doing it on their home field is very poor sportsmanship, and I would never acknowledge that type of behavior.

After that game was over, when they attempted to shake hands with us, I refused to do so and sent our team to the locker room. I knew this would draw some controversy, but the only people I was concerned with were my players, that they understood why I had us do what we did and that I would never allow anybody to treat us in a disrespectful fashion no matter what the score was. They got it, and the president got it, but our no-knowledge-having Athletic Director didn't get it. He couldn't wait to write me a three-page memo on how I embarrassed the university by my actions. The ridiculous part of this was that he wrote this memo on Monday, but being the asshole that he was, he presented it to me as I was getting on the bus the following Friday to depart for the game at Virginia Union University. That was his usual mode of operation. He would do things at the last minute with the attempt to disrupt your train of thought with controversial nonsense. He was notorious for this. That week, he even had the locks changed on the equipment room door, which meant we could not get the needed equipment to travel, including, of all things, footballs. That was how he behaved, and the relationship, which there was none, was unhealthy, and not only me, but the other coaches in the department felt the same way. I put up with all kinds of crap from this guy, but soon, my focus would move away from him and his antics.

My usual schedule on Friday was, if we were traveling, we would be leaving around noon. If we were at home, I would give the coaches the morning off and be in by noon. The third week

JOHN STEPHEN PARKER

of the season, my brother Tony decided to fly in and see me and in one of our games. That morning, I got up a little later since I was staying home. Laura said she would fix breakfast since she appeared to feeling OK. She was nine months pregnant, and it had gone pretty smoothly. Went upstairs and proceeded to take a shower. About three minutes into it, she came into the bathroom and said, "I think my water just broke." I asked if she was sure, and she didn't know really, so I told her to call the doctor. I finished my shower, and she came back to me and said the doctor wants her to come in for a checkup. We got ready and went into his office. While we were sitting there, I told her that I needed to get Tony from the airport. She said to go ahead and go. "Nothing was happening here, and there probably wouldn't be anything happening today. Just come back after you pick him up." Well, that all sounded easy, so I proceeded.

I got to the airport and picked up Tony and headed back to the hospital. In the back of my mind, I knew what was happening, but it just was not in my face yet. My thought process was right on point because when I arrived back at the doctor's office, I asked where she was, and the receptionist said they had taken her up to the birthing center because she was in labor. My jaw almost hit the floor. The reality of the situation was truly whacking me in the face. I was going to be a father. I went upstairs, and there she was, lying in bed. I was surprised by the fact that she was just lying there watching television. We had been to the crazy birthing classes and watched the two films. If you have never seen them, one was like the love scene in the film *From Here to Eternity*. It was all nice and sweet, with no agony whatsoever. Just a couple of pushes, and the baby comes out very easy. The other, well, the only way to describe it was *Armageddon*. It was a woman in labor for about forty hours, in a great deal of pain. They had even gotten her out of bed and walked her around, with the hopes that gravity would help the situation. I mean, I am not even female, and it was painful to me. But here she was, just relaxing and watching game shows.

The nurse came in and told us it was going to be a while, so I decided, since we lived very close to the hospital, that I would take Tony to our house and let him get settled, and I would come right back to the hospital.

I took him to our place. He said he just wanted to drop his stuff off and go straight to the golf course. I thought that was prefect, and it was right down the street. We got to my house, threw his baggage in the door, and ran up the block to the golf course. Now by this time, I had been gone from the hospital about fifteen minutes, but when we pulled up at the golf course, my pager started going off like crazy. I returned the call, and it was Laura telling me that whatever drugs they gave her kept her from taking the epidural and sent the labor process from zero to sixty in thirty minutes. She said she was at nine centimeters, and if I don't get back to the hospital immediately, I would miss it. Well, I must have broken every speed law in the state of Pennsylvania as I drove up Baltimore Pike.

When I arrived back at the hospital, I ran up the stairs into the room and found it full of people. My first thought was something had to be wrong. I mean, I had seen the delivery process on television, and it looked nothing like this. There were always one or two people in the room. This room had five or six people in it, and I was not sure why they were all needed. I asked, but they reassured me that everybody there was needed. I immediately went over to the bed, and I heard "You almost missed it." There

JOHN STEPHEN PARKER

was no way I was going to miss it. I was really glad that we had a home game because I might have really gotten squeezed if we had been on the road, but I was there, right there in that moment.

I stood at the top of the bed and tried to be as helpful as possible, but I had also been warned that women can be quite irrational and strangely emotional during childbirth, and I should be aware should the situation begin to go down the "coo-coo" road a bit. The doctor told me that this was not going to take a very long time. And he was absolutely right. I was in the room for five minutes when he said, "Get ready to push!" I was in the middle of something I was really excited about but really didn't understand. That was probably the same feeling that every man has when he is in there.

After the first push, the doctor looked at me and said, "Wow, she has a lot of hair. Do you want to see?"

I said, "I don't think so, I am just going to hang up here right now. You look like you know what you are doing, and I don't want to get in the way."

I do not have the strongest stomach in the world, and there was no way I was getting anywhere close to the end of the bed. The best place for me to be was right where I was. The doctor then said, "We are going to push again, ready?"

She pushed for about three seconds, and I heard a baby beginning to cry a little. She was finally here. Andrea Janae Parker was in the world, and looking very, well, oatmeal covered. The doctor asked, "Do you want to cut the cord?" and I stated to him, "There are at least five or six other people in this room right now who are more qualified than me to do that, so please take care of it." He just laughed and cut the cord. He then asked if I wanted to hold her. I said to him, "You are full of questions, Doc. Please take my daughter over to that hamburger-warmer-looking thing, rinse off some of that oatmeal, wrap her up, and bring her back to us, and we will be holding her then. Can we manage that?" That brought an even larger chuckle from him.

Through all the commotion, I realized we had a new member of our family. She was absolutely perfect, with a whole head of hair. She was the most beautiful thing I had ever seen, and I didn't get emotional on the outside, but I was welling up on the inside like nobody's business. I was happy and terrified at the same time. I am not going to lie. When I first found out I was going to be a father, I was really hoping for a boy, as most guys would. I just believe that all kids should have big brothers to watch over and protect them. I even took Laura to have two ultrasounds to be sure that it was a girl because I needed time to warm up to having a daughter first, but when I saw her for the first time, that all went away. She stole my heart away, and has continued to steal it every day since the day she was born. The thing about that day was I still had football practice. All that had happened in less than ninety minutes, and I still had to go to work. She told me to go and take care of what I needed to and just get back as soon as I could. I left the room and could literally feel myself skipping down the hall of the hospital when I left. I was so happy and could not wait to tell the world. I first ran to pick up Tony from the golf course. I told him and took him back to the hospital to sit with Laura while I went to practice.

I then headed to practice, and I have to admit, for the first time in my career, I really didn't want to be on the football field. It was the day before a game, and in the past, I wouldn't even sleep because I would be thinking about the game plan the night before. Right then, I was thinking about how fast I could get through practice and get back to the hospital and be with my daughter. I hate to say it, but I think maybe I may have checked out for the week. In a way, I let the team down, but on this day, it didn't matter. I had always made everything I do about someone else. I was always about my players, my program, and the school I was at. This time it was about me and my feeling for the moment and my little girl.

As I went through my preparations for the game the next morning, it really hit me that my life had changed in a matter of hours. It did make it a little easier to get fired up for a game. Although we did lose again, the loss didn't hurt as much that time. There was some added pressure, though, because Prairie View A&M University in Texas, who had the longest losing streak in the country at eighty-something games, had gotten a win this same weekend, which meant that this dubious distinction had now been put on our doorstep. We were sitting at fifty-two games of not winning and for thirty-nine games of losing. They couldn't call it fifty-two games of losing because they had tied a game about three years prior to this, long before I was here and before I ever knew where Cheyney University was on the map. Nevertheless, it was important that we get busy getting past this fact, and the only way to do that was to hurry and get a win and the proverbial monkey off our back. That was an albatross around the team's neck, and it was all anybody on campus or in both the local and national media could talk about. By the time the Mansfield game rolled around, I was so tired of hearing about the streak. It was consuming everything we were trying to do, and it became larger than the program itself.

When Mansfield University came in to play us, I made a point of not answering any questions with reference to losing or the streak. I focused on winning the game only. By the end of the first quarter, I knew we were on the right track. The players could feel that this was the day to change their reputation, and they could begin to get past the stigma. By the end of the day, we had done what they had failed to do for a number of years: they were able to get a victory. That was something that was desperately needed around there. When you have lost for as long as these guys had lost, an inferiority complex sets in, and I didn't know if I could ever bring them out of that, but this win was exactly what the doctor ordered. Nate Floyd-Ingram was my strong safety, and Pierre Campbell was my starting outside linebacker. These two guys became more than just players to me. They were like my sons. They had seen so much turmoil in both their personal lives and their life at Cheyney. It was so important to me that these two guys get a chance to experience what it was like to win a game and have others look at them in a successful light for a change. I had never seen players cry after a win like I saw that day. It brought so much joy to me to watch these guys finally get some much-needed admiration from their fellow students on campus. They had never experienced this.

As we progressed through the season, clearly, breaking the longest losing streak in the country would be the highlight. Injuries had forced us into some incomprehensible situations, and we were looking to finish with the players we had. Still, I was unwavering on my commitment to this program. Even with Dr. Smith continued his ridiculous antics of trying to create more conflict in the program, I managed to keep moving forward. I had even put myself on the college coaching map, and other schools were calling and inquiring about me. That made me feel good. We started recruiting for the next season with much, much more effort. However, I had no idea that this profession was beginning to take a toll on both my health and my personal life. I was always the ultimate workaholic, so the idea of putting in one hundred hours a week didn't bother me. I just drove myself all the time, but this was the type of position where you were almost forced into doing that. These guys had more issues than just not winning football games. Their home lives were in turmoil. Between guns, drugs, AIDS, and general crime itself, these players had real problems in their lives. When I say that "winning is not everything," I mean that trying to keep their heads above the water and surviving was much more important.

Dr. Smith was in his usual asshole stage. He was trying to make my life as hellish as possible. He had gone to one of the alumni meetings and told them that I was not the man that should be running the football program. Now in most situations, your Director of Athletics is in the public eye, supporting both you and your program. He stands up for you and fights for your needs and the needs of the program. Not this guy. He would get in the public eye and bad-mouth the entire Athletic Department staff and, in particular, me more than anybody. It all came to a head one day in his office. We had a departmental staff meeting. Previously, he had gone out and scheduled future games for me without telling me. That was a complete breach of trust in the athletic business. That was even more of a sore spot with me because this person not only had no knowledge of the program I was running, but also no knowledge about scheduling opponents. His whole idea was to try and schedule as many tough out-of-conference opponents as possible so that when we lost to them, he would be justified in recommending my termination to the president.

In this meeting, which was always as "enjoyable" as it could be, he stated to all the other coaches to please make out their future schedules and get them to him as soon as possible. I found this to be extremely aggravating, seeing as how he had made out my schedule for me without even checking with me to see how I felt about playing certain teams. As I heard him say this, the anger in me began to just rage. How could he be as stupid and inconsiderate as to think that I would sit here while he did this, and not think that I was not pissed, or that I would not speak up? Well, as I am always prone to do, I spoke out, and it had no signs of political correctness. As he gave out the deadline for him receiving this information from the rest of the coaches, I, without warning, said, "This is rather funny. You request their schedules, and yet you make mine out for me. Wow! I guess I am supposed to sit here and smile while you bend me over and push your dick in and out of my ass, and I would not say anything except thank you? Well, I can assure you that it is not that simple!" Clearly, this statement took everybody by surprise. Tara Owens, who was the assistant AD and women's basketball coach, just dropped her head. I looked at Harold, and he looked like he was going to fall out laughing. I have to admit now, it was pretty shocking, but I didn't care. It needed to be said. It was out, and it was not coming back.

When he heard the comment, he asked everyone to leave the room because he and I needed to have a "conversation." I, in turn, told everybody, "Sit the fuck down. If you have anything you need to say to me, you can say it in front of these people." He again directed all the other coaches to leave the room "as a directive from your supervisor." Well, I knew they would leave on that note. Once they left the room, the tension rose immediately. He asked me what my problem was, and again, I spoke about my complete dissatisfaction with him, his knowledge, and his ability and disrespectful behavior in scheduling my team for contest without any consultation by the person who is running the program. He began to tell me in no uncertain terms that I was not a good coach, and he would have me out of here soon. I said, "We will see." As I began walking away, he asked, "Where you going?" I said, "Think it's best now that I leave because if I don't, I will put my foot in your ass so far that you will think that it grew there."

As I walked out the door, there was the entire staff standing there in the hallway. They were smiling at me. I thought it was over, but I was mistaken. As I left the office of this asshole, something hit me like a brick. It was like a big fishhook, and my mouth was open like a big bass. I got hooked by a comment, and it reeled me back in. As the door closed, I heard the words "Why are you running away?" Well, being the hothead that I was at that time, that was all I needed to get me going again. I went after him with the intent of beating the living shit out of him. The only thing that stopped me was Milt Colston, the assistant men's basketball coach. He saw me and the look of rage and anger in my eyes and grabbed me immediately. As Milt ushered me out the back door, I shouted a vast amount of expletives at him. If I had gotten free, I probably would have choked the life out of him. After it was over, I immediately got in my car and drove to the president's office. I knew I was in serious trouble, and I needed him to hear about this incident from me first. That was the only way I knew I could keep my job. I mean, let's face a fact. I went after my immediate superior with the intent of doing serious bodily harm to him. Obviously, I could be terminated on that alone.

I went to the president's office, and since he was not in, I waited outside to see him. When he walked in, he could see the look on my face. He told me to follow him into his office, where I told him about the incident. He dropped his head as he did on many instances when I gave him news. He then did something that I had not anticipated. He asked me if I had hit Dr. Smith, and I told him no, I had not. He then came back at me and said, "John, this is nothing more than a heated exchange between two employees of the university. I need you to go back to work and just stay away from Dr. Smith." I was completely blown away with the fact that there wasn't even a reprimand of any kind. This clearly drove up my stock in Dr. Pettus. He, to me, was a guy that, although his hands were tied in many different ways, had the ability to see right from wrong and knew when there was behavior deserving of the type of reaction I gave. I also believed that he and I were on the same page about how to operate a program. Something that Dr. Smith really had no clue about.

Over the course of my stay at Cheyney, he would help me tremendously, not only as an administrator, but also as a person. In the world of college athletics, most college presidents are trying to run your ass off because truthfully, you cost way too much money. I actually had one that was doing everything he could to keep me around, and I could appreciate that. That, in turn, made the AD even more pissed off at me. After the incident, I received a memo in the campus mail from him, in which again he made a futile attempt to intimidate me. His final statement was that my rude and inconsiderate actions and behavior would no longer be tolerated. He would also send a copy of all memos to the president just to be sure there was a paper trail. As soon as I saw the memo, I immediately called the president and asked what he wanted me to do. He told me that because it was a memo from my supervisor, I needed to respond to it, but he instructed me to make it short and to the point. Well, being the occasional prick that I can be sometimes, I responded as only JP would do. I wrote, "In response to your memo I received, SO FUCKING WHAT?" I also sent it to the president so that he knew I responded. He called me and, with a chuckle, said, "Well, I guess you did what I asked you to do. Now go back to work, get me some recruits, and win some ball games."

We got through the spring practice sessions. Recruiting had gone as well as you could expect. Cheyney was the kind of place that you could get into with a blood test. The requirements were not very high. It was understandable. Because of the fact that enrollment was so low, Cheyney would let you in school. They really didn't care what your grades were. As long as you had your financial aid in order or you had the cash on hand to pay the bill, you were in. You found out that there were more issues over the summer than there would ever be during the year. You had grade issues, class issues, family problems, and hundreds of personal problems with your players. It was never ending. I was also trying to be a new father. Andrea was getting bigger and walking everywhere. She was a funny baby, but she was mature even at a young age. She never took a baby bottle at all. In fact, she went from taking the breast to drinking out of a cup. She was and is still an amazing person.

About this same time, I began to notice a change in Laura. I understood that life as I knew it before would be changing. A new baby gets and deserves a great deal of attention. I understood this, but it was important that we not lose each other, and I could tell that if I didn't attempt to right then try, curb this mind-set,

I probably would be headed down a bad road. You never know what kind of premonition you are going to have or how much of a reality it will become. Little did I know that this one would eventually come true.

CHAPTER TWENTY-SEVEN

Bitterness is like cancer. It eats upon the host. But anger is like fire. It burns it all clean.

—Maya Angelou

SECOND-YEAR BLUES

GOING INTO THE second season, I made some changes not only in players, but also within my staff makeup. I hired Darryl Mason as my new offensive coordinator. Darryl and I had been together at East Tennessee State, and I knew him to be a great coach. He would be a great influence on these impressionable young black men.

I still was dealing with the issue of Dr. Gregory Smith. He was going to be an even bigger thorn in my side that second year, but I just decided to keep my head down and continue working as hard as I possibly could. We started off the season with a couple of wins over Bowie State and over another school in North Carolina. After which the season went downhill a little bit, and we took some major losses. I had a couple of other issues come up the second season also, and really found out what kind of coach, and what kind a person I was going to be. These players, as I've said before, had a broad range of problems.

One in particular was a young man by the name of Eric Washington. Eric was a rebellious young man. Eric was from Pittsburgh, Pennsylvania. He would occasionally go home to Beaver County. Lots of the players thought he was going home to sell drugs all the time, but he was really going home for another reason; Because his mom was a drug addict, Eric had this unique obligation to her and wanted to see her protected and, eventually, off drugs. One night, I had received a phone call at about 3:00 a.m. It was Eric telling me that he was in serious trouble. He had been arrested, and he was in the Beaver County jail.

Eric wanted to protect his mother, so this time, when he got home, he went into her room and took her gun, her drugs and left the house. She called the police and had Eric arrested in the street. When I hung up the phone, I went to my car, and made a five-hour trek across the state of Pennsylvania. I met up with Eric's lawyer and the prosecuting attorney in Beaver County. The prosecuting attorney explained the circumstances to me and told me that he wanted Eric to work for him. Now as most people who are familiar with the drug business, when you become a snitch for the law, you can virtually never come home again. It's always funny where a lawyer, who has no experience in simple street justice, can possibly come up with an idea like this. This is a clear example that the judicial system in the United States is, in a word, sucks. Instead of trying to prosecute a twenty-year-old black college student, who was trying to do nothing more than simply protect his mother, they should be focusing on the real criminals of the drug trade. I'm talking about the people and companies, most of them being white and white-collar, who have the resources and the means to bring this poison into our country. But instead, their focus is on the people, most of them being young black men who were simply dealing on the streets and picking up their 10 percent.

Eric had nothing. I had to bring him a coat and tie just so he would have something to wear in front of the judge. When I walked into the jail, I saw Eric sitting in the cell with his head between his hands. He saw me and broke down crying immediately. I knew Eric Washington was not a bad kid. He was like many young black men, and many young men in general. He was looking for some direction in his life. I said this before. I am a firm believer that most young people want, and even crave, discipline in their lives. Many of them just have never had it, which means they have no idea how to accept it. Eric was one of those young people. Now I am not going to sit here and tell you that Eric Washington was a saint. He was not, but at twenty years old, I don't know many people who were. He was a frustrated and angry young black man who had no idea about his future or where it would lead. The only thing Eric knew was crime and drugs. And when that is your only frame of reference in life, your outlook wouldn't be very bright either.

I went before the judge with Eric and his lawyer while the prosecuting attorney sat at a table adjacent in the room. Eric's lawyer said nothing as he wanted me to do all the talking. At this point in time, I put on my best *L.A. Law* routine and pleaded Eric's case. What happened next came as even a surprise to me. The judge heard my case, and at the end of it, he released Eric to me. But there was a stipulation. If Eric got into another incident or had another run-in with the law of any kind, the judge would put both of us in jail. When it was stated to me, I looked at Eric, and he could see the look on my face. He knew that it said "If you mess up on that, I will have your ass in my back pocket."

I had no other problem with Eric Washington for the rest of my tenure at Cheyney University. He would get frustrated. He would even get angry sometimes, but when he got angry and frustrated now, he would come to me and we would talk about it. Eric is now the executive director for a company in Philadelphia. That young man, like many of the young men at Cheyney University, became my son. They knew that regardless of how bad something got or how crazy a circumstance was going on in their lives, they could always come to me. There's no other feeling in the world like that. I've never experienced that with anything else in my life except with my own children.

That second season moved forward. We won games, and we lost games. But on homecoming of that year, I had another loss. I received a phone call from my then sister-in-law at about 2:00 a.m., the morning of our homecoming game. My mom's husband Millard, who had been on kidney dialysis for about six years, had passed away. That man, who had come into my mom's life at a low period, had become everything to both her and me. Millard loved my mother and protected her with everything he had. He had also become a father to me. I loved him, but more importantly, I respected him for who he was, for his philosophy of life, and for being a strong black man. When I was told that he died, it shook me at my core. I had no idea how I was even going to function on that day. It's funny how you can go about your everyday life and sink so much stock into game preparations, equipment issues, and the everyday operations of a football program, and just when you think you have a grasp on everything, real, true hard-core life continues to hit you right in the face.

I arrived on campus that morning. I went straight to my office to start my regular routine in the preparation. As usual, Dr. Smith started his usual shit to distract me from the process of getting my team ready to play. Usually, I would have been OK, but that day was different. That day, I had no patience or tolerance for any of his crap. I immediately went to find the president and try and get his assistance in game management for the day. The weight of my stepfather's death was heavy on me, and I didn't want to lose it with the players around. When I found Dr. Pettus, I explained to him that I needed help with some issues athletically related. I could feel the agony building in my heart. When I saw Dr. Pettus, I barely got the issues out concerning Dr. Smith, when I broke down and started crying. I explained to him that I had lost my father last night and that I was in no mood or shape to deal with the antics of Dr. Smith today. I headed back to my office where Tara Owens, who was the assistant athletic director, came to see if I was doing OK. The president followed shortly behind her. Dr. Pettus walked in, and the first question he asked was "What is the penalty for forfeiting a game?" I told him that we were not going to forfeit a game. There was no way I would leave players hanging on game day, especially on a homecoming game. He told me that there was no requirement for me to coach today, and if I wanted to leave and be with my family, it was entirely up to me. I told him I would coach and after the game I would begin to make arrangements to get to St. Louis as soon as possible. He told me, "That would be fine, but please, let me help you."

We went into pre-game meetings, and somehow I got through all of them. At some point in time, word got out to the team about my situation. During my talk with the team, I told them that I had never asked them for anything, but I needed this one really badly. Before I could get all the words out, I was beginning to break down. When that happened, I heard Nate Floyd-Ingram in the back of the room say "we got your back coach". Just hearing those words come out of his mouth brought so much support to me at that moment. In all your efforts to get your team to gell, and to get them to put their individual needs to the side, for the greater good of the team, you never realize that maybe they are buying into you as a coach, and as a person. That day did more for me than they could ever know. I will always love that bunch of players.

We went out and played a great game. Eric Washington, my prodigal son, even scored the opening kickoff for a touchdown. After the game was over, the teams had left the field, and I manage to make it back to my office. When I walked in, there was a note on my desk. The note was from Dr. Pettus, and it said, "We are in no rush. Please come back when you're ready. You have an unlimited amount of time. Anything you need, call me." Underneath the note was a first-class plane tickets to St. Louis. I had done a good job of keeping my feelings under wraps, but when I saw the plane ticket, I actually lost it. It was a good thing the players were not around to see me blubbering like a two-year-old. I probably would have lost their respect that day.

Being at Cheyney University was simple routine. It was only when life threw you a curveball that things would change for you. We got through that year, recruiting, and preparing for spring football. I again made a couple of changes on the staff. Then Dr. Pettus decided to make some changes within the department. One morning in the summer, I received a phone call from his secretary, and she asked me to have all Athletic Department staff members in the present conference room at 9:00 a.m. We all walked into the room, and the president wasn't there, but there was a speakerphone in the middle of the table. Once we

JOHN STEPHEN PARKER

were all seated, the president told us that this morning he had removed Dr. Gregory Smith as Director of Athletics at Cheyney University. That meant two things for the Athletic Department. It meant that one, he was aware of all the disruptions that this man had caused in his short tenure as Director of Athletics, and two, that now there was no excuse for us not moving forward as a department. He placed Tara Owens in the position of interim director of athletics. I was so happy I could hardly stand it, but I also knew that any reason for distraction from the program's progress had just been removed.

During the third season, the stress and anguish of the job began to take a toll on my health. I was now putting in more hours and more time than I ever put in my entire career, and it was wearing on me. Shortly after the third season was over, I had come home from the national convention, and I was not feeling well. Lots of things were going on at home. We were now expecting our second child, which was a boy. I was excited, and at the same time, I could feel my body breaking down. I came home early from the office. It was about 8:00 p.m. Laura knew that if I was home at 8:00 p.m., something must be wrong with me. I told her I wasn't feeling well and then went to bed. I woke up from a very light sleep with a raging headache. It was not one of my usual headaches, so I knew something was wrong. Laura, at this time, was about six months pregnant with our son, Jordan. I was really concerned that whatever I had I could pass it to her. I got out of bed and drove myself to the hospital. That was where I became a fan of any type of health-care bill that could possibly be passed that would make emergency room workers be more observant.

I sat in the emergency room at this hospital for over three and a half hours before I got attention from a doctor. At this time, my temperature had risen to 104.7 degrees. They finally brought me in and placed me on a bed, where I lay for another hour before I got tended to. The doctor said he wanted to run some tests to determine if I had spinal meningitis. I had no idea what type of test he would run until the nurse came in with a needle that was about eight inches long. I stared and asked her what she was going to do with that. She told me that she was going to need to drain spinal fluid off of me to determine if it was meningitis. My exact words to her were "If you take one more step at me with that needle, I will take it out of your hands and stab you in the fucking heart with it." She looked at me like I was a bit crazy, but she had a clear understanding of what would happen to her if she continued on her course. She told me to come up with another way of getting the spinal fluid that she needed. I didn't think she knew that I had a little medical background and was very familiar with certain drugs. I told her, "I need 175 milligrams of Demerol, IV push. Once I am passed out, you can feel free to stick that needle wherever you feel like you need to, to get whatever fluid you need, but until that happens, don't come near me."

I think she found that a little offensive, but honestly, I didn't care how she felt. It was my body, and I was not going to let anyone do anything to me that I didn't like or was not under the circumstances that I wanted it to happen. She did return with a small needle that had the 175 milligrams of Demerol, and she put it right in my arm directly. I instantly passed out, at which time they performed the spinal tap. After waking up, I found it was determined that I did in fact have spinal meningitis, and now, the determination had been made to see if it was viral, which basically means you just have to ride out, or the deadly bacterial, which, if you have, means you can pretty much cancel Christmas.

Many thoughts would pass through my mind in the next few hours. Obviously, I was thinking worst-case scenario. If it was bacterial, the entire university would have to be quarantined because anyone in contact with me would have been affected. I immediately contacted Dr, Pettus to let him know of the situation. He said, "Just keep me abreast of the situation." The next thought I had, which was actually my first thought, was about Laura, Andrea, and my unborn son. So the question of it being viral or bacterial was of the utmost importance. I needed to know as fast as possible. Not to mention this was not the most modern hospital to wake up in after being administered Demerol. I woke up in what was an old padded room, which had been turned into a storage closet. It had wheelchairs, crutches, prosthetic limbs, and various medical, equipment hanging from the walls. It was also very scary. It was like something out of a medical horror movie.

The test results came back, and it was determined that the spinal meningitis was in viral form and that they would be admitting me to the hospital where, basically, I would be on pain medication for the next eight days. I was relieved to know that I had not passed this on to any of the students or faculty at the university, and that my own family would not be affected by this. But I also realized that, at that point and time, I do not have long for this profession or for this world if I did not change my work life and my personal life as a whole. I spent the next eight days in the hospital receiving pain medication. I realized that was such a bad hospital, because one evening, Laura thought she was going into labor and was taken to the hospital. I called one of my assistants and had him come to the hospital and pick me up at the side door. He took me to the other hospital where Laura was being taken to. I got the information I needed and found out that she was not going into labor. I managed to get back to my own hospital. I went back up to my room and back in the bed, and the nurses and doctors never even knew I had left the hospital. At that point in time, I knew I needed to hurry up and go home. The day I returned home, we received some more news. Again, at one moment, just when you think life hasn't thrown you enough curveballs, you get hit smack in the face with another one. Laura's father, Walter, who had been ill for a while, had passed away. Walt was a great guy and another man whom I have the utmost respect for.

He had a brilliant mind and a great sense of humor, and we got along very well. Laura was absolutely crushed, just as I was when Millard passed away. I could barely stand up because of the pain from the meningitis, but we now had to make a trip to Ithaca, Michigan, in the dead of winter to attend the funeral. I guess it was right after this time that I began to see a light at the end of the Cheyney tunnel. I started thinking in my mind that I wanted more out of life and more of a life for my children than to be mad, sick, and tired all the time. So in my mind, I made a decision, without telling anyone, that the following season would be my final season at the university. That decision was made even easier for me when, in March of that year, my son, Jordan, was born. He was beautiful, just like Andrea was. He had a healthy head of hair on him. He was everything I wanted. It was really amazing that we ever had another child.

Something happened to Laura after Andrea was born. I don't know, but she changed. She never wanted to do anything anymore at all. Again, I knew life would change, but this was different. The only thing I can describe it was that she had turned into her mother almost overnight. Her mother was a sweet woman who, at one time, was studying to be a nun but eventually changed her mind. She did, however, stay in the church and married a great guy. But even as wonderful as a woman that she was, I did not want to be married to her. Slowly, I could see that Laura was turning into her. Even when I would suggest that we do things together, she would say no or "I don't feel like it." I just let it go with the hope that she would grow out of it. Maybe it was some form of postpartum depression that she was going through, and hopefully, over time, she would get past it and maybe there could be time for just her and I again soon. Sometimes, life is written on the wall right in front of you, and you are just too damn blind or hardheaded to see it. Sometimes, if you would just slow down, listen, and pay attention to the signs that life is giving you, you could save yourself and the people around you a great deal of pain. Many of us choose to cover our face and even sink our head in the proverbial sand with the hopes that the situation will change when we know deep down in our hearts that the situation will never change and, in many cases, will just get worse. Funny how life works that way.

CHAPTER TWENTY-EIGHT

*Man's feelings are always purest and most glowing in the
hour of meeting and of farewell.*

—Jean Paul Richter

THE CHEYNEY SWAN SONG

I STARTED THE year with a few more changes. Cheyney
had done a real search this time for the search for a new
director of athletics, and they narrowed it down to two individuals.
One black man named Patrick Simon, and the other was, get this,
a white woman from Easton, Pennsylvania, named Eve Atkinson.
When Eve was interviewed, Dr. Pettus summoned me to the
office. I was asked to give her the nickel tour of the campus. By
the time we were finished, I owed her at least four cents. Cheyney
University was not a very big campus, so the nickel tour was well
overpriced. Eve and I discussed a lot of things that day, but the
one thing I did convey to her was that I didn't think Cheyney
University was going to hire a white woman as the next Director of
Athletics. With that being said, I took her back to the president's
office, where I expected that to be the last time I laid eyes on Dr.
Eve Atkinson. About three weeks later, I received a call from the
president, telling me that Dr. Eve Atkinson had been hired as
the new athletic director at Cheyney University. It took me by

a huge surprise, but in all reality, it was probably the best thing for the Athletic Department. For the first time in my career, I felt like I was going to be working for someone who understood how athletics should be run at a university. She was sharp, very authoritative but had a sense of compassion about her. I believe she deeply cared about the staff of coaches that worked with her. I was happy to have her there.

Unfortunately, in my mind, I had already made a decision not to return. When I acquired spinal meningitis, what I failed to notify anybody about was that I also had a small stroke at the same time. The feeling in my left side had gone numb, and stayed that way for quite some time. On my subsequent visits to the doctor, I indicated many difficulties with my equilibrium. After running a battery of tests, the doctor did determine that I had a small stroke. I never made this public to my family or to the administration at Cheyney. I always try to live by the fact that a true gentleman never reveals his illness to the public, but instead handles them in a more private manner. Because of the meningitis and a stroke, I felt like I needed to step away from this game and this profession until I felt like I could return with some confidence in my health. All I can tell you is that the feeling was a huge sign on the wall, and I probably should have stepped away right at that moment.

We started the season with a visit to North Carolina Central University. Needless to say, we got the living crap kicked out of us. We had good kids and a good scheme, but we did not have the kind of horses that they did. As every coach in the country does, I put everything into my team and my work. And just like every other coach in the country in this profession, I enjoyed what I was doing, never realizing how much real time I was putting into work. I came to a huge realization after that game was over, when I was walking off the field. I began to get a tingling sensation in my left shoulder. And it was quickly moving down to my fingertips. I stopped in my tracks and bent over because I could feel my left arm tingling, and becoming very sore. The next thing I knew, I was on one knee, with an unbelievable amount of pressure on my chest. I then went down on my back, and the only way I can describe it was that it felt like a four-hundred-pound man was standing on my chest, and he was quickly gaining weight. Before I passed out, I saw the paramedic units running across the field at me. They put me on a stretcher and took me off the field, where they placed me in an ambulance, placed nitroglycerin tablets underneath my tongue, and took me to the hospital in Durham, North Carolina.

After running tests on me, it was determined that I did have a heart attack. How amazing was that. At this point in my life, I am less than forty years old, I have now had meningitis, a stroke, and a heart attack. Not to mention I have survived a head-on accident at high speed. If this does not make me the poster boy for both luck and prayer, I don't know what does. I made three phone calls from the hospital. First I called Laura to let her know what had happened and that I was all right. The next person I called was Eve and let her know what happened. Looking back now, it's kind of amazing that Eve appeared to be more upset than Laura. That was a clear indication that I needed to finally take a few steps backward, regroup, and rethink my time and commitment to this profession. I now had two small children, and I felt like I really wanted to be around for them. My father died when he was fifty-four years old because he never took care of himself. He was angry and stressed out constantly over

JOHN STEPHEN PARKER

things that in the grand scheme of life really didn't matter. I was determined that I would not go out the same way. Right then, I made a decision to take better care of myself, to be around for Andrea and Jordan.

That season was much of a disaster. The unsuccessful nature of the program kept taking a toll on me. Finally, after the last game, Dr. Atkinson and I came to a decision that I would step down as head football coach. We called a press conference for Monday afternoon. I met with the president earlier that day, and we looked back at the highlights of the things we had accomplished. When I first came there, we were losing players to drive-by shootings, to drug usage, to academic retention, and a broad range of issues. During my tenure there, we had a 97 percent graduation rate, the second-highest grade-point average of any organization on campus, and the discipline issues were almost completely negated. As I got up and left the president's office, he looked at me and said, "We may not have won a bunch of football games, but we changed a lot of lives. You've gotten a bunch of young man to turn right when they could have turned left, and because of that, you should be very proud of yourself because I'm very proud you."

Now you have to understand, in the business of college athletics, football coaches are what you would call a necessary evil. It costs an ungodly amount of money to operate a college football program. Then when it comes to the salary, you have to pay not only the head coach but his entire staff. I had a guy who, in spite of the fact that on many occasions his hands were tied financially, he would go out of his way and figure out a way to maybe not get all the things I wanted, but to at least get the things that I needed to have, to operate the program. When he said those things to me, I almost broke down and cried right there in his office. If he and I were in at a different university, under different circumstances, and in a different financial situation, there's no doubt in my mind that we would have won a national championship. To this day, I can honestly say that I really miss Dr. Pettus.

I told Dr. Atkinson that I would stay on and help her with the search for my replacement, and I would also stay on for two weeks after he was on the job. I wanted to be sure that the new guy would get help becoming acclimated to the lay of the land. This was something that nobody was ever did for me, not to mention, I wanted those players to understand how much they were cared for. Although we didn't win a bunch of games, we were able to change some lives. That alone makes you feel pretty good.

That was one instance in my coaching profession, and in the profession overall, where the adage of "winning isn't everything" was really true. It was more important to me that these young men not only have some success on the football field, but also gain some professional life skills. This was Division II football. The chances of any of those young men making it to the NFL were not very good. I know they all had a dream, and it was the same dream that I had as a young player, but it was more important to me that these young men understood confidence, presentation and know how to speak to people about any subject at any time, in any place. I made them understand the basic things that they were going to need in the business world, which is where I hope they would all end up. Things like how to tie a tie, how to wear a suit, how to wear your hair, what things people might find offensive in your look. I had fights about this with many of the administrators, and even a few of the parents. They would always ask me what any of that has to do with playing football. And my answer was always the same. I would tell them "We're going to sit in restaurants and in hotel lobbies, and these young men may be sitting next to someone who is the president of a major corporation. That president may begin to have a conversation with one of these young men. If that president is impressed with the young man, that could possibly turn into an internship, or even a future job. If that same president is set off by the fact that this young man has earrings, or braids in his hair, or lots of gold chains around his neck, or the diamond-and-gold grill in his mouth, they have now lost that opportunity to make a good impression."

I would then let them know that I was not willing to risk any players future in the business world over facial hair or an earring in his ear, and I would hope that they were not either. Most of the parents got the message, but there were few that I really didn't understand why they would not get on board. There was even a couple who complained to the president of the university that I was doing this. Once again, I had the support of Dr. Pettus. I truly believe that we did change a great deal of lives. I was always told that whenever you come into a job, you should always try and leave it better than you found it. I truly believe I left this place significantly better than the day I walked in.

CHAPTER TWENTY-NINE

*But friendship is precious, not only in the shade, but in the
sunshine of life, and thanks to a benevolent arrangement
the greater part of life is sunshine.*

—Thomas Jefferson

YOU CAN GO HOME AGAIN

I GOT READY to make the move back to St. Louis. I took
that spring off, and I'm not going to lie, I did search for
a couple of new positions, and I even landed one in Texas, but
unfortunately, the circumstances surrounding the job all changed
and I ended up taking Laura and the kids and moving back to
Missouri. I became a manager working for Pete Gallagher. It was
a little out of my element. I had been used to running football
programs for almost twenty years, and now, I was in the business
world where things did not operate quite as I was used to. I did
long for the field, but I did need to take some time off and get
my health issues back together. I thought I would be out of it
for a year or two, but it's funny, when you're not looking for a
position, somebody will find you.

Warren Powers, who was the former head football coach at
the University of Missouri, called me one day. He asked me one
question. He asked me, "John, do you know anything about

arena football?" I told him no, that I knew nothing about the game or the rules. Arena football was played on a smaller field with fewer players, and I knew nothing about it. He then said to me, "Then come out here and be my associate head football coach and defensive coordinator, and let's see if we can screw this thing up together."

I was not overly excited about the idea. I had come back to St. Louis to kind of sit back and rest a little bit from the game. The idea of grinding away in game plans and practice schedules really was unappealing. But the idea of getting an opportunity to work with Coach Powers, Steve Miller, and a number of other good coaches got the juices flowing again. So instead of a much-short-lived hiatus, I was back in game plan sessions, coaching an indoor football-league team in St. Louis. Who would have thought that would have happened?

Being in St. Louis, was always very comfortable for me. Even today, I know the lay of the land very well. Working for Pete made things easier. I knew I had a constant paycheck and benefits, plus I was getting a chance to coach in my hometown again. Laura was not that comfortable there. Nothing really changed in her demeanor. She was still very, very focused on the kids, whom I was always running a distant second to. It was almost like she had given up on any kind of real relationship with us, because she threw everything into always doing things with and for the kids. Even then, I could tell that this was the beginning of the end. I figured we should try and make a go of this, but in the back of my mind, I knew that I was not done moving in my career, and that on top of having kids now, I was going to make it more difficult.

I went to work for Warren Powers, coaching the indoor team in St. Louis. Warren had recruited me at a high school, and I felt like it was a great opportunity to work for a great guy and to learn a great deal of football. I knew it would not last long because indoor football was a fading fad. We were hired by a guy named Ed Watkins. He was a very spiritual guide, or at least I thought he was. I lasted about four games before he fired me as associate head football coach. It was about the same time that I met a guy named Randy Gardner. He was a media guy who was doing high school games on the weekends, and had his own television station and studio in the basement of the city of Black Jack City Hall. Randy asked me to join him, and do a couple of high school games with him on the weekends. That turned into a full-fledged television sports show opportunity. *Primetime Sports* was the name of the show, and it became unbelievably popular in the same area. I can truthfully say that if I had not met Randy, I would not be in the broadcasting business, or the public speaking business today. He is an unbelievably brilliant person who locked himself into this station, and passed on many opportunities. I always gave him a boatload of shit for never leaving the area, but I admire the fact that his family was here, and as he began to have children, he wanted them to have the ability to see their grandparents.

The funny thing was, the day I was fired from the indoor team, we were actually on set doing interviews. Gary Pinkel, the Head Football Coach at the University of Missouri was on set with us, and I received a call from Coach Powers. He told me that I had been fired, and that Ed sent the message through me. I thought it was kind of a chickenshit way to do it. Any time I have ever had to fire anybody, I have always done it face-to-face. If that was the way they wanted to conduct business, I didn't like it, but I didn't have much choice in the matter. All the spiritualism and good-heartedness that he had completely went out of the book as far as I'm concerned. I took the firing in stride and kept working for Pete and constantly looking for a new position. I was a football coach. I knew that would be the only thing, at that time, that I would be happy doing. Nobody—not Laura, not my mother, and none of my friends—could really understand my obsession with a career, in a profession, that had not been very kind to me. It affected my health greatly, and was driving a wedge in my family life. Sometimes, instead of sharing your beliefs that you also keep enduring in your heart, it's better to keep them in the compartments that life has provided you. Only later in your life will you realize that the compartments that you choose to keep separate will eventually all run together, and the delusional control factor will begin to fade away.

Working for Pete was a great thing in the beginning, but that eventually began a stressful relationship between he and I. Pete had been like a father to me. He had counseled me a number of times on just about every life issue that exists in the universe. People always say that you should never hire your family or your friends in business. I completely agree with this statement because when my tenure was up working for Pete, our relationship would never be the same. Although we haven't really spoken in many years, he is still one of the most important people in my life, and even after all these years, I could never replace him. I guess this will be a great time in this compilation that I would just say I am sorry for anything that has ever happened that put us in the relationship that we have today. I love him more than life itself, and maybe a little forgiveness is appropriate on both our parts now. It's very tough when you have someone in your life for over thirty-five years, and then one day, they're just gone. Wherever he is, I hope he will be reading this someday and realize just how I feel about him.

I continued the job search and, finally, got lucky, or at least I thought I was getting lucky. I was hired by Washington and Lee University. It's a small school in western Virginia. I was in a hurry to get back to the realm of college football. It's difficult when you're out and you're trying to get back in. I managed to find this position, and I jumped at it, but in looking back, it was probably a huge mistake.

Washington and Lee University was one of those rich uppity places that I knew that I was never going to fit in. All the kids who went to school there were very well-off and what I would call spoiled brats. The atmosphere was a bit ridiculous. It's the only place that I've ever been where after a game, even if it was a major loss, they would have a tailgate spread for the whole team. Now when I say tailgate spread, I mean a gourmet chef slicing two or three different kinds of meat. It was a fully catered the event. These kids were babied beyond belief. They were even able to hang their laundry on their dorm-room doors every Tuesday for laundry service. The big joke was that you could throw a bomb into the middle of the student parking lot and destroy about $400 million worth of vehicles. The lot was full of Mercedes-Benz, BMW, Jaguars, and Range Rovers. I knew that I was not going to be there very long. The guy whom I was working for was not very intelligent about the game of football. Again he appeared to be a good guy but at the end treated me like absolute crap. After this season was over with, I began looking around for a new position.

The other thing was when I found this position in Virginia, Laura and I were at a little bit of a crossroad. We decided to separate for a while. She took the kids and went to Michigan, to stayed with her mother, while I went to Virginia and coached the team. They say it takes a separation to bring appreciation. That was never as true as it was when we were separated for that six months. When she and the kids moved to Virginia after Christmas, I thought things would be better. But they were not. I was still very focused on my career, and she was just as equally focused on the kids. It's amazing how two people who were so in love with each other at one time completely fall off track. I guess the sad thing was we fought and tried to keep it together, but even then, it was clear that we probably wanted different things out of life.

The Washington and Lee stint was not working out. And it was the same old thing for me. I needed to be a head coach because it comes down to a trust factor. I have never really trusted, with the exception of Larry Kindbom, any head coach that I ever worked for. He was the only guy that I always felt, not only had the best interest at heart for a team, but also looked out for his coaching staff. I guess I spent my entire career trying to find a Larry again, but I knew it would be impossible. It's amazing how someone can touch your life and your career in that way. I always thought it was something special. I put the feelers out for a vacant head-coaching position at Cumberland University in Lebanon, Tennessee. It was a small NAIA school in middle Tennessee that had not had any recent success. Since this was my specialty, I leaped at the opportunity, and as usual, I should've probably looked a little closer before I leaped.

CHAPTER THIRTY

Society is one vast conspiracy for carving one into the kind of statue likes, and then placing it in the most convenient niche it has.

—Randolph Bourne

THE DOGMAS OF SOUTHERN LIVING

I WENT OVER and got interviewed for the position. As usual, my interviews were outstanding as I was very well prepared. When I arrived back in Virginia after the interview, I did not hear from them for a number of weeks. Finally, one Wednesday afternoon, the Athletic Director, Patrick Lawson called me and asked me to come over and get this thing sealed up. They formally offered me a position and wanted me there by Friday for a press conference. The scheduling issue had been some indication that they were disorganized, considering that it was already Wednesday. I packed up Laura and the kids, and we headed to Lebanon for the press conference. Now I believe that it was quite a shock when I walked in with my six-feet-tall, white, Polish wife and my two interracial children. My beliefs were really confirmed when my wife sat in a section directly in front of the podium where I was speaking, and no one sat within three rows of her. That was your ultimate "guess who's coming to dinner" moment. I got through the press conference as I always do and moved on to quickly try assessing the team. Let me remind you, I was hired the first week of May, after spring practice had taken place. So going into the fall, I knew then that I had no idea what kind of hand we had been dealt. All I can tell you is that it turned out to be the worst I had ever been dealt.

I had to hire a staff, and the first person I picked was Matt Hall. Matt was an army reservist who was a graduate assistant at Washington and Lee University with me. He was smart about football, but his greatest asset was the fact that he was extremely efficient. I knew that nothing would ever get messed up, especially in recruiting, if Matt was in charge of it. He and I were putting our heads together at getting this thing off the ground. The problems that we faced were a bit different than the problems most teams face. Instead of half a dozen bad players, we had about sixty. The problem when you have that many is that you can't cut all of them. So you have to figure out the best way to use those players, because all they are going to do is use the program. Man, did we ever have some assholes. It didn't help that neither the president nor the athletic director had any kind of athletic background. They were administrative bureaucrats that would nitpick at some of the most ridiculous issues. Not to mention they would very rarely support you in a project, that they did not have control over.

When I came to Cumberland, I wholeheartedly believed that it would be my last position as a coach. My kids were growing up, and I wanted them to have friends, establish relationships, and be around some of the same people all the way through their school life as I did. I think it's kind of special that I have the same two or three friends in my life today that I had when I was in the second and third grade. I wanted my children to have that same opportunity. I was also tired of dragging Laura around from city to city in search of the elusive "championship." I moved them from Virginia with the hopes that this would be it, and I would coach there for the remainder of my career. I should have played baseball because life was always throwing the curveballs, and I was always struggling to hit them.

I met some great people at Cumberland. David and Anne Whitefield, who became my second set of parents. Beth Alpert was Vice President of Institutional Advancement and became one of my best buddies. Beth had worked in South Africa, and in Washington, under the Clinton administration. She was smart, cute and unbelievably funny. We used to laugh for hours together, and we also shared a few tears from time to time. Renee Gill was the president's secretary and eventually moved over to be Anne's secretary. Debbie Patterson was the Director of Human Resources, and was a great person to be able to vent to. Being around these people was one laugh after another. It's funny that within one year's time, all of us would be gone from the university.

Matt and I struggled day in and day out with that program. Most of the struggles that we had, though, had nothing to do with football. Most of them dealt with the administration issues, bureaucratic red tape surrounding the fact that nobody ever wanted to pull the trigger over at the university, or the childish behavior of our players. It's amazing when you say that you're in the business to support young people and educate them about life, when most of people working at the university were more or less collecting a check. The fact that you had a president that was so much of a control freak, made it even more difficult to get things done. I tried to work within the system, but I always believe this. It is easier to ask for forgiveness after you have done something, than it is to ask for permission before you do it. We ordered equipment, uniforms, and supplies that we needed to operate the program. I did not have time to wait for people, who had no concern for the well-being of our players, to sign purchase order forms. I would not be held up by the annoyances, and the red tape of paperwork. That was a very frustrating thing to deal with.

That also had an immediate strain on the relationship I had with the Athletic Director. When he would be sitting on his ass, in his office, doing anything, I was out raising money, politicking, and trying to get interest back in the program. As an Athletic Director, if you don't coach anything, and you don't teach anything, then I should never find you in your office. You should constantly be out in the public selling the athletic programs. This guy would never do anything, and I found that completely unacceptable. I am sure he thought that I was the biggest crazy man on campus from time to time, which I was, but I had a method to my madness. My method was to build this program into the best that it could possibly be, and I was not waiting for him to get in line. These players deserved more. Looking back on it, I am sure that if he could have gone back, and hired someone else after about three weeks, he would have. Instead, he began to mount a black-eye operation campaign against me, that would have to be battled on a number of different fronts.

As I was not hired until May of that year, and not knowing or realizing the lack of talent that we had, we went out that fall and lost every game. This was both good for us and bad for us. It was bad for the handful of players that you were very happy were with the program. It was good for what was about to happen to the players, that I needed to get rid of. At a team meeting following the last game, I cut nearly forty-five players from a football team. These guys were nothing more than a growing cancer, that was infecting the team every day that they were around. And as with all cancers, it is important that you cut them out and relieve yourself of them as soon as possible. I did that, and at the same time, I put the remaining players on notice that things are changing. I always told the players that the train moves, not the station; you can either be on the train or be at the station. Please don't stand in front of the train, because the train will move and run you over.

We started a brand-new campaign after that season. It started with a new facility, or what I would call a facility upgrade. It was important that we begin to change the thought process of the players, who were on that team, and the incoming players who were joining the program. We brought in new staff members, and we changed the uniforms and logos. Little did I know that the covert operation conducted by the President and the Athletic Director was mounting against me.

After the spring, I personally raised about $150,000, and had the locker room renovated. I knew that they were mounting a witch hunt against me, but as long as I was raising money, and kids were going to class and not causing trouble on campus, I could get past all of it and deal with the administration for a while. They hated the fact that I was married to a white woman, and they were never going to allow that to continue, as long as I was the Head Football Coach. It sucks that as far as we have come in society, we have not come far enough to understand the fact that we are all God's children, and that when we bleed, it is always red. These people were still stuck in the era of lawn jockeys, field hands, and referring to black men as "boy." The most-feared person in the South today is still an educated black man, and for that reason, the change to keep one down, unambitious, and uneducated is what appeals to many in the South. I heard someone say that General Colin Powell "speaks so well." My question is "What do you expect?" He is a retired army three-star general. How the hell would you expect him to sound?

CHAPTER THIRTY-ONE

The years teach much which the days never know.
—Ralph Waldo Emerson

PROFESSIONAL AND PERSONAL VALLEYS

AS THE SEASON began, things between Laura and I were going downhill. She never wanted to do anything, and if I didn't initiate it, it never would happen. The only thing she ever wanted to do was church, which she has always taken great pride in. Dancing with Andrea was the second obsession. After that, it was about her, not her and me. I was not of any help either. I tried to spend time with her, and tried to communicate, but there were times when I would just give up and go out and find my good time and communication outlet. I just wanted my wife back, and for her to give me some type of attention. She devoted every waking moment to all those other things, and I no longer had a place. Although this went on for a number of years, eventually, we knew that the writing was on the wall, and us being apart was eminent. We would eventually grow completely apart. All the fighting, bickering, and crap would need to just stop, and we need to make our lives separate, but at the same time, focus on Andrea and Jordan, and do whatever we needed to do to make sure that our children would be OK. Although many events would happen, both triumphantly and tragically, we would eventually get away from each other, and try to be happy apart. I believed it was important that as our children grew up, they needed to see two parents that were happy apart as opposed to being miserable together. We just needed to have some peace.

As the second season was progressing well, we were beginning to make a dent in the program. We brought in a truckload of new, young players. We did win a few games, and the future was very optimistic for us, but on the morning of the last game, I was on my way to breakfast when I was stopped by the athletic director in the parking lot. He told me after the game that we were going to make some changes. I asked what changes he was going to make, and he stated, "We are probably going to go in another direction." Well, anyone that has ever had a job knows that when those words are stated, then somebody is getting fired. I asked him flat out, "Are you trying to say that I am getting fired?" He said, "Yes." He said that the season had not gone as they had hoped and that they felt it was warranted.

I stood there completely flabbergasted. I had been on the job for less than two years. I was hired in May of the previous year, after spring practice was over, and had one season to bring in a recruiting class. I also raised over $150,000.00 for the program in less than a year, something that had never been done. Did I win a bunch of games with seventy-five freshman players? No, I did not, but anyone who understands college football, business, or the concept of team building knows that it takes time, and as long as progress is being made, you have to be patient. For them to do this, and the manner which they did it was completely unprofessional.

I went to breakfast and sat at the table with my coaches. I gave them the news, and they were all just as taken back as I was.

I then picked up the phone and called Laura. When I told her, she just freaked a bit, but then told me to come home and not coach today. I knew I could not do that. I made a commitment to the players from start to finish, and what kind of example would I be showing if I completely bailed on them on game day? I elected to stay, but I made sure that they knew what had just happened. I was upfront with them about the situation. I told the team during the ten thirty meeting that morning. It was a very emotional moment for me. I really had never been fired before from a position that I was really in to, and the way this was done caught me completely off guard. When I told them, I did well up a bit. I had just sunk the last eighteen months of my life into this deal. I had sacrificed time away from my own kids, and energy for this program. I truly believed this would be my last job, and went into building it as such. I made relationships with businesses in the area, and built a foundation that I knew I could construct on. The thing that I was most disappointed in was the fact that I was a company man. I spoke always highly about the university and the administration. Even in corners of the town that the President knew nothing about, and among people who were talking about him like he had a tail attached to him. I represented him and the university with honor and integrity. I felt unbelievably betrayed by these people, but it was not going to keep me from doing the job that I was hired to do. I needed to finish my job and just move on.

That evening, Laura and I went to Anne Whitefield's home. She and her husband, David, were waiting for me. They were a support to me like nobody else ever was. We talked about a lawsuit, because David was an attorney, and he thought I probably had a potential suit. He took me to meet with some

JOHN STEPHEN PARKER

representation prospects. I remember walking into the office of a guy named Doug Janney. He was a short little guy with a big smile, but something in me told me that Doug was a bulldog of a lawyer. I explained the situation, the mounting evidence I had, and he agreed to take my case. We were going to file a lawsuit against the Cumberland University for racial discrimination. I knew that if I did that, it would probably eliminate me from ever coaching again. Nobody would take the chance on me if they knew I might play the race card against them, but this was a risk I was going to have to take. I also knew it was going to be a long wild ride, but I also knew that if I didn't do it, one day, my daughter or son would read about this or hear about it from someone. I wanted to be sure that there was a footprint that I was here, and that there was an accurate account of the facts, and that they could be proud of their father for standing up for his rights and the rights of his family.

While the process took many months, I bounced around from a few jobs. I took a position at Dell Computers as a sale consultant. I didn't make much money at first, but I knew I could sell pretty much anything. I worked there for about sixteen months, and I sold almost thirteen million dollars worth of computers and equipment for them, but unfortunately for me, Dell pays less than 1 percent to its sales team members. So I really never made any real money. The division that I worked in got completely shut down and eliminated. There I was again, laid off and out of work.

I have always worked hard and pursued streams of income to keep myself and my family afloat. This time was no different. I got into the contract business as a negotiator for coaches and their contracts. I was also bird-dogging players for various agents. Because I knew or had access to almost every program in the college football, and guys would call me to contact various staff members from different schools. It was easy for me, and it kept me in the game also. The suit was beginning to come to a head, but I had no idea when it would be finished. There were numerous depositions, and crap like that, but I knew it would eventually come to fruition. I was confident that we would settle on something. Also, because there were so many compartments in my life, I decided to begin writing. Just when I thought I would never get another opportunity, I got a call. I was in the airport in Bangor, Maine, when James Webster, Head Football Coach at Tennessee State University, called. He had a position available and wanted to hire me. I was really excited about the possibility, not to mention I did not have to move. TSU was in Nashville, which was about a twenty-five-minute drive each day. It was also a Division I-AA school in the Ohio Valley Conference, where I had been interviewed many times in my career for various positions.

I accepted the position and was very excited to be back on the field. I did, however, forget that TSU was a historically black University, and I had not been at one in almost ten years, since I left Cheyney. I had to readjust my mode of operation because everybody knows that an HBCU does not operate like mainstream universities. You have to prepare for your own mind to operate under those circumstances. I was, however, happy at the moment to be moving back into the world that I was used to.

I remember reporting to work. I met with Rod Reed, who was the defensive coordinator. He was a good guy, who was a TSU alum. He had played there, and was actually a great player. He was also a legacy there, as his father had also played there before going to the NFL. Rod had a great reputation on campus, and was a very good football coach that, at the time, I believed I could both learn a lot from. I thought I could teach him a few things, and it was a good to be working with him. He did have one flaw, though, and it is the same flaw that every coach has a bit of. He was very territorial. Everybody at TSU knew that he would be the Head Football Coach there someday if he just stayed around long enough.

The suit did come to fruition, and Cumberland University did settle with me although the settlement was no admission of guilt. That is always the chicken-shit way of admitting you were wrong without truly admitting you were. I was a black coach, with a white wife in Tennessee. They didn't like it, and they can say anything they want, but I know the truth. Clearly, their attorney didn't think it was worth taking to a courtroom, so we just settled and walked away. I was finally done with the saga know as Cumberland University, and none too soon because I was on my way to soon face another battle that I would again compartmentalize. I always felt that there was nobody I could turn to, who would not necessarily take my side, but would at least show compassion for what I was going through. I know that this is a two-way street, and, with the way I have lived my life in a very black-and-white manner, unless someone was willing to put the time in, they would probably never get close to me.

I have had people tell me that I was very cold, but they never understood, and in a way, I guess I never really did either. I guess it stemmed from my childhood experiences. When you are a victim of the things that I had experienced, I guess you become very guarded. The people who really know me, like Jimmy and Michele, know that when I am truly a friend to someone, I am a friend through everything to the end. No matter what happens,

I would never leave you. In my fifteen years of marriage, I never felt that I had that closeness with Laura. I was always desperately seeking that from her, but when I would tell her what I needed, she would somehow just blow off how important it was to me, and to the relationship we had, and the one I really wanted to have in my marriage. If I was not receiving what I needed to mentally survive, I was almost forced to seek that security in my work, in other people, or in whatever activity I could, to get what I needed to keep my head above the water mentally. At times, I knew I was compromising myself, but it was difficult not to have something so basic as intimacy and conversation. I am not talking about sex and affection. I am talking about the kind of intimacy you have when you can just sit and talk with someone, or laugh about something funny and borderline stupid. That was what I wanted. I had that with my close friends, but not in my marriage. I hated that, but there was nothing I could do.

I did continue with the broadcasting jobs with Randy. We had done the show in St. Louis for going on eight years now, off and on, and had built a nice following to it. There was also a conflict developing with Rod and I at Tennessee State. As I said, he was very territorial and becoming a bit of a hardhead. It didn't help that Coach Webster was not what I would consider a strong Head Coach. I loved him, and appreciated him offering me a position on his staff, but when it came to running a football team, it was like the inmates were running the prison. Rod understood the players because he was once one of the inmate-type players we had at TSU. When the season was over, I got out on the road, but began making plans to find another position. There was way too much disorganization in the program, the department, and in the university as a whole. I am the type of coach that does not

JOHN STEPHEN PARKER

do shady deals or, have ideas that need to be acknowledged. I would prefer that administrators get right to the point with me and not talk to me in code. When you give me a partial answer or a partial direction, it is aggravating. And when I decide that I don't like something, and I get right to the point in a conversation, it is taken by people as being rude.

When I got back from a road trip after Christmas, I met with Coach Webster, and we agreed that I would leave the staff. I was OK with that. The University was making cuts anyway, and I was on the block. I did not fit in with the staff very well anyway. I was not a ghetto guy, or as Rod said, I was not "hip" enough. Those guys wore sweats all the time, and I came to work in business casual attire. They would always say "Why are you so dressed up?" which I never understood. I only tried to be as professional as I could. I did not want the last football position I had, to be at Tennessee State University, and I didn't want to spend my career on the "Chitlin Circuit". I had my own ambitions, and all of them required me getting off the circuit.

I left there and dove back into the contract business as fast as I could. My writing was taking a bit of a backseat right then also. Toward the end of my tenure at TSU, I developed a mass on my left testicle. I kept it to myself as not to worry anybody, especially my home life. It was already going down the drain, and I was not going to add to it. I saw my urologist, who had snipped me a couple years before, and he suggested I see an oncologist, which I did. He did some tests and determined that it was stage 1 testicular cancer. It was quite a shock, but he said it was stage 1. There really is no reason to worry or panic. He put me on a drug called Vepesid. It was a pill form of chemotherapy used for small-cell lung cancer, but was used for other types of cancers if they were in the very early stages. The only thing the doctor said was that it would make me sick. Man, was he correct. I took it for a short period of time, and I did lose some major weight then because my appetite did decrease. I went back to the oncologist months later, and after they ran their test, I was told that it had been virtually eliminated. Man, you have to love modern medicine.

I moved on from TSU, and kept operating the company I was slowly building. I kept writing the book, and coaches were always calling me because I knew where the next opening was coming in college football. I was still a wealth of knowledge for young coaches who, to this day, still call me on a regular basis either looking for answers to football-related questions, trying to get their first position, or seeking an advancement in their career. I have stepped away from organizations such as the Black Coaches Association, of which I was on the Board of Directors for a few years. I got fed up with the leadership of the organization, and the fact that they were never accomplishing anything. I was a more deliberate person than the people they wanted on the board. The executive director was a man named Floyd Keith. He was a former football coach at the University of Rhode Island. I was instrumental in getting him that position, because I thought he would not be so much of a politician, more of a pit bull, and begin to expose institutions on their blatant racism toward black football coaches. Instead, he chose to be the bureaucrat that would never make a real stand about the subject.

It all came to a head with me when Tyrone Willingham was fired at the University of Notre Dame. Many people were upset about it, and publicly voiced their displeasure. His own secretary, a black woman, even shaved her head in protest. The

JOHN STEPHEN PARKER

one organization I never heard from was the Black Coaches Association. Two of the board members had degrees from Notre Dame, and were in non-coaching positions in athletics, but neither one of those two people, nor did the executive director of the organization, open up their mouth to voice any displeasure. When you are in a position to speak out, when something is wrong, and you choose not to, then you are just as much to blame as the people who are actually committing the injustice. I did not want to be a part of that board any longer, and I let that be known. To this day, no matter what you hear, the fact is that the Black Coaches Association has never gotten, or been instrumental in getting any black coach hired. While I was on the board, I even helped to develop a Coaches Academy to train young coaches, who had ambitions to become a Head Coach. I really did find out what hypocrites they were when after I left the board, I applied for the academy, and my application was quickly rejected by the BCA. Now I had really given up on those people. Don't get me wrong. I will always believe in the true mission of the organization, I just will never support the leadership. I don't believe that the leadership of the organization has the best interest of the membership at heart.

CHAPTER THIRTY-TWO

Most people can look back over the years and identify a time and place at which their lives changed significantly. Whether by accident or design, these are the moments when, because of a readiness within us and a collaboration with events occurring around us, we are forced to seriously reappraise ourselves and the conditions under which we live and to make certain choices that will affect the rest of our lives.

—Fredrick Flack

EPILOGUE OF A COMPERTMENTALIZED LIFE

THIS HAS BEEN a journey filled with a vast amount of experiences that have affected my life. So many things that affect people every day go completely unnoticed to the ordinary eye. I was asked once, if I could go back in time at a random point in history, where would I go? That is a difficult idea to ponder because there are so many instances that I knew I could affect. I would tackle whoever the shooter was in the sixth floor of the Texas Book Depository on November 22, 1963. I might have gotten the wire to President Roosevelt on December 6, 1941, informing him of an eminent attack on our nation. I would probably have liked to have been at Logan Airport in

Boston on September 11, 2001. I would like to have warned the airport security of a plot to virtually destroy our country. And yes, I would go back to that traumatic summer of my childhood when my innocence was taken. I would have gotten away from home even faster before I was ever touched, for that has affected me and every relationship I have ever had.

I have also read that if you go back and change history, you would also change the current life you are living in. My guess is that if I could have stopped an assassination, maybe the war in Vietnam would have ended sooner, but maybe not. If Roosevelt had gotten the wire sooner, the war may have never happened, but that would mean that the era of the New Deal would have been delayed, and the Depression would have continued. And yes, if the hijackers had been stopped, three thousand Americans would not have lost their lives, but that would have also delayed a time in this country where, for a moment, Americans united as one, out of sympathy and anger, and decided that today we are all on the same team. There was no time to segregate or for petty prejudices. Firemen, police officers, pilots, mothers, fathers, and children of this melting pot of a country had been killed. There was no time to feel like that. And maybe I would not be the man I am today, possessing both the good and bad qualities I have, if I could have prevented what had happened to me. Maybe I would not have the ability to compartmentalize life, which is truly not a great quality. Unfortunately, none of us has that wonderful gift, and hindsight will always be twenty-twenty. This ability has saved me from a great outpouring of heartache and pain throughout my life, but has also kept me from enjoying things that most people enjoy. It has affected me with my communication, both with my children and their mother. It has kept me guarded, and reserved from almost every relationship I have ever had. I have never been able to express how I feel about certain issues. Recently, I lost both my twenty-year-old niece Alex and my seventy-one-year-old uncle Herschel. I cried and got emotional, but I held much of it back because it does not help me when I think about it.

I have had love in my life. I was in love with someone when I was fourteen years old. To this day, I am still in love with her, although we have gone on in our separate lives. She will always be a special person to me. I have had the same best friend since the third grade, and although we have had our disagreements over the years, it has never put us in a position where we did not love and care about what was going on with each other's lives. I know that will never change. I have many other friends that although maybe we don't see or speak to each other very often, I know if we run into each other, we will have a difficult time walking away because we will have so much to catch up on. Thank God for the social networking abilities of the twenty first century!

The same men, whether they know it or not, are still the major influences in my life. I have had an extraordinary and unique career path that continues even today. Through that career, I have come in contact with both the average person, and people of influence, who were just like me. I have wonderful children who are growing up around me as I write this, and I want to thank their mother for doing an outstanding job of raising them while I was off doing what I needed to do. One day, they are going to pick this book up, and maybe they will think that their dad was a great man. I, of course, will settle for the hope that they thought I was a good dad. And of course, there will always be my mother, who has been—and no matter where she is, either on this earth or in the ever after—will always be my rock and cornerstone.

My only assessment of this compartmentalization of life is that it works for me. I would never recommend it to anyone. My advice would be to open up the corners of your life to the world. Not only do you let people into thought processes, but you also give the world an opportunity to know you. We are all incredible creatures of a wonderful god. We owe it to the world to share ourselves, and the different compartments that we all dwell in. They say life is like a circle. Everything you do comes back to you. Look back and ask yourself, "Would that be so bad?"

Good luck!

INDEX

C

Campbell, Pierre, 245, 266

Caven, Mike, 206-7, 210-11

Chrisco, Lisa, 121

Clark, Betty, 23

Clark, Brian Preston, 14, 23-24, 26, 88

Clark, Doug, 86, 138

Clark, Mildred, 13, 22, 25

Clay, John, 121

Coats, Darryl, 245

Coe, Charlie, 93, 95

Colston, Milt, 269

Comegies, Rick, 253

Connors, Gary, 147

Courtright, Jim, 179

Craig (Mary's boyfriend), 179

Crandall, Ken, 225

Crone, John, 99

Crutchfield, Chris, 197

Curtis, Brian, 237

D

Dawn (female friend), 105

Dew, Sam, 60

Doobie Brothers, 59

Dooley, Vince, 210

Dopp, Dan, 196

Dr. White, 243, 249

Dunk. *See* Smith, Robert

E

Elam, Lisa, 39

Engebretson, Pam, 227, 248

Engelmann, Glennon, 22

Essen, Eddie, 121

F

Farrier, Steve, 116

Ferrante, Kim, 63

Fields, Wayne, 89-90

Floyd-Ingram, Nate, 245, 266, 277

Fohl, Mark, 219, 222, 227-28, 230, 234, 237

Foster, Julie, 193

Fouches, Kamic, 40

Fozzard, Ron, 41, 68

Frey, Bob, 170

Furch, Randolph William Jr., 39

G

Gallagher, Caroline Devlin, 94

Gallagher, Pete, 7, 47, 49, 86, 290

Galloway, Dominique, 95

Garvey, Carey, 155

K

Kaminski, Mary, 178
Karnes, Karree, 108
Keith, Floyd, 310
Kilgore, Phil, 128
Kindbom, Larry, 7, 167, 175, 295
Kottila, Geoff, 186-88, 190

L

Laura (wife), 187, 282
Lawrence, Wayne, 205
Lawson, Patrick, 296
Lewis, David, 87
Lewis, Harold, 218
Liepold, Lance, 197
Linnenbom, Harry, 83
Linville, Howard, 28
Lloyd, Ronnell, 58
Lorraine (John Wesley's girlfriend),
    69-70, 72
Lowell, Kevin, 80, 91

M

Mangelsdorff, Laura, 121
Marker, Denny, 112, 155
Mason, Darryl, 211, 214, 273
McCarthy, Lisa, 149-50

McDonald, Michael, 59
Mellencamp, John "Cougar," 134
Mierhoff, Glen, 74
Mitchell, Judith, 79
Mitchell, Vernon, 79
Moore, Johnnell, 85
Morgan, Nolan, 63, 80
Mr. Bates (barber), 25-26
Mr. Dean (barber), 24-25
Mrs. Crouch (teacher), 39-40
Mrs. McDonald (math teacher), 59
Mueller, Mike, 82-83

N

Nolan, Bill, 74
Nordman, Gerry, 84
Nowlin, Cheryl, 77

O

Oliver, Jappy, 238
O'Neal, Alexander, 121
Osborne, Tom, 197
Otten, Orv, 229
Owens, Tara, 268, 277, 279
Owens, Terrell, 218

P

Parker, Andrea Janae
  birth of, 263
Parker, Barbara, 13, 22, 35-36, 97
Parker, Felice, 20, 97, 116, 125,
  130
Parker, Frank, 51
Parker, John Stephen
  Ball State University experience
    of, 101, 104-5
  Cheyney University experience
    of, 241, 243, 253, 265, 267,
    273, 276, 278-79, 284, 287
  child abuse experience of, 52
  childhood of, 15, 26, 29-30, 37-
    38, 42-43, 46, 53, 70-71, 74
  death of father of, 124, 126,
    138-39
  East Tennessee State University
    experience of, 206, 208, 210
  employment with Pete Gallagher
    of, 290
  fatherhood of, 240, 261-62, 264,
    271
  football coaching philosophy of,
    288
  friendships of, 100
  Good Samaritan encounter of,
    219, 221

  health problems of, 279-80, 285-
    86, 309
  hobbies and interests of, 133-34,
    136-37
  life in Baldwin County of, 156,
    158, 160, 162
  Mac Murray College experience
    of, 170-71, 173-75
  marital life of, 194, 200, 202-3,
    205, 291
  McCluer Senior High School
    experience of, 65-67, 72-73,
    75, 77, 80, 83-84, 87, 90,
    124
  Michigan Tech University
    experience of, 173, 175, 177,
    180, 182-83, 186, 192
  Missouri Valley College
    experience of, 107-8, 152,
    155
  pot experiment of, 110
  quest for independence of, 218
  quest for self-discovery of, 101
  racism experience of, 191
  relationship with Michele Henke
    of, 63-64, 113, 119, 145,
    147, 152
  relationship with Susan Walters
    of, 91-92, 106

Rosary High School experience
of, 164-67

Tennessee State University
experience of, 306, 309

University of Minnesota-Morris
experience of, 222, 224, 228,
230

vehicular accident of, 142, 144

Washington and Lee University
experience of, 294, 297

Parker, John Wesley, 51, 55, 69,
96, 123

Parker, Jordan, 282

Parker, Tony, 20

Pennington, Charles, 31, 39

Pennington, Charles Sr., 32

Pennington, Jean, 31

Peoples, Nannie, 16-18

Peoples, Pony, 16-18

Peoples, William, 85

Pettus, W. Clinton, 240, 244

Pilgrim, Rick, 74

Poe, Fielding, 33

Poenicke, David, 63, 92

Powers, Warren, 35, 117, 290-91

Q

Qualls, Angie, 77

Quigley, Bill, 7, 60-61, 82, 124,
163, 205

R

Ramsey, Bob, 225

Redd, John, 121

Reed, Fred, 209

Reed, Rod, 306

Reese, Doug, 228

Renner, Charlie, 111

Reynolds, Debbie, 149

Robinson, Eddie, 11

Robinson, Steve, 40

Ross, Al, 127

Ross, Diana, 131, 138

Russo, Tony, 86

S

Satchel, Ronnie, 122

Scales, Burrell, 127

Schneider, Debbie, 63, 77

Scott, Michael, 118

Serling, Rod, 129

Shannon, Ed, 72

Shannon, Terry, 72, 77

Simms, Steve, 115, 117

Simon, Patrick, 284

Simpson, Nicole, 212

LaVergne, TN USA
21 January 2011
213368LV00002B/18/P